Creating a Mentoring Culture

Creating a Mentoring Culture

The Organization's Guide

Lois J. Zachary

Foreword by Peter Koestenbaum

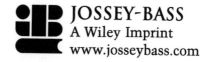

JOSSEY-BASS
A Wiley Imprint
www.josseybass.com

Published by Jossey-Bass
A Wiley Imprint
989 Market Street, San Francisco, CA 94103-1741   www.josseybass.com

Jossey-Bass books and products are available through most bookstores. To contact Jossey-Bass directly call our Customer Care Department within the U.S. at 800-956-7739, outside the U.S. at 317-572-3986 or fax 317-572-4002.

Jossey-Bass also publishes its books in a variety of electronic formats. Some content that appears in print may not be available in electronic books.

Credits on p. 299.

Library of Congress Cataloging-in-Publication Data
Zachary, Lois J.
  Creating a mentoring culture : the organization's guide / Lois J. Zachary ; foreword by Peter Koestenbaum.— 1st ed.
     p. cm.
  Includes bibliographical references and index.
  ISBN 0-7879-6401-8 (alk. paper)
  1. Mentoring in business. 2. Corporate culture. I. Title.
  HF5385.Z33 2005
  658.3′124—dc22
                              2004030323

Printed in the United States of America

HB Printing   10 9 8 7 6 5 4 3 2 1   FIRST EDITION

The Jossey-Bass Higher and Adult Education Series

Contents

Exhibits and Figures

Exhibits

Appendix

Figures

Foreword

LOIS ZACHARY'S *Creating a Mentoring Culture* is a timely and towering piece of work. It covers the full spectrum of mentoring and furnishes a complete recipe for establishing and sustaining a comprehensive mentoring culture in organizations. As a philosopher in business, I insist emphatically on both *practicality* and *insight*. This book does both, does them well, and is likely to get impressive results. These are far from easy tasks to accomplish.

Mentoring makes the full human available to the most basic strategic needs of an organization. But mentoring is more. It requires that we be sensitive to the highest ethical considerations of which human beings are capable—something desperately needed in today's organizations. This is far from being soft. Quite the contrary; this sensitivity helps organizations face confrontation and tough choices. It is today's task of the leadership consultant to support people who are under uncanny stress and to empower them in the face of demotivating defeat. Today's is not an easy economy. Neither being employed nor being an employer is straightforward. There is no simple way to succeed in a tumultuous global political climate. *Creating a Mentoring Culture* addresses itself meaningfully to precisely these central themes in today's organizations.

This book meets the core criteria of organizations that truly understand what it means to concentrate on authentic character values. These criteria can be clearly identified: focus on the person, on dialogue, on accountability, on the art of co-creation, on taking individual responsibility for the welfare of the whole, and on the image that life is a journey more than a destination. Last, but not least, the book offers practical steps for implementation. Indeed, it accomplishes all of this with an array of extraordinary exercises and activities.

What strikes me as memorable about this book, and what sets it apart from most others, is that it recognizes the meaning of *depth*—helping an organization dig several layers below the surface—in creating effective intervention programs. This sensitivity to depth is the critical success factor, for depth means results, whereas superficiality alone means frosting and no substance. Zachary offers substance and the opportunity for substance. To me this is true professionalism, genuine value for intervention.

Professionals understand that, after all is said and done, leadership is about character even more than skill, about emotional maturity even more than competence, and about the capacity to stand up to defeat even more than best practices. Zachary goes beyond techniques and best practices to the very core of human character. Her imaginative and tested exercises tighten the essential connection between thought and action, concept and results.

Executives, managers, and human resource practitioners will be exceptionally well served as they follow Zachary's guidelines and her treasure chest of activities to develop an organization's strategic intent for establishing a powerful mentoring culture. Zachary shows how to do it, step by step, in chapters that make splendid reading, especially for a reader concerned with greatly improving the quality of life within a company, and in such a way that we are not talking about charity but about strict business effectiveness. The focus is on the person; the emphasis is on interaction and dialogue. What matters is that people take responsibility for themselves and for participating in creating wholeness across the organization.

Zachary is aware of the enormous gap between thought and action, theory and practice, strategy and implementation—a chasm that is usually bridged with one more theory and nothing approximating authentic commitment and engagement. She achieves this transition by detailing how mentoring programs can be introduced into an organization, nurtured, protected, adapted, and made to be ongoing. Yet this is not just one more book on technique. Techniques alone are not enough. Zachary knows that the difference between an organization that does succeed in sustaining organizational mentoring and one that does not is whether or not a flexible and alive approach to mentoring is created. It is this ability to create transformational experiences—for individuals and their organization—that supports a mentoring culture. It is these experiences that engage people's heart and soul in the work and enterprise of mentoring. This book, written with the sure hand of an experienced and accomplished practitioner, constitutes the action link between theory and practice that is often missing. It even uses poetry to help people connect and engage with the hallmarks of a mentoring culture. It raises the level of thinking and practice by providing practical tools that engage people and their organizations, tools that are sustainable but supportive of flexibility. Reading—and above all using—Zachary's book is easy, effective, and a pleasure. *Creating a Mentoring Culture* truly deals with the many facets of establishing a mentoring culture.

I believe you will be convinced that the idea of a mentoring culture is a perfect solution to some of the most pressing leadership problems facing modern corporations, institutions, and organizations. There may be no better solution to the need to focus on the person than to establish a mentoring organization and do so in the detailed fashion Zachary recommends and facilitates. If you are a professional interested in mentoring, then this book is for you. It tells you all you need to know to move your culture from good to great.

Peter Koestenbaum

Peter Koestenbaum is the founder and chairman of Philosophy-in-Business (www.pib.net) and the Koestenbaum Institute, headquartered in Stockholm and Los Angeles. He has consulted on leadership, management, marketing, and strategy implementation in more than forty countries with such Fortune 500 companies as IBM, Ford, and Xerox. He is the author of many business and philosophy books including The Philosophic Consultant: Revolutionizing Organizations with Ideas (Jossey-Bass/Pfeiffer, 2002); Leadership: The Inner Side of Greatness (Jossey-Bass, 2002); *The Heart of Business*; and *Freedom and Accountability at Work: Applying Philosophic Insight to the Real World* (Jossey-Bass, 2001).

Preface

MENTORING IS an organizational practice whose time has come. In today's competitive business climate, the need for continuous learning has never been greater. At the same time, the hunger for human connection and relationship has never been more palpable. Because mentoring combines the impact of learning with the compelling human need for connection, it leaves individuals better able to deepen their personal capacity and maintain organizational vitality in the face of continuous challenge and change.

Mentoring is also a smart way to do business. Organizations that continuously create value for mentoring achieve amazing results. They report an increased retention rate, improved morale, increased organizational commitment and job satisfaction, accelerated leadership development, better succession planning, reduced stress, stronger and more cohesive teams, and heightened individual and organizational learning.

My travels have taken me many miles since *The Mentor's Guide* first appeared in 2000. My thinking about coaching leaders and their organizations in designing, implementing, and evaluating learner-centered mentoring has traveled quite a distance as well. Now, more than ever, I am convinced that organizational leaders must learn to think seriously and systemically about mentoring and create a mentoring culture to support and strengthen all the mentoring that goes on within their organization. Applying the richness of adult learning theory to the planning, creating, and delivery process elevates the process.

How This Book Came to Be

As a leadership development consultant and adult learning specialist, I consider myself first and foremost to be a student of culture. Understanding an organization's culture clarifies how and why things get done the way they do. This is important to me in my work because my clients include an array of for-profit and nonprofit organizations, all with a variety of subcultures within them.

I have been thinking about the importance of creating a mentoring culture for almost a decade and writing about it for nearly as long. I have learned that the difference between an organization that succeeds in sustaining organizational mentoring and one that does not lies in creating a viable and dynamic mentoring culture. All too often, people in an organization that spends valuable time, energy, and resources in building a mentoring program end up feeling disappointed, frustrated, and dissatisfied because of their inability to sustain either the program or its results. I have consulted with many organizations that started out with success initially but missed the mark when it came to sustainability. Some viewed their mentoring program as the cure-all for everything that had previously gone wrong and yet committed no funding to support mentoring. In some, mentoring failed to take root because of inadequate support from an already overextended organizational leadership. In others, there was a blatant cultural mismatch between the mentoring program being put in place and the organization, either because the program was too structured and formal or it was too informal for the organizational culture.

If a mentoring program is not sufficiently embedded in a supportive organizational culture that values learning and development, it rarely flourishes. The program may enjoy short-term success but then disappear. It becomes the whipping boy for other initiatives and problems. It competes for dollars, attention, participants. The program fades in and out. It becomes too easily expendable.

A mentoring culture strengthens the mentoring capacity, competence, and resilience of an organization. There are two categories of best practices that a mentoring culture exhibits: building blocks and mentoring hallmarks. The building blocks—cultural congruence and learning, and infrastructure— are the foundation supporting the process of creating a mentoring culture. The hallmarks are clusters of mentoring practices that relate to alignment, accountability, communication, value and visibility, demand, multiple mentoring opportunities, education and training, and safety nets. It is attention to these building blocks and hallmarks that enables an organization to create and sustain a vibrant and full mentoring culture.

Defining and Practicing Mentoring

There is no one universally accepted definition of mentoring, but many variations on the theme. The current definition has evolved along with enlightened practice. It focuses on facilitating learning and requires growing a partnership. Each mentoring partner is unique. This uniqueness—all the experience, history, diversity, and individuality that the learner brings to the relationship—must be honored and appreciated. It is the context within which the relationship lives and grows.

The practice of mentoring has evolved to the point where traditional one-to-one mentoring is only one item on a menu of organizational mentoring options. Lateral mentoring groups (that is, peer mentoring, mentoring forums, team mentoring) are becoming more commonplace among work groups and special-interest groups. New business and development needs have given rise to new forms of mentoring, such as reverse mentoring and the mentoring board of directors. There is also great variation in how mentoring is conducted. Face-to-face mentoring has been augmented and often replaced by distance mentoring. Distance mentoring itself has many permutations, among them videoconferencing, electronic expert mentoring, and e-mail; the list continues to expand, along with the technology.

Purpose of the Book

In *The Mentor's Guide,* I wrote about the mentoring journey. This metaphor of a journey is also appropriate for creating a mentoring culture, for it too is a journey and not a destination. Creating a mentoring culture is a journey of organizational learning in which mentoring competency and mastery are enhanced at all levels: participant, leadership, administrative, and institutional. The challenge of creating a mentoring culture is huge and can be somewhat intimidating. My personal challenge has been to provide a concrete, manageable roadmap for creating a mentoring culture without overwhelming you. I urge you to consider the building blocks and hallmarks as signposts to help you establish or reestablish organizational readiness, create appropriate opportunities, and build ongoing support.

The journey requires work. It is not easy; I encourage you to stay with it. Enlarge your thinking and sense of what is possible, and be persistent and steadfast in your effort. The payoff is a more integrated approach to mentoring that enhances the mentoring thinking and practice within your organization. The questions and exercises presented throughout this book are designed to stimulate a higher level of consciousness about the practice of mentoring in an organization. The insights you gain by answering the questions and completing the exercises create value far beyond the scope of mentoring.

Who Should Read This Book?

This book is a practical guide to building the framework that supports and sustains organizational mentoring. Whether your organization is thinking about starting a new initiative, implementing an existing one, jump-starting a stalled one, institutionalizing process improvements, or keeping mentoring fresh, this book is designed to broaden and enlarge your thinking so that you can take mentoring in your organization to the next level. The book helps senior organizational leaders more fully understand the scope and commitment required for mentoring to thrive. It also brings home the potential benefits of mentoring that can redound to the organization as a whole by embracing a thoughtful and systematic approach. *Creating a Mentoring Culture* is of particular interest to organizational leaders charged with strategic mentoring launch and implementation, change agents, mentoring leaders, mentoring program developers and administrators, program managers, and members of a mentoring taskforce. Faculty and staff development specialists as well as people in a corporate human resource department will find tools, templates, and tips that can be used as they are or adapted.

How to Use This Book

This book is a pragmatic guide for assisting organizations and individuals as they implement the work of creating a mentoring culture. It is also a sourcebook for analyzing existing mentoring efforts. The chapters include examples from organizations I have worked with and researched. In some instances, these organizations are identified; in others, the stories are representative and an amalgam drawn from several organizations. The book and its accompanying CD contain information, guidelines, assessment tools, and resource materials consistent with principles of adult learning. A variety of exercises are included to expand your thinking and elevate your mentoring practices. There are many ways to use the exercises; you may want to complete exercises individually or work through the process of completing particular exercises together as a group. There is much here to guide the journey. Choose what works for you and what feels right to you given your organizational context and culture. You will want to begin by taking stock of your organization, particularly if your organization is just getting started or finds itself stalled.

Creating a Mentoring Culture is a comprehensive guide for thinking about mentoring from a broad and deep strategic perspective, for creating a culture in which mentoring is a well-honed and practiced competency. It is a guide to creating a culture in which mentoring lives because mentoring itself is natural and normative, and in which mentoring excellence is the standard. In addition to the big picture, you will find detailed materials that have helped many organizations in developing and refining transformative mentoring programs. You may also find that these materials serve as a lens to examine and improve other organizational processes. I hope you use this volume to stimulate purposeful reflection and action, raise the level of discourse and dialogue about mentoring, and enhance mentoring practices within your organization.

Overview of the Chapters

The chapters in this book are divided into two main parts and an epilogue. Part One, "Taking Stock: Mentoring's Foundation," defines mentoring and considers how it adds value to the organization. The chapters lay the groundwork for understanding mentoring and its importance to the organization. Chapter One explains the importance of embedding mentoring in the culture. Chapter Two helps you discover where your organization is along the mentoring continuum. Then it moves toward helping you connect your organization's culture and mentoring by digging into the dynamics of the wider culture in which mentoring grows. The chapter includes specifics about raising cultural consciousness, mapping the culture, understanding cultural ecology, identifying cultural anchors, establishing the learning anchor, and testing for cultural congruence and deciding to move forward. Chapter Three focuses on planning implementation, specifically the people and process (a recurring theme throughout the book), and doing the groundwork necessary to develop sound mentoring processes.

Part Two, "Moving Forward: Mentoring at Work," introduces the concept of infrastructure and the eight hallmarks. A mentoring infrastructure is critical to a mentoring culture. The infrastructure and its components are described in Chapter Four, together with examples of mentoring practices. Chapter Five delves into the concept, challenges, characteristics, and process components of alignment and presents a mentoring alignment model. As the chapter explains, mentoring alignment promotes consistency of practice, cultural fit, and coordination. The more aligned mentoring is with an organization, the more it strengthens the learning that takes place within the entire organization. Chapter Six explores the framework for mentoring accountability by first broadly addressing the concept and then focusing on specific accountability processes. Some of the communication challenges that occur in organizational mentoring are presented in Chapter Seven. The chapter also identifies specific criteria for producing effective mentoring communication.

Chapter Eight includes a discussion of how to demonstrate and stimulate value and visibility for organizational mentoring. It focuses on the practices of role modeling, reward, recognition, and celebration. Chapter Nine looks at the impact and indications of demand and identifies levers for success in creating demand. Chapter Ten identifies an array of mentoring opportunities for learning outside of the formal structure of education and training. Formal and informal approaches are described, along with one-to-one, group, distance, and cross-cultural mentoring models. Strategies for supporting the learning that goes on within these types are outlined.

The structural frameworks for mentoring education and training are presented in Chapter Eleven, along with a sampling of training exercises that can be customized to specific situations. Chapter Twelve identifies some potential stumbling blocks *and* roadblocks that derail mentoring partnerships and jeopardize mentoring efforts within an organization. It also addresses how safety nets can be used to proactively and reactively manage those obstacles and sustain a mentoring culture. All twelve chapters conclude with a section for reflection on practice, designed to stimulate your thinking about next steps for your organization.

The Epilogue, "Moving on: Mentoring and the Future," acknowledges the everyday work, the struggle, and the joy of sustaining the mentoring effort. It offers implementation strategies for successfully moving from the seed of the idea of mentoring to a blossoming mentoring culture that is both nourished and nourishing.

Some themes and topics recur throughout the book, to highlight their importance, interdependence, and integration. The ideas behind mentoring are not intended to be discrete. For example, the topic of language is particularly relevant to both alignment and communication. I have intentionally selected only some aspects of the overarching topics that relate to organizational mentoring.

Two appendices, a wealth of forms on the CD, and an extensive reference list supplement the text. The first appendix sets forth the Mentoring Cultural Audit that you can use to assess where your organization is and what steps you might take at the outset. The second appendix is an annotated reading list, grouped by chapters, that you can use to dig more deeply into the topics.

Moving on as a Metaphor for Growth

The simple phrase "moving on" is a powerful metaphor for describing individual growth and learning. In our personal lives, moving on signifies growth and readiness for change. When we move on, we acknowledge our past and present (what it is we have learned and who we are) and move to a higher level, integrating what has come before with what is to be.

Creating a mentoring culture has much to do with moving on too. In a mentoring culture, transforming learning and leveraging experience are a way of being and a gateway to becoming. The nature of organizational life is often fast-paced, but if the opportunity to discover and make meaning out of daily experience is present and valued, an organization's collective level of performance is raised—with remarkable results.

Mentoring contributes to shaping this reality. Mentors come in and out of our lives and leave us with an insight, a kernel of truth, a piece of wisdom. They plant seeds that germinate for a lifetime. They challenge us to move on and help our organizations grow and embrace new possibilities. Their very presence enriches the workplace within which we work. They remind us of the profound power of learning and the promise of moving on.

Acknowledgments

MY HUSBAND is a baseball nut. He lives and breathes the sport. Finally, after thirty-three years, he convinced me to read a book about the game of baseball while we were on vacation. The one he gave me contains a juicy nugget that has stuck with me ever since. It reads, "it takes a lot of sentences to make a book, and it takes a lot of time to find them and try to get them down on paper" (Benson, 2001, p. 127).

I was in the midst of writing this book, and the quote resonated for me. As I continued to write, I slowly began to add items to my personal "what it takes to make a book" list. It grew to include the people I want to acknowledge here. I know how important it is to cover all the bases, so:

- First base: I acknowledge the love and support of my husband, Ed, and my children, Bruce, Lisa, and David. I couldn't have gotten to first base without them.

- Second base: I acknowledge the understanding and consideration of friends and special colleagues, particularly my dear friend and colleague Lory Fischler, for whom no request was too small and no task too much. There were times when I was halfway home and the game was delayed by rain; her constancy and support kept me in scoring position. I am also grateful to my C2 colleagues who understood my need for space, honored it, and stood by me.

- Third base: I acknowledge the wisdom and feedback of some smart people—Marge Smith, Amy Webb, and Martin Parks among them. When I was out in left field, they pulled me back with candor and thought-provoking advice. Their encouragement pushed me closer to home.

- Home plate: I acknowledge the guidance and assistance I received in completing this book. I thank Larry Daloz, a mentor and friend, for his keen insights and challenging questions. I appreciate Peter Koestenbaum's support and very gracious words in the Foreword. I pay special tribute to David Brightman, my editor, who is indeed a bright and patient soul; I thank him for his confidence. I am grateful to my development editor, Jan Hunter, and my permissions editor, Veronica Oliva, who waved me around to home.

Last but not least, I acknowledge my granddaughter, Tali, who brought joy and a happy ending to Mudville.

About the Author

Lois J. Zachary is president of Leadership Development Services, a Phoenix-based consulting firm that provides leadership development, coaching, education, and training for corporate and nonprofit organizations nationwide.

Zachary's innovative mentoring approaches and expertise in coaching leaders and their organizations in designing, implementing, and evaluating learner-centered mentoring programs have made her a nationally recognized expert in mentoring and an award-winning consultant. Zachary consults with multinational, Fortune 500 companies; national associations; and nonprofit, education, government, and health care clients to improve organizational leadership practices. Her approach of integrating sound principles of adult learning and development has been proven to enhance organizational effectiveness and improve business results. Her consultation services, workshops, seminars, and keynotes combine opportunity for self-reflection with interactive group learning and practical application. Individual and organizational clients value her skill at asking relevant, timely, and often challenging questions that stimulate new thinking and help organizations move to the next level.

Her previous, best-selling book, *The Mentor's Guide* (Jossey-Bass, 2000), has become the primary resource for organizations interested in promoting mentoring for leadership and learning. Additional publications include articles, columns, and monographs about mentoring, leadership and board development, staff development, consulting, and adult development and learning. She coedited *The Adult Educator as Consultant* (Jossey-Bass, 1993).

Zachary received her doctorate and master of arts degree in adult and continuing education from Columbia University. She holds a master of science degree in education from Southern Illinois University.

Part One

Taking Stock
Mentoring's Foundation

MENTORING IS NOT NEW. Informal mentoring relationships have existed for centuries. However, the concept of formal organizational mentoring *is* relatively new. When organizational mentoring first became popular in the mid-1970s, many considered mentoring programs just another management training fad. Some organizations ignored it, and others immediately got on the mentoring bandwagon for fear of missing out on something their competitors were doing right. Mentoring programs for select populations (mostly elite, high-potential and high-performance leaders) seemed to be the spirit of the day. Some programs were successful; others were not. The mentoring management fad seemed to fade away for a period of time, replaced by more "critical" programs.

A decade later, many more organizations began to focus on mentoring as a vehicle for transferring or handing down organizational knowledge from one generation to another. The predominant model was the mentor as "sage on the stage," with the mentee's role a passive receiver of knowledge.

Since then, the practice of mentoring has evolved in lock step with the expanding knowledge of how to best facilitate learning. Mentoring practice has shifted from a product-oriented model (characterized by transfer of knowledge) to a process-oriented relationship (involving knowledge acquisition, application, and critical reflection). The hierarchical transfer of knowledge and information from an older, more experienced person to a younger, less experienced person is no longer the prevailing mentoring paradigm.

Organizations engage in mentoring for a number of business reasons, many of which relate to the need to cultivate or manage knowledge and relationships. The emphasis is not on making available a mentoring program but supporting mentoring efforts throughout the organization.

The best chance for fulfilling the promise of mentoring within organizations today, I believe, lies in creating a mentoring culture. Organizations must create readiness, provide opportunities, and build in support so that mentoring can have a profound, deep, and enduring impact on their people. The extent to which an organization can accomplish this depends on its ability to take stock. Creating a mentoring culture begins with looking in the organizational mirror: reflecting on people and processes, culture, and the vision of what your organization might become. Every organization has its own unique ways of conducting business. In any organization, "the way things get done" is demonstrated in thought and deed every day. For a mentoring culture to be sustained, the mentoring effort, the culture, and the organizational practices must be aligned with one another. Taking stock begins with full understanding of mentoring and the mentoring process.

What Is Mentoring, Anyway?

Mentoring is best described as a reciprocal and collaborative learning relationship between two (or more) individuals who share mutual responsibility and accountability for helping a mentee work toward achievement of clear and mutually defined learning goals. Learning is the fundamental process, purpose, and product of mentoring. Building, maintaining, and growing a relationship of mutual responsibility and accountability is vital to keeping the learning focused and on track.

Mentoring often involves skillful coaching. Although the two terms *mentoring* and *coaching* are often used interchangeably, it is important to understand the difference. They are two distinct practices, but in process very much kindred spirits; ideally, they work together to support organizational learning.

Mentoring, at its fullest, is a self-directed learning relationship, driven by the learning needs of the mentee. It is more process-oriented than service-driven and may focus on broader, "softer," intangible issues as learning goals (getting to know the corporate culture) as well as "harder," more tangible goals (learning how to manage one's direct reports). Generally speaking, there is more *mutual* accountability in a mentoring relationship than in a coaching relationship. Both mentoring and coaching focus on expanding individual potential by enhancing development and performance success. Coaching focuses more on boosting performance and skill enhancement; mentoring, on achievement of personal or professional development goals. Mentoring relationships are voluntary (they may be assigned and enhanced by individual preparation and training but are not-for-hire); in contrast, coaching relationships are often (but not always) contractual (for pay). Coaching is a burgeoning professional field with certification, established ethical standards, and protocols of practice. Coaches are often hired outside an organization, while mentors usually come from within the organization. Although there are many mentoring best practices one can point to, mentoring lacks standardization and is not a professional field of practice (even though professionals practice it). Mentoring relationships evolve organically over time. The type and number of people involved in a mentoring relationship can vary (from formal mentoring to informal group mentoring or peer mentoring, for example), and multiple learning opportunities (shadowing, project development, conferences, meetings) are used in a mentoring relationship. In contrast, most coaching is carried out one-to-one, typically using one or two learning venues.

How individuals and organizations define mentoring depends on past history, training, and experiences. Without establishing some common enriches the vibrancy and productivity of an organization and the people within it.

Creating a mentoring culture enables an organization to enrich the learning that takes place throughout the organization; leverage its energy; and better use and maximize its time, effort, and resources. Launching a mentoring program without simultaneously creating a mentoring culture reduces its long-term effectiveness and sustainability and decreases the likelihood that a program or programs will grow and thrive over time.

A mentoring culture sustains a continuum of expectation, which in turn creates standards and consistency of good mentoring practice. A mentoring culture is a powerful mechanism for achieving cultural alignment.

How Do We Start?

The chapters of Part One help you take stock and prepare your organization to actively engage in the work of creating a mentoring culture. Chapter One illustrates the importance of embedding mentoring in an organization's culture. Using the fictional example of Ideal Organization, we see what a successfully implemented, integrated, and aligned mentoring culture might look like in practice and how the phases of a mentoring relationship progress. Chapter Two presents tools to help you take stock of your organization's culture as it currently exists. It introduces a framework for connecting the mentoring program to the culture and what you want for your organization. Chapter Three helps you focus on the future and sets out a model for effective change. It offers strategies for planning and aligning mentoring initiatives and then going forward with implementing those plans.

Creating a mentoring culture is a work-in-progress. To begin the process, let's get started by seeing why mentoring works best when embedded in the culture.

Chapter 1

Mentoring, Embedded in the Culture

Along the way

places and people

planted seeds in my soul and in my spirit

and added stones to the foundation

I was trying to form

—LISA FAIN

AN ORGANIZATION'S CULTURE profoundly influences its people, processes, and business practices. Its impact is felt and expressed daily, in many ways. Culture also has explanatory value. It explains why things are done in a specific way in an organization, and why specific rituals, language, stories, and customs are shared. In addition to explaining behaviors, culture also sets boundaries and offers stability. Culture is rooted in behavior based on shared values, assumptions, and practices and processes, all of which live within a mentoring culture.

Mentoring requires a culture to support its implementation and fully integrate it into the organization. Without cultural congruence, the challenge of embedding mentoring into the organization is daunting. Any mentoring effort will continuously face challenges that have an impact on its viability and sustainability. For example, an organizational culture that fosters learning strengthens mentoring; if learning is not valued, learning is stifled and mentoring efforts are undermined. As the work of creating a mentoring culture unfolds, mentoring integrates itself more deeply into the organization's culture and becomes embedded in the fabric of the culture. Alignment between the organizational culture and the mentoring effort must be well established in order to promote cultural integration.

A congruent organizational culture becomes the placeholder for mentoring by maintaining its presence on the organizational agenda. It helps ensure its viability and sustainability by making mentoring a cultural expectation and organizational competence. Mentoring is so tightly woven into the fabric of organizational life that it seamlessly informs the way business is accomplished.

In this chapter, we examine some of the more compelling reasons mentoring works best when it is embedded in organizational culture. We see how a fully embedded mentoring process might look in an ideal scenario and look at what mentoring is in the real world of today.

The Importance of Embedding Mentoring in the Culture

The importance of embedding mentoring in the organization's culture cannot be overemphasized. Today more organizations are embracing mentoring than ever before, because it adds value for organizations, individuals within the organization, and others with whom they interact. There are compelling business reasons to warrant the effort. Embedding mentoring into an organization's culture

- Establishes ownership. It ensures that mentoring is vested in the many rather than the few. People outside the immediate circle of implementation feel a sense of ownership and responsibility and hold others accountable.

- Promotes shared responsibility. The success of mentoring is explicitly linked to the organization's wider strategic agenda.

- Maximizes resources. Duplication of time, effort, and dollars is minimized because mentoring is integrated with the organization's infrastructure.

- Maintains integrity. Cultural integration helps maintain the integrity of the mentoring practice by ensuring that there is always readiness, opportunity, and support for mentoring.

- Facilitates knowledge utilization. Cultural integration enables an organization to create opportunities to integrate new learning and leverage knowledge gained as a direct result of mentoring.

- Supports integration of key processes into the organization. Mentoring competencies such as feedback and goal setting often improve performance throughout an organization because of the insights gleaned from mentoring training and practice.

- Creates openness to learning through mentoring. People trust mentoring because they know it is a valued practice and see it demonstrated daily.

- Shortens ramp up time. Cultural congruence facilitates creation of a mentoring culture because there is always a level of readiness in the culture.

Some of the many mentoring benefits for individuals are accelerated learning, expanded and diverse perspectives, increased tacit organizational knowledge, additional insights about other business units, and improved skills in specific areas (for example, listening, or building relationships). Mentoring also offers individuals a trusted sounding board, role model, or go-to individual. Individuals often say that as a result of mentoring they feel more self-aware and self-confident; they are more closely connected to the organization, and they find work more satisfying and meaningful.

Not surprisingly, the mentoring benefits realized by individuals redound to the organization on a larger scale. A mentoring culture helps people meet adaptive challenges (Heifetz and Linsky, 2002); it facilitates new learning and organizational resiliency in the face of rapid change. Because it is tethered to the organization's culture, it contributes to organizational stability by managing knowledge and facilitating communication. If workers find work more meaningful and satisfying, retention and organizational commitment are increased, ultimately saving on the costs of rehiring. Increased confidence results in improved performance and quality of work. Individuals become more adept at risk taking. The more positive attitude contributes to increased trust and morale. Expanded perspectives trigger more global and visionary thinking. Mentoring helps manage and maximize knowledge, connecting and pooling pockets of organizational knowledge that strengthen and speed up organizational learning. It facilitates leadership development by building the internal capacity of leadership. Mentoring humanizes the workplace by building relationships of head, heart, and soul.

The benefits of mentoring can have a profound impact on those whom an organization touches: its customers, clients, and the community. The learning gained through mentoring has a ripple effect because it affects others, including those outside of the mentoring relationship. It helps people build new relationships and strengthen existing ones; people become more collaborative in their performance and learning, and individuals feel more prepared to offer themselves as mentors to others.

An Ideal Scenario

The benefits of embedding mentoring in an organizational culture and the mentoring best practices that contribute to creating a mentoring culture are showcased in Ideal Organization*, an example drawn from the best practices of mentoring cultures. Learning has long been a high priority at Ideal. The chief executive insists that all senior managers participate in annual executive training, hire an executive coach, and attend seminars at a nearby

---

Note: All names of companies, organizations, and schools used in this book are fictitious unless otherwise noted.

university. Their direct reports and all managers are required to complete at least thirty-five hours of continuing education annually; this requirement is tied directly to cash compensation and advancement.

The organization recently opened Ideal University (IU) to supply and manage all of its internal continuing education and training needs. This new line of business serves for-profit and nonprofit organizations in the vicinity of its corporate office. Ideal's blended learning programs, which combine state-of-the-art online and face-to-face learning venues, are highly regarded and often used by others to benchmark their organizational learning best practices.

Ideal's internal "Gateway to Learning" Website posts regularly updated information about IU programs and courses as well as a directory of external educational providers. In addition, Gateway houses self-assessment tools to facilitate analysis of individual learning needs and planning of self-directed learning programs. Employees who desire additional assistance access an online learning mentor who is trained to match employee development needs with educational institutions.

Mentoring is a cultural expectation at Ideal. The commitment to mentoring aligns with Ideal's core value of "building bridges of opportunity for employee development." Mentoring grew out of a formal program for high-potentials that began ten years ago. The program created such a buzz throughout the organization that the excitement it generated is still talked about today. The fact that so many "graduates" from the mentoring program commit to mentoring others and seek to initiate mentoring opportunities in their own organizations speaks to its continued success.

Several years ago, an organizational practice survey revealed that in addition to one-on-one informal mentoring and formal mentoring programs, multiple groups were actively engaged in mentoring on the corporate and local level, including women's executive mentoring, technical mentoring, and cross-functional mentoring. Currently, 87 percent of all employees are engaged in at least one informal or formal mentoring relationship. Those who participate in mentoring take it very seriously. Leaders regard it as part of their role as leader to informally mentor employees who show promise.

Today, all new employees are assigned mentors to help them navigate the organization and familiarize them with Ideal's history, values, practices, and policies. Most new employee matches are made using an automated mentoring tool to ensure an optimal learning match. Mentors must attend trainings and are given a list of topics and timelines for covering specific organizational content during the first year of a new hire's employment. At their first annual review, many new employees voice appreciation for the experience and remark on how quickly the mentoring program enabled them to feel confident, comfortable, and connected to the organization. Mentoring has given them an opportunity to connect with more people and to jump-start their productivity. Once launched, many choose to participate in a formal mentoring group or one-on-one relationship and to find an informal mentor.

All employees, not just new hires, are encouraged to seek mentoring partners and build mentoring partnerships. Everyone knows how and where to find mentoring partners when they need them. Ideal has its own virtual mentoring center, which periodically posts "mentoring want ads." An online mentor directory assists mentees who want to self-select mentors to help them achieve their learning goals. Human resource specialists or department heads make themselves available to help facilitate mentoring selection and matching.

Senior executives lead the way by finding internal and external mentors to expand their perspective and increase their technical knowledge. Internally, these same executives facilitate mentoring groups and formally and informally mentor employees. One of Ideal's best practices in this regard is group mentoring sessions; they are so widespread that they are a familiar item on monthly staff meeting agendas. Group mentoring is clearly seen as a valued-added tool for leveraging mentoring success from one department to another. A system is being established so that mentoring can be used to teach best practices across the organization as a new line of business is rolled out.

A full-time mentoring director and support staff are charged with managing, supporting, and coordinating mentoring efforts at Ideal. They monitor progress, measure results, and work with teams throughout the organization to integrate mentoring process improvements. In addition to keeping an internal focus on mentoring, these people work hard at ensuring that all mentoring programs align with each other and with the organizational culture.

An annual "mentoring boot camp" is available to employees who choose to advance their knowledge about the mentoring process, improve their mentoring skills and relationships, or network with other employees who may be potential mentors. Each year a keynote speaker kicks off the week at camp, setting the tone and theme for the week. In addition, a basic core curriculum is offered through IU, consisting of skill building and mentoring-specific content courses that align internally with the content of other IU courses. Advanced mentoring and refresher modules are offered cyclically.

Approximately 15 percent of Ideal's managers are certified mentoring coaches and often initiate mentoring events in their own departments.

Mentoring coaches must commit to annually upgrading personal mentoring knowledge and practice by attending twenty hours of continuing education as well as meeting once a month as a peer mentoring group.

As good as Ideal's mentoring culture and practices are, the picture was not always so rosy. There were false starts resulting from disparate assumptions about what mentoring is and ought to be. Leadership musical chairs at the top of the organization restructured some of the original mentoring champions out of the organization, thus upending some of the initial efforts. Those who remained were convinced that mentoring would be another corporate fad and didn't feel fully committed to the mentoring planning work they had been charged to deliver. The team regrouped several times and finally created enough common ground to move forward. A task force studied Ideal's culture to determine how to best align the program with corporate values and mission. It was clear to everyone that to successfully launch mentoring, Ideal's culture required a means for financially motivating and rewarding participation. Today, mentoring is so embedded in the culture that the financial incentives have disappeared, and emphasis is placed mainly on public reward and recognition.

Ten years ago, Ideal's technological capacity was quite modest. The mentoring pool was harder to identify, and making matches was a nightmare. Ideal had to struggle with the complex process initially set in place to make it manageable. As the organization grew, so did the capacity of its technology. Overcoming resistance to using technology for the very human task of matching mentor and mentee was difficult. At first, it seemed far too complicated. Yet over time technology has become the primary mentoring communication vehicle, offering a fast and expedient way to collect data, disseminate results, and make information about mentoring readily available throughout the organization. Monthly e-bulletins and quarterly e-newsletters about mentoring are distributed on line.

Initially, the task of establishing feedback and evaluation systems was a struggle. The competitive nature of Ideal's culture led to mistrust, fear of how the data might be used, and anxiety about the repercussions that might follow if confidentiality were ever breached. Today, feedback is a critical component in ensuring that learning from each phase is incorporated into the next phase. The mentoring director and her team methodically gather regular feedback, which in turn enables best practices to be shared and process improvements to be implemented.

Annual surveys reveal that mentoring, both formal and informal, has had a tremendous influence on Ideal's bottom line. Because employees are integrating their learning, they end up working smarter and faster. This enabled one group to close a major deal (beating out a competitor) that will generate revenue for several years. The speed and quality of the group's proposal process continues to yield major dividends that are directly attributable to the mentoring they have received at Ideal. These are not isolated experiences. In fact, mentoring is seen by many as the main impetus for a steady rise in productivity over the last four years.

Employees report increased collaboration; they are able to better navigate the organization because they know more about it. The retention rate is consistently high. Many point to mentoring relationships as a critical satisfier for them at work. People are committed to the organization; they feel valued by it and value relationships they have formed. They say that the opportunity to engage in cross-cultural mentoring made them feel more comfortable with and connected to one another, and more effective in developing and maintaining relationships with customers from around the globe. There has been a subtle shift from a once internally competitive culture to a trusting and collaborative one.

Ideal continues to build bridges of opportunity internally and externally. It offers reward and recognition to departments that build such bridges by creating innovative mentoring opportunities with demonstrable results. A once-a-year occasion, called "Building Bridges of Opportunity Through Mentoring," is dedicated to celebration of mentoring excellence, personal and organizational mentoring milestones, and recognition of mentoring bridge builders at Ideal. A new corporate bridge-building initiative includes formation of a strategic alliance with six external organizations to create a mentoring consortium for sharing best mentoring practices.

Mentoring at Ideal is always in motion. The continuous momentum builds learning bridges to the future through mentoring and empowers individuals to transform Ideal to live up to its name. Ideal did not arrive here in one leap; it had to work through a number of steps and phases in developing its mentoring culture.

Phases of a Mentoring Relationship

Understanding the predictable cycle of the mentoring relationship helps organizations meet the learning and relationship needs that may require support from the organization and its culture. The four phases—preparing, negotiating, enabling, and coming to closure—build on one another to form a developmental sequence. The length of each phase varies with the relationship and is influenced by the culture.

The preparing phase incorporates two components: self-preparation and relationship preparation. Training, materials, and coaching are often needed to get a relationship started off on the right foot.

The work of the second phase, negotiating, results in well-defined learning goals, success criteria and measurement, delineation of mutual responsibility, accountability, protocols for addressing stumbling blocks, consensual mentoring agreement, and a workplan for achieving learning goals. HR can support the goal-setting process by coaching on goal setting or helping to ensure that the learning goal aligns with other development goals.

Most of the work of the relationship is accomplished in the third, and typically longest, phase of enabling. The enabling phase offers the greatest opportunity for learning and development, yet mentoring partners often face challenges during this time that make them vulnerable to relationship derailment. This is the phase where support in the way of networking and sharing best practices is most helpful.

The final phase, coming to closure, presents a dynamic learning opportunity for mentors and mentees to process their learning and move on, regardless of whether a mentoring relationship has been positive. The focus of coming to closure is on reaching a learning conclusion so that learning is elevated to the next level of application and integration. Success is celebrated, the relationship is redefined, and mentoring partners move on. Just-in-time training to support mentoring partners as they prepare the relationship for closure helps ensure a good experience. An organized mentoring celebration affords the opportunity to share best practices, encouraging networking around mentoring and supporting people as they take their learning to the next level.

The people at Ideal understand the phases of the mentoring cycle and the importance of embedding mentoring within the culture at large. They know, from experience, that mentoring requires a lot of work, from the organization and the individuals. They know, also from experience, how worthwhile the effort is.

Embedding Mentoring: Reflection on Practice

Whether your organization is large or small, it is important to be able to stand back and look at your organizational culture analytically—to be fully aware of the "soul" and "spirit" that forms its cultural foundation. Without some degree of cultural consciousness, it is impossible to do the cultural due diligence required to embed mentoring into your organization. Effective mentoring initiatives can and do exist without the support of an established mentoring culture, but inevitably they require more work, a longer ramp-up time, and unwavering and conscientious persistence to maintain and ensure programmatic growth and long-term continuity. The struggle to create a mentoring culture—the challenge—can actually drive the alignment process. The struggle will be continuous unless mentoring itself is congruent with the culture and has meaning for it. Creating a mentoring culture is well worth the effort, especially in a world in which constant learning and change are the foundation.

Chapter 2

Connecting Culture and Mentoring

> The first step in finding your way somewhere is to discover where you are, to begin with.
>
> —POLLY BERENDS (1990, p. 8)

THE IMPACT OF CULTURE is omnipresent; it has both a conscious and an unconscious influence on human behavior (Kotter, 1996; Schein, 1992, 1999; Galpin, 1996; Phelan, 1996). It influences what and how individuals think (their assumptions and mental models), what they say (their philosophy and values), and what they do (their behavior). Similarly, an organization has a culture that influences closely held assumptions about the organization and the people within it, values, and practices and process. Yet most organizations and their leaders remain unconscious of its powerful and dominant influence.

Grounding the Work

Creating a mentoring culture begins by engaging in a discovery process to solidly ground the work of mentoring. The discovery process focuses on understanding the dynamics of an organization's culture from multiple perspectives and determining its cultural readiness for mentoring. Discovery includes raising cultural consciousness, mapping the culture, understanding cultural ecology, identifying cultural anchors, establishing the learning anchor, testing for cultural congruence, and deciding to move forward. Some organizations begin the process of creating a mentoring culture with cultural consciousness and a well-established learning anchor already intact. Some have minimal awareness and lack understanding of the dynamics of their culture. Some have thoroughly considered the cultural fit of mentoring within their organization; others have never considered the impact of culture. If your organization has made progress along this continuum, you might skim through the first few sections that follow; if that's not the case, you'll need to take the time to assess your organization's readiness for learning. As in any discovery process, knowing "where you are, to begin with" may reveal some surprises, validate some hunches, and open up new possibilities. Focus on what is doable and appropriate to your organizational context, and remember that the task of grounding the work is best addressed in conversation with others.

Raising Cultural Consciousness

If there was any doubt that culture matters, consider this illustration of the pervasiveness and explanatory power of culture. An accounting firm of fifty certified public accountants (we'll call it Alpha Organization) was founded seven years ago by five ambitious, smart, and charismatic men who had worked for a large accounting firm in a nearby city. The founders brought the command-and-control culture of their previous employer to Alpha. Today, decision making is closely held, and the five founders exert a heavy hand in operations out front and behind the scenes. Those within the organization describe the culture as a no-nonsense, impersonal, entrenched, highly individualized culture of "boutique silos." Each CPA is expected to function independently and conform to the standards and practices of the firm, including a requisite number of billable hours. Most of the interaction among the accountants is done via fax and e-mail; in fact, all communication other than annual reviews is done by way of memos. The language of the culture is straightforward and no-nonsense. People treat each other courteously and with respect. Employees who produce are treated well. Those who don't get fired or leave volitionally.

There are many small cliques within the firm, and most of the accountants would agree that they don't know many of the other CPAs. Few "corporate" events or celebrations are held. All that counts are productivity and dollars generated. The firm's governance is locked-door and legislated.

This description reflects the culture and explains (1) why new employees might experience difficulty integrating into the Alpha firm, (2) why an accountant from another firm might not understand a colleague's resistance to teaming on a new matter, and (3) some of the potential hurdles Alpha might face in setting up a mentoring program.

Becoming more attuned to organizational culture is a positive step toward gaining cultural consciousness. Lack of cultural consciousness results in wasted human and financial resources. Deep understanding of the culture requires an expenditure of time and effort since culture is inherently complex; yet the return on the investment can be significant.

Organizational culture and the assumptions that go along with it have been studied in great depth by Edgar Schein (1999), Timothy Galpin (1996), and John Kotter (1996). In short, cultural consciousness isn't about what gets accomplished in an organization. It is about how it gets accomplished—the specific assumptions (what people think consciously or unconsciously—their mental models), values (what people say—the philosophy and mission), and behaviors (what people do—the practices and processes they use) that inform practice. These factors in turn have an impact on how mentoring is experienced in the organization.

Mapping Organizational Culture

The Spanish philosopher and politician Jose Ortega y Gasset is quoted as saying, "Tell me what you pay attention to and I will tell you who you are." A mapping of culture defines what an organization pays attention to. It is a handle for understanding a system that is as unique as a fingerprint (Phelan, 1996) and yet inherently more complex. One way to align individual mental models about corporate culture (Senge, 1990) is with a map of current reality. This map becomes a tool to focus thoughtful discussion about future alignment of the current culture.

Mental models are "semi-permanent tacit maps" (Senge and others, 1994, p. 237) that consist of the unexamined stories, images, and assumptions we hold about the world in which we live. They inform what we think, how we act, and what we do. One of the core tasks of "the fifth discipline" (Senge, 1990) is to surface mental models by reflecting on the assumptions we hold so that we can validate what we believe with current reality.

The challenge of understanding cultural complexity is enormous—and one that we need to embrace, because it influences and permeates the work we do at every level of our organizations, formally and informally (Schein, 1999). The map of a culture paints a picture of an organization as a whole. How are things done in an organization? What are the habits? What is it that people think (their cultural assumptions), say (their espoused values and beliefs), and do (how their assumptions and values are expressed in terms of behavior, practices, and processes)? Exhibit 2.1 illustrates input information for a cultural map for Alpha Organization, where each person is focused on the bottom line.

A blank version of the form used for Alpha is in Exercise 2.1, Cultural Mapping; use it as a guide to examine the layers of your own culture. First complete the exercise individually or as a group. Try to gather diverse perspectives. To deepen the process, you may want to conduct focus groups to gather data. Make sure you allot enough time to analyze results and note synergies and gaps. In time you may find that the same themes repeat themselves from group to group.

EXHIBIT 2.1

Cultural Mapping: Alpha Organization

Cultural Dynamic	Descriptors from the Culture
Think What are cultural assumptions, beliefs, and mental models about our organization's culture?	*I need to generate X dollars.* *Productivity is important.* *The bottom line is all that really counts around here.* *I really need to keep my nose to the grindstone.* *I can't afford to socialize too much with others around here or I won't be able to make my numbers.*
Say What are the espoused values, philosophy, and mission of our organization?	*Productivity should be rewarded.* *We do whatever it takes to satisfy our clients.* *The fewer people involved in governance, the easier it is to keep control.* *We don't encourage fraternization of employees.*
Do How do cultural assumptions and espoused values get played out on a daily basis? What behaviors, norms, language, rituals, processes, and practices describe our culture?	*We are a formal culture.* *We are a formal culture. Everyone is left to do his or her own job without intervention, unless there is a problem.* *Interpersonal communication is fairly impersonal and mostly accomplished through fax or e-mail.* *There is no venue for sharing best practices or professional development.* *Many employees have never met one another.*

Corporate culture is, by definition, sui generis. At the same time, it is embedded in a system of differentiated subcultures that combine to form a larger, more complex system of interrelated cultures. Subcultures exist in layers and "nest" within a larger organizational context. Nested cultures share many of the same espoused values, cultural assumptions, and established processes and practices. Yet each is held together by its own cultural glue, consisting of assumptions, values, and practices and processes. Understanding the dynamics at play within an organization rests on awareness of the nested cultures that contribute to the organization's culture as a whole. They may or may not be reflected in the structural framework of the organization.

EXERCISE 2.1

Cultural Mapping

Instructions: Describe how each cultural dynamic is expressed or demonstrated in your organization. Review your answers and determine the consistency of practice among the dynamics. Where do gaps occur? Where are the synergies?

Cultural Dynamic	Descriptors
Think What are the cultural assumptions, beliefs, and mental models about our organization's culture?	
Say What are the espoused values, philosophy, and mission of our organization?	
Do How do cultural assumptions and espoused values get played daily? What behaviors, norms, language, rituals, processes, and practices describe our culture?	

Yours may be a culture of few subcultures or many. Drawing an organizational map of nested cultures can help you analyze the dynamics of the system of cultures operating with your organization. For example, even though there appear to be similarities within the entire culture of Alpha, there are variations on those themes in its nested cultures. These variations offer an opportunity for the company to find venues for building cross-functional relationships that would maximize the strengths of each and establish a sense of wholeness in the organization. Mentoring might be such a venue.

To begin the process in your organization, start where you are (including the information you gathered in Exercise 2.1) and build outward—expecting revisions. The size of your culture map depends on the size and complexity of your organization. The intention is for this exercise to be a work in progress. You don't want to overanalyze, but you do want to define the current reality. To do this, you should get feedback and input from others to check on the validity of your own assumptions. Recognition of the diverse cultures (formal and informal) that exist within an organization—what each looks like and contributes to the greater culture—deepens understanding of the culture and identifies opportunities and readiness for mentoring as well. Once you feel comfortable with your map of nested cultures, you are ready to explore the dynamics of those cultures.

Understanding the Cultural Ecology of the Organization

Cultural consciousness involves more than understanding cultural assumptions, espoused values, and established practices and processes. Grounding the work for mentoring also requires knowledge of what Maxine Greene calls the interstices (1988) and Marilyn Ferguson (1980) names "the place in between." An understanding of cultural ecology (Zachary, 2000; Daloz, 1999)—the "surround sound" and "undiscussables" of what is going on in the background of the culture—provides clues about other factors affecting the organization. Examples are reorganization, talk of merger or acquisition, leadership succession or transition, political climate, power plays. Whenever ecology is ignored, dismissed, or disregarded it eventually ends up costing time and money to get back on track.

Exercise 2.2, Identifying the Ecology of Your Organization, presents a framework to help identify organizational ecology. It involves asking and considering two sets of questions: (1) What keeps people awake at night? What worries them? What problems do they puzzle over? (2) What gets people going in the morning? What are they energized and excited about at work?

Identifying the Ecology of Your Organization

Instructions: Identify what is going on in the organization's ecology that could potentially affect your mentoring efforts. In the space in question one, describe what they worry about or puzzle over. In the space in two, identify what energizes and excites people at work. For each item you identify, describe the potential to directly affect mentoring, the potential to indirectly affect mentoring, and implications of each factor for organizational mentoring.

	Direct Impact on Mentoring	Indirect Impact on Mentoring	Implications for Action
1. What keeps people awake at night?			
2. What are people energized and excited about?			

Once you have identified internal and external surround sound and undiscussables, consider the implications and impact each factor could potentially have on organizational mentoring efforts. An analysis of cultural ecology is a useful tool for anticipating and proactively addressing resistance and pressure you may encounter while creating a mentoring culture. It also increases awareness of how to help jump-start mentoring efforts.

Identifying Cultural Anchors

Cultural anchors are the moorings of an organization's culture to which a program, process, or initiative is tethered. Without strong cultural anchors, an organization may embark on or engage in organizational mentoring but easily drift away from its intended purpose. Mentoring, when unconnected to something larger than itself, gets buffeted by changing tides and sometimes even cast out to sea. Cultural anchors help stay the course and ensure cultural congruence. They are inextricably linked to an organization's cultural assumptions; espoused values; and established behavior, practices and processes, and ecology.

The cultural anchor for Ideal Organization is learning and development. In fact, it prides itself on its reputation as a learning organization. Growth and development targets are set for each employee, who then selects appropriate learning modalities to accomplish her targets. Some choose coaching, some training, some e-learning, some mentoring, and others a combination thereof. Every employee is guaranteed one day a month for training and development activities. An hour is set aside every Friday at noon for employees in each department to share how they are applying their learning.

In contrast, a local management consulting firm decided to institute mentoring throughout its organization. Having completed their cultural groundwork, they discovered that there was so much cultural dissonance among divisions that it would be a mistake to roll out a one-program-fits-all to the entire organization. Instead the organization focused on launching its mentoring program in the division that was most like the culture they wanted to create.

As you review Exercise 2.1, you may find that there are clear, common cultural threads that run throughout the organization. If not, your task may be to discover a likely starting point. Once you have created an organizational map and compared the nested cultures within your organization, you are ready to begin identifying common culture threads; these lead you to cultural anchors. Grounding the work in the culture is a prerequisite to sustainability for organizational mentoring. It takes time, conversation, and analysis to understand the many factors at play. A cultural anchor in learning is the leverage point for mentoring.

Establishing the Learning Anchor

Without the presence of a learning anchor, it is virtually impossible to create a sustainable mentoring culture. Mentoring must be grounded in the anchor of individual and organizational learning. Learning constitutes the grounding for systems thinking, for process improvements, and for strategy. Both individual and organizational learning must be grounded in sound learning practices and principles. These very practices and principles inform action, whether it is taking mentoring (or any other initiative) from idea to development, or to implementation or evaluation.

Knowles's framework for understanding how adults learn is just as relevant to organizational learning as it is to individual learning. According to Knowles:

- Adults have to know why they need to learn something before undertaking it.

- Adults have a self-concept of being responsible for their own decisions, for their own lives.

- Life's reservoir of experience is a primary learning resource for adults.

- Readiness for learning increases when there is a specific need to know.

- Adult learners have an inherent need for immediacy of application.

- Adults respond best to learning when they are internally motivated to learn. (See Knowles, 1980, pp. 43–46; Knowles, Holton, and Swanson, 1998, pp. 64–69.)

Take some time to evaluate the extent to which your organization adheres to principles of adult learning as espoused by Knowles. Certainly his is not the only theory of adult learning, but it is the seminal work that informs much of current theory. You need to consider whether these principles are reflected in daily practice in your organization. If they are not, you have some work ahead of you.

By the mid-1990s, learning no longer "belonged" strictly to academe. Organizations began to formally claim learning as their own. Organizational learning became imperative in order to grow people, stay competitive, and achieve business results. The learning organization (Senge, 1990) became a fixture in organizational life, and organizations began investing in the concept of the corporate university (Meister, 1998). As learning gained a foothold, the concept of a teaching organization began to emerge. Organizations discovered that applying adult learning theory to organizational learning had a multiplier effect, resulting in the budding, building, and boosting of relationships.

A learning organization positions learning as a core asset (Knowles, Holton, and Swanson, 1998, p. 141). Its focus is on capacity building. There are many operational definitions that speak to this point (Garvin, 1993; Senge, 1990; Tobin, 1993; Watkins and Marsick, 1993) but few organizational archetypes. Senge (1990) popularized the concept and envisioned the learning organization as the paradigm shift needed to fuel organizational transformation. Together with his colleagues, he developed *The Fifth Discipline Fieldbook* (Senge and others, 1994), a toolkit to enable organizations to create their own individualized learning organization.

The core of learning organization work is based on Senge's five learning disciplines: personal mastery, mental models, shared vision, team learning, and systems thinking. According to Watkins and Marsick (1993), continuous learning takes place at all levels of a learning organization—individual, team, and organizational. Six action imperatives characterize the learning organization: "creating continuous learning opportunities, promoting inquiry and dialogue, encouraging collaboration and team learning, establishing systems to capture and share learning, empowering people toward a collective vision, and connecting the organization to its environment" (p. 11).

For Daniel Tobin, a learning organization requires reeducating the corporation so that "ideas and solutions come from everyone in the company, no matter what their functions, job descriptions or locations. The organization taps into the cumulative knowledge of its entire value chain, suppliers and customers included, to create value" (1993, p. 4). The key is to create a learning environment in which employees constantly pursue learning. Tobin identifies five foundations for the learning organization, which together create "a proper learning environment": "visible leadership, 'thinking' literacy, overcoming functional myopia, building and sustaining effective 'learning' teams, and managers as enablers" (p. 166).

The learning organization is a compelling concept that has gained currency and momentum over the last decade. Watkins and Marsick (1993), Senge (1990), and Tobin (1993) take different but entirely complementary approaches to understanding the dynamics of a learning organization. Together these models paint a picture of what is required in terms of action, processes, and outcomes to create a learning organization.

Use the questions given here as a guide to help you steer reflective conversation about the learning that goes on in your organization. The focus of the discussion should be on promoting shared understanding so that you can apply your insights as you begin to create a mentoring culture.

- How would you describe the learning style of your organization, your department, your team? How are those learning styles demonstrated? What similarities and differences exist among the organization, department, and team?

- What opportunities for learning exist within your organization? within your department? your team?

- What organizational systems and practices help sustain learning in your organization?

- What gets in the way of effective learning in your organization?

Applying lessons learned is the crux of action learning. When lessons learned are used to inform planning and implementation, they enrich the process and the product—whether it is mentoring or anything else. Reflecting on lessons learned from your past experiences, positive or negative, is a catalyst for learning. Begin by listing the major organizational projects, initiatives, and changes that have occurred over the past several years. Take care not to evaluate items as you list them. Use the items on your list to inform your thinking as you answer these questions:

- What lessons, positive or negative, have you learned from your experience initiating and implementing organizational initiatives?

- What key issues is your agency or organization dealing with now, or in the foreseeable future, that could possibly affect your work in creating a mentoring culture?

- Where are you likely to find the greatest resistance?

If you are part of a small organization, you can answer these questions on your own to gain greater insight. It is best done, however, in a group setting, with the exercise first completed individually. Answers to the reflection questions are then shared round-robin or used to brainstorm ideas. With a larger group, this exercise can be completed in teams first and then shared. The point is to come up with a solid list of criteria that can be turned into a checklist to guide creation of a mentoring process.

Exhibit 2.2 illustrates how one organization maximized the lessons learned from previous experiences. They turned their lessons-learned questions into a checklist and used it to guide and monitor their mentoring planning process. The checklist became a helpful reminder to help keep them focused and on track and not to fall back into old habits.

EXHIBIT 2.2

Application of Lessons Learned

This exhibit demonstrates how lessons learned were converted into a checklist to ensure conscious application of lessons learned to the process of developing and implementing a mentoring initiative.

Has our mentoring initiative taken lessons learned into account?

Lesson Learned	Yes/No	Suggestions for Improvement
Need to be inclusive	No	We need to let people know this is a pilot and that our intention is to learn from the experience and offer opportunities to others.
Give it time to take hold	No	We need to hold back on other initiatives and slow things down for a while.
Get group feedback	Yes	And we need to go broader and deeper on this. Jenny will come up with a strategy by the next meeting.
Spend time getting people on board	No	By our next meeting we'd better attend to this. Mark has agreed to develop presentation material and talking points by the next meeting.
Make involvement compelling	In progress	See above. Now that we're so excited, we've got to share that excitement.
Get buy-in at the top	Yes	That's what got us here in the first place.
Make resources available	Some	We're set financially, but we need to access other institutional resources. This should be easier once Mark and Jenny make the rounds.
Clearly define what we are doing	Yes	Our goals are crystal clear.

Have we avoided these pitfalls in our planning?

Lesson Learned	Yes/No	Suggestions for Improvement
Made mentoring seem like one more task	Somewhat	At first, mentoring seemed just another task. Now we are all invested. We've got to figure out what engaged us and make it feel like a priority for us.
Got to implementation too fast	Yes	We're really trying to think this one through—carefully.
Didn't articulate a clear vision	No	We are aware that this is a priority and we are working on it.
Failed to build a sustainable infrastructure	Yes	We were ensured funding for the next five years. Each department is represented.

Lesson Learned	Yes/No	Suggestions for Improvement
Didn't connect mentoring to the work of leadership	*No*	We've emphasized that mentoring is part of becoming a leader in the organization, but we haven't yet linked it to the work of current leaders.
Valuing the intangible as well as the tangible aspects	*Yes*	We've built in rewards and included a mentoring networking forum to create value and share best practices.
Didn't make sure what we are doing is universally understood	*No*	We are working on this.
Made it too structured	*Yes*	We've decided to use a facilitated process and encourage participants to avail themselves of the opportunity. People have to volunteer. We're not going to force it.
Overplanned for the exception	*Yes*	We've maintained our focus on the big picture.

Testing for Cultural Congruence

After identifying cultural anchors and establishing learning anchors, there is usually increased cultural consciousness about the organization. The next step is then to test for cultural congruence to see if there is a learning fit.

Cultural congruence does not mean that the entire organization has to be in alignment. If your organization lies within a larger organization structure and there is relative independence, you would likely focus on your organization, the nested cultures within it, and the ecology surrounding this culture to determine culture congruence.

As an example, consider Fox Trot Association, a nonprofit organization with seventeen chapters located throughout the United States. In its national office, which is the coordination and information center for its chapter affiliates, style of dress, attitude, and chain of command are assuredly formal. When members of chapter affiliates visit the national office, they remark that there is a big difference in how things get done in the affiliate chapters. The difference and uniqueness among the chapter affiliates is pronounced as well and is readily apparent to the diverse group of delegates who attend the annual conference. Each chapter functions independently. Some chapters serve college students; others predominantly attract retirees. Many chapters operate by a seat-of-the-pants culture. Although they espouse the same values and financially support the national office, they are quite slow to adopt national initiatives—if they do they adapt them. There is little patience for prescriptive oughts and shoulds. The reality is that Fox Trot is a collection of loosely linked cultures. There is little nesting of cultures, and the common link is financial. The only anchor among these diverse local organizations is their commitment to the mission of the organization. This commitment is strong enough to serve as a learning anchor for the organization at large. Similarly, Ideal Organization's well-established learning anchor was a key factor in continuously supporting its efforts to create a mentoring culture.

Deciding to Move Forward

Readiness to learn expands when there is an anchor for mentoring that is congruent with the existing culture. In fact, there is a direct relationship between the degree of cultural congruence and the time it takes to create a mentoring culture.

The experience at Ideal underscores the importance of establishing cultural congruence. At the very beginning of its mentoring efforts, Ideal had a number of false starts and had to regroup several times. Once it aligned the program with corporate values and mission, it was able to address the roadblocks that were getting in the way.

Ideal was a highly competitive culture with lots of employee rewards and incentives built into the system. Without incentives for mentoring, it was impossible to successfully launch mentoring. Neither evaluation (other than dollars generated) nor feedback were part of the culture. When it came down to anything soft (like relationships), resistance and skepticism often sabotaged the process before it began. The challenge was to grow mentoring so that that it would enrich the culture and at the same time be supported by it. It could not succeed without being in sync with the culture. Focusing first on areas with the most cultural congruence enabled Ideal to get mentoring on more solid footing so that people would trust it. People trusted it because mentoring made sense in the culture. This synergy enabled the planning and implementation process to move forward with integrity and coherence. For this to happen, Ideal's leaders needed a clear picture of where they wanted the organization to be.

The most common cultural anchors found in an organization with a sustainable mentoring culture today are learning, development, diversity, knowledge management, and leadership.

Where Do You Want to Be? Aligning Organizational and Mentoring Goals

Transparent alignment between mentoring and business goals builds a solid foundation to support the mentoring platform and strengthen organizational mentoring practices. For mentoring to gain credibility, the leadership at Ideal needed to align mentoring goals with the organization's business goals and strategy. This meant identifying the clear and precise business reasons for engaging in mentoring so that results could be measured. The value that it could potentially create for the company was self-evident.

Since I spend so much time sitting on runways, airport choreography is the image that first comes to mind as I think about alignment. Picture the dance that takes place when airplanes take off and land on the runway. A bird's-eye view reveals a complex series of simultaneous alignments. Precise timing and sequencing allow planes to take off and land safely. Symmetry of movement gives the necessary flexibility to allow each plane the space required to maneuver separately and yet move synchronously with others. Focus on direction makes it possible for planes to line up in an orderly fashion on a runway with noses pointing in the same direction. Leadership in the omnipresent control tower permits seamless orchestration. Nonnegotiable ground rules promote consistency of practice and independent judgment within specific parameters. In a mentoring culture, multiple components must work together reliably, seamlessly, and with efficiency. Alignment between goals and mentoring makes it possible for this to happen.

Connecting Culture and Mentoring: Reflection on Practice

Lack of cultural congruence—a cultural mismatch—is one of the primary reasons that mentoring fails to take hold in an organization. Far too many mentoring programs fail (or merely survive) because they were not sufficiently embedded in a supportive organizational culture. It is well worth taking the time to discover where you are to begin with and learn about your organizational culture. The understanding that emerges from this learning helps ensure that mentoring is fully embraced and sustainable.

If, despite a cultural mismatch with mentoring, the organization still wants to create a mentoring culture, a cultural anchor that supports the culture must be established. You must consider organizational horsepower and the amount of time and energy you are willing to invest in developing the people who are the lifeblood of the organization. If your organization does not value learning, it is going to take time. Even if a learning culture exists, it can take time if the prevalent values, assumptions, and behaviors are incompatible with mentoring.

At its core, mentoring is about learning. The needs of the individuals engaged in a mentoring culture on every level (as participants, planners, coordinators, leaders) must be considered, and adult learning needs must therefore be accommodated. Mentoring must honor the best principles and practices of adult learning to go forward with integrity. Then, with cultural congruence, a learning anchor, and specific goals in place, the traction for creating a mentoring culture can take hold. The next chapter lays out a roadmap to ease implementation of your plans.

Chapter 3

Planning Implementation

At each moment you choose the intentions that will shape your experiences and those things upon which you will focus your attention....
If you choose unconsciously, you evolve unconsciously. If you choose consciously, you evolve consciously.

—GARY ZUKAV, *THE SEAT OF THE SOUL*

THOSE WHO ENGAGE in planning implementation of mentoring must focus their attention on the cultural context in which mentoring takes place. The dynamics of culture affect how implementation work goes forward, regardless of the scope of the mentoring effort.

Ideal Organization (described in Chapter One) illustrates a flourishing mentoring culture that is well embedded in an organization. Ideal's initial expectations for mentoring continue to exceed expectations. Mentoring has permeated the entire organization; ownership is embraced across and through the organization. It has support from the top of the organization all the way down to its grass roots. By everyone's account, mentoring is hugely successful, and other organizations look to Ideal as a benchmarking organization.

Ideal's strategic commitments to organizational learning and employee development anchor its mentoring initiatives. Even when people are engaged in other learning activities and projects, mentoring remains a personal priority and responsibility. In fact, many individuals are involved in several types of mentoring relationships.

Mentoring has increased connectivity across and within the various layers of the organization. Regular mentoring networking sessions link people together who otherwise might have no reason to connect with one another. People come back from mentoring activities energized, excited, and filled with new and practical ideas.

Ideal's reputation for supporting new hires through mentoring has been a strong recruiting and retention tool. Employees know that there is support for them in the organization. The mentoring training process has strengthened existing feedback practices by teaching the feedback process, fostering safe opportunities to practice and hone skills, and reinforcing the importance of feedback as a personal process improvement tool. Those who support the mentoring efforts in a leadership, management, or coaching role are more engaged than ever in learning and mentoring and increase their long-term personal and professional commitment to the organization.

Organizations spend significant time in planning for mentoring implementation. In some, as in Ideal, mentoring programs continue to thrive and grow. In other organizations, mentoring efforts barely get off the ground: they are short-lived and achieve only a modicum of success. Some mentoring efforts roll out to great fanfare, raise the level of expectation, and suddenly disappear. Far too often, organizational mentoring programs fail (or merely survive) because their planning did not factor in the culture. A primary reason that mentoring fails to take root in an organization is lack of cultural congruence (a cultural mismatch). It can't be overstated: a cultural fit must exist between mentoring and the organization to achieving consistency of mentoring practices within an organization's culture.

As we have seen, culture is complex and mediated by many interacting elements. The implementation planning process acknowledges and honors this complexity. Understanding organizational culture offers important insights about whom to include in the planning and how to best engage them. Here are some questions to ask:

- Are the right people included and engaged in planning the work needed to create a mentoring culture?

- Is there a trusting climate among those doing the planning?

- Is planning, implementation, and follow through a deliberate and deliberative process?

Mentoring can, and often does, become an impetus for understanding culture and promoting culture change.

Readiness, Opportunity, and Support: A Model for Change

I use a model consisting of three elements—readiness, opportunity, and support (ROS)—as part of a disciplined approach and process tool for developing a mentoring culture. The ROS model can be used as a diagnostic tool in evaluating a mentoring initiative within an organization. It is also helpful in the planning process in that it frames three important questions:

1. How will we go about creating readiness for this initiative within the organization?

2. Which specific opportunities have we built in to engage people in mentoring?

3. Which structures and practices have we put in place to support mentoring?

Just as readiness to learn is necessary to facilitate adult learning, readiness is also essential in regard to organizational learning. In fact, readiness may be the most important element in the early development stage. Creating (and often recreating) readiness is also absolutely imperative for a mentoring culture and the mentoring initiatives that go on within it. This is particularly noteworthy when new players come on board and organizational circumstances change.

In a mentoring culture, learning opportunities abound. A business opportunity, a new CEO, loss of a customer, implementation of a new curriculum, relocation . . . any or all of these present a need and therefore an opportunity for organizational learning. A mentoring culture enhances substantive learning opportunities and uses action learning (learning about the learning as it takes place) to inform process improvements. A mentoring culture generates multiple learning opportunities, settings, and processes to foster cognitive, affective, and behavioral learning.

Organizational mentoring requires multiple supports, some visible to the eye and others not so. Daloz (1999) defines the functions necessary to support mentoring relationships as listening, giving structure, expressing positive expectations, serving as advocate, sharing ourselves, and making the learning relationship special. These are the same support functions that come to the fore when managing the mentoring process.

To use the ROS model in the planning process, consider these questions:

- On the basis of past experience, what are our strengths and weaknesses as an organization when it comes to creating readiness?

- What have we learned from our experience that helps us create readiness for mentoring in our organization?

- Which specific opportunities currently exist or are emerging to engage people in learning through mentoring?

- Which structures and practices currently exist that function particularly well to support learning?

- What additional structures and practices do we need to put in place to support mentoring?

If a mentoring culture already exists, the planning work is that much easier. Questions that should then be asked include:

- How is mentoring adding value to the institution? (Examples are retention of key players, development of new talent, faster solutions to business problems.)

- What contributions does mentoring now make consistently that add value to the institution? (Mentoring might, for example, ease collaborative networking, promote knowledge of the organization across silos, or help people feel more connected to the organization as a whole.)

Program planning models offer guidelines for success, not guarantees. It is not the plan but the planning that is most important. As this chapter explains, the planning and implementation of organizational mentoring require a balance between people and process. Both are essential to creating and sustaining a mentoring culture.

People and the Plan

Organizations come together in their own ways to plan and coordinate mentoring. Familiar configurations are committees, task forces, workgroups, advisory teams, and design teams. Occasionally an organization divides responsibility for the work of development, implementation, and maintenance and assigns it to groups and subgroups. Whatever the configuration, planning the mentoring work involves careful preparation, bringing the right people to the table, establishing a climate of trust, finding common ground, and creating a learning community.

Preliminary Planning: Setting the Stage

Successful implementation requires careful preparation for planning. Team member roles and responsibilities should be clearly delineated. Ground rules for communication, decision making, and conflict resolution must be established early on. Accountability mechanisms have to be put in place. In practice, here is how it works.

A single individual (or group of individuals, or organization) realizes the need for mentoring to meet specific business targets or goals. For example, a need for increased retention may be the impetus, or mentoring might be part of a larger organizational initiative such as executive development. An exploratory meeting is set up to discuss the idea, and a work team is identified. The scope and purpose of the work involved are clearly defined and anticipated outcomes or deliverables identified. A budget is prepared, the financial and human implications are explored, and a financial commitment is made.

Lima Agency's cofounders were nearing retirement age and eager to leave the insurance company's business to the next generation. They realized, belatedly, that there were not nearly enough people ready to assume leadership. Senior management met and decided that a mentoring program was the remedy. They also realized that what they wanted and what their direct reports desired did not always match. Rather than legislate a mentoring program, they set in motion a process so that the idea and ownership for mentoring would come from within their leadership. They called their managers together to discuss the idea of installing a formal mentoring program. It wasn't long before it became apparent that the idea of mentoring carried a lot of old baggage with it. Many thought that embracing a formal program would take away the power of personal choice, the natural spontaneity and informality of the business. A few feared that formal mentoring would be exclusionary and overlook some people, thereby potentially creating a kind of caste system. It could also be a disincentive for low-potentials. All the arguments pro and con were raised. As they surfaced, the group began to understand that they could launch a formal program and still preserve what they valued and at the same time overcome the elitism some feared.

Bringing in the Right People

Bringing people to the table can be challenging enough. However, the biggest challenge is bringing the right people to the planning table at the right time. The individuals developing the program may not be those who actively implement or eventually "own" the program.

Cervero and Wilson (1994) use the term planner to describe "the broad array of people who are involved in deliberating about the purposes, content, audience and format of educational programs for adults" (p. 6). When it comes to mentoring, planning groups should consider individuals who

- Reflect the diversity of the groups and constituencies

- Include the various points of view of key stakeholders

- Hold the organizational power to make commitments

- Bring rich and diverse perspectives

- Are open to learning and considering the thoughts of others

- Act in the best interests of the organization

- Are willing and available to commit to the task force or committee process

- Can work collaboratively with others as a group

The reality is that seating of a committee is often political. Just as there is a hidden curriculum in education, there may also be a hidden agenda behind including or excluding certain people from the planning process or from collaborative groups. For example, a manager might put together a mentoring team to see how certain individuals work together, or to test out future leaders, or to make "busy work" for someone who has too much time on her hands.

Planning the Initial Meeting

Not every program planning committee starts from the same place. Some organizations do more extensive advance work and already have a consolidated vision of what they want their program to look like before they invite people to the table. Others bring people together to decide whether or not to build a program or implement a decision made by someone else.

A well-planned and well-executed first meeting is necessary to attain the level of trust needed for planning and team success. A well-defined stage-setting process helps level the playing field and creates common ground so that the team members can work together more productively.

Setting the stage is frequently overlooked because most people assume they understand the work to be done by the team, either because information was sent ahead of time or "everybody just knows." In point of fact, everybody may know what but not fully understand why. Understanding the rationale, circumstances, and needs that led to the decision to build a mentoring program helps create common ground on which to move forward. In addition to understanding the rationale and establishing a process agenda, it is imperative to have some knowledge about who is in the room and the assumptions, experience, and expertise they bring with them.

Knowledge about what is needed from an internal organizational perspective is of paramount importance. The information that results from conducting this type of due diligence ensures that the program meets the needs of the organization and its participants. In addition to understanding the internal needs of the organization, information gleaned from best practices should inform (but not dictate) program development.

The mentoring vision must be clear and shared by team members. Without such alignment, effort is often duplicated. Team members may end up working at cross-purposes, and energy and enthusiasm may wane. Lack of a shared vision makes it difficult, if not impossible, to define critical success factors. By focusing on what people see as desirable, rather than what they think is possible, a creative and open atmosphere can be generated in which new ideas emerge and underlying assumptions are identified (Senge and others, 1994).

A shared vision frames a context for decision making. Like a compass, it sets the direction for a planning process by helping individuals create the future program they want and to develop action goals to achieve that future. Shared vision paints a vivid picture, thus offering a starting point for building consensus about how to move forward and avoiding stops and starts in planning.

Process is a prerequisite to ensuring that the team achieves positive results. Taking time as a group to reflect on the learning is a way to foster understanding and reinforce the learning that has occurred during the meeting. Building into an agenda explicit reflection time for shared insights and learning helps validate the process, motivate ownership, and move the group to its next step. It is also a useful way of summarizing the learning so the group can decide which key messages it needs to communicate to which segments of its organization.

Exhibit 3.1 displays a sample mentoring task force agenda that illustrates how each of these points can work together to establish the level of trust and understanding needed for effective planning. Since this agenda is quite ambitious, it might take the better part of a day to complete. However, dedicating this much time in one sitting is not always possible. Practice teaches us that it is better to do the work well than to rush through the agenda. Hence, it might make more sense to spread out the work over two sessions. In this case, items one through four might be completed in the first session. The second meeting could then focus on items five through eight.

Creating a Learning Community

When the planning incorporates learning into its deliberative process, organizational mentoring is likely to be stronger because the group is able to work more collaboratively. People who sit together as a task force or development team forge a learning community as they work together to achieve desired results. The team leader becomes a facilitator for team learning. It is for this reason we do well to remember that those who engage in the design and development process are adult learners themselves. Therefore the processes that facilitate learning in a mentoring relationship should inform the work of the team(s) charged with planning and implementing mentoring within an organization. In my experience, the learning (both content and process) that takes place on a mentoring development team or task force cascades down into the organization.

Exercise 3.1, Enabling the Process: Establishing Planning Group Guidelines, presents a list of questions for clarifying group behavioral expectations and operating principles; doing so helps maintain a climate of trust by keeping communication channels open and frees people to think together as a group. Defining operating principles helps a group maintain its focus by delimiting the scope of the work. These principles are referred to throughout the group's work so that planning maintains alignment with the operating principles.

EXHIBIT 3.1

Sample Mentoring Planning Task Force Agenda, Meeting Number One

The objective of the first meeting is to lay solid groundwork for planning by building the team through communication, accountability, and feedback. The topics on the left frame the agenda. The processes needed to accomplish tasks, on the right, are named; the task column describes the specific group tasks that need to be addressed under each agenda item.

Agenda Topic	Process	Task
1. Setting the stage	Review	Background
		Link to organizational strategic vision
		Task force charge
		Member responsibilities
2. Enabling the process	Establish	Ground rules
		Operating principles
	Discuss	Hopes
		Expectations
		Concerns
3. Getting connected	Share	Mentoring and mentoring experiences
	Check out	Assumptions about mentoring
4. Examining results of organizational needs analysis	Discuss	Outcomes from data, due diligence report, consultant input
	Clarify	Desired goals and outcomes
5. Learning from mentoring models and best practices	Present	Hallmarks
		Best practices (i.e., sustainability indicators)
		Benchmarks
	Discuss	Organizational and programmatic implications
6. Envisioning the program	Share individual perspectives	The "ideal," on the basis of needs and best practices from the field
	Identify	Common themes in visions
	Build	Shared vision
7. Gathering learnings and insights	Dialogue	Learnings and insights
8. Defining next steps and key messages	Identify	Next steps
		Communication messages and timeframes

EXERCISE 3.1

Enabling the Process: Establishing Planning Group Guidelines

Instructions: At your first planning meeting leave time on the agenda to discuss guidelines for the group (ground rules) and for development of the program (operating principles). Come to consensus, and then continue with your meeting agenda. At the end of the meeting, check back and see how you did with the ground rules that were created and if the group would like to amend them. Once people have agreed on the ground rules, adopt them and use them at subsequent meetings. Refer to the operating principles as you plan your program.

Group Guidelines	Questions for Discussion
Ground rules: What are the norms and guidelines we will follow in our process?	What kind of meeting guidelines do we want to put in place? What decorum and conversational courtesies do we want to enforce? Is there a minimum level of participation that we expect from team members? How will we go about making decisions? For example, what constitutes agreement? consensus? majority wins? If agreement cannot be reached, then what should we do? What does it mean to back a decision once it is made? Are there confidentiality considerations we ought to take into account individually and as a group? How will we hold each other and ourselves accountable for the work that needs to be done?
Operating principles: What are the principles we will use to guide and focus our thinking, our actions, and our decisions about the mentoring initiative we are about to develop?	What works in our organization? What are our best practices?

At the first team meeting, a set of ground rules and operating principles are defined. The task force should adopt and use them and hold themselves accountable for enforcing them. When first adopted, they may seem awkward and "different." It is best to use the rules and principles and then evaluate them. In this way, the group is able to really gauge if they are working or need to be modified. When used consistently, ground rules and operating principles maximize the contribution and efforts of team members, focus and guide the work of the group, and ensure that meetings are productive. Exhibit 3.2 offers an example of the guidelines one group completed for itself.

People come to the table with differing assumptions. Sharing these assumptions at the beginning of the planning process allows diverse points of view to be aired and opens up a group to consider options.

EXHIBIT 3.2

Planning Group Guidelines: An Example

Group Guidelines	Questions for Discussion
Ground rules: What are the norms and guidelines we will follow in our process?	Everyone participates. Go for consensus. If that doesn't work talk it out until we get there. Respect timelines. Cell phones off. Check out assumptions. Keep an ongoing list of important issues that need to be discussed at a later time. Wear your organizational hat. Check our egos at the door. Keep it simple.
Operating principles: What are the principles we will use to guide and focus our thinking, our actions, and our decisions about the mentoring initiative we are about to develop?	Align with culture and processes that are in place. Keep our messages consistent and clear. Hold each other and ourselves as a group accountable. Maintain flexibility. Honor the uniqueness of our culture. Maximize existing organizational resources. View implementation as a work-in-progress. Communicate the same messages at the same time. Don't go public until we are ready.

The Process of Implementation

Planning mentoring implementation requires the best possible combination of people and process. Bringing the right people to the table and creating a collaborative and trusting team lays a sound foundation for planning mentoring implementation. Ongoing attention to both people and process enhances mentoring planning and implementation efforts. Chances are, if you have tried implementing a mentoring initiative and it didn't succeed, one or more of these reasons ring true: lack of time, untested assumptions, inadequate training, lack of thoughtful pairing, failure to act on past lessons, a feeling of being blindsided, unclear program goals, failure to monitor mentoring implementation, breach of confidentiality, failure to anticipate resistance, lack of internal alignment, and lack of cultural congruence.

Creating a mentoring culture requires focus, discipline, time, and patience. It is a process of ongoing movement, of creating and recreating. It requires continuous tending and learning. Exercise 3.2, the Action Step Accountability Checklist, itemizes the steps you can follow to proactively address many of these potential stumbling blocks. It is also an accountability tool to help you ensure the integrity of your people and process as you work toward effective execution of your implementation plan. These are described in more detail next.

• *Define the purpose, scope, target population, learning outcomes, and benefits.* Doing so creates a level of readiness and a set of expectations for those involved in the planning process, for those affected by it, and even for those who are interested or invested in the outcomes of the program. The purpose of the program must be crystal clear and the intent of the program unambiguously defined. Clarity of purpose and program intent delimits the scope and the target population and drives further definition of the learning outcomes. Since there are many stakeholders who might benefit from a mentoring program, care must be taken to first identify them and then to project the benefits for each of them as realistically as possible.

• *Identify success factors.* To successfully achieve a program's intended purpose and desired outcomes, it is not sufficient to merely enumerate success factors. They must be clearly described and mutually understood since they define the work and what will become the basis of success measurement. An example of a success factor is "Eighty percent of our managers are promoted within the next three years."

• *Articulate roles and responsibilities.* One major impediment to achieving success in a mentoring program is failure to clearly define and articulate the roles and responsibilities of the various program participants. If roles and responsibilities are not defined, multiple (and often unrealistic) expectations

EXERCISE 3.2

Action Step Accountability Checklist

Instructions: Refer to the discussion in the "Process of Implementation" section of the chapter to guide you as you work through each action step. After it is complete, check it off the list.

Action Step	Complete
Define purpose, scope, target population, learning outcomes, and benefits of the program.	
Identify success factors.	
Articulate roles and responsibilities.	
Establish mentee and mentor criteria.	
Develop pairing protocols.	
Assign accountability for managing, overseeing, and coordinating implementation.	
Prepare a marketing and communication strategy.	
Establish continuous feedback loops.	
Ensure visible support from the top.	
Design education and training opportunities for the organization as a whole as well as for mentors, mentees, coaches, and key support personnel.	
Set up a reward, recognition, and learning celebration plan.	
Map out a contingency plan that addresses potential obstacles.	
Plan rollout and full implementation.	
Gather and share stories and best practices.	

An earlier version of this checklist appeared in Zachary (2003b).

are created. The result is chaos and confusion arising from untested and often erroneous assumptions. Roles and responsibilities should be defined for all those who participate in or relate to program participants regularly (HR manager, supervisor, direct report) and those who relate on an ad hoc basis (mentoring coaches, mentor managers, mentoring task force or committee members).

- *Establish mentee and mentor criteria.* Identifying the target population takes an organization only so far. It is important to clarify just who is eligible to participate in mentoring. In other words, what are the criteria used for inclusion in the participant pool? Of those included, what is the ultimate basis for selection? Establishing criteria is not an issue for an organization where everyone is expected to participate in mentoring. Organizations with a solid infrastructure have both eligibility and selection criteria, as discussed in Chapter Four. For example, one organization requires its mentors to be in a managerial position for two years before they are eligible for the mentor pool. At another, all new employees are automatically assigned a mentor.

- *Develop pairing protocols.* Regardless of whether mentoring partners are self-selected or determined by a third party or committee, the selection process should proceed proactively according to criteria for the best learning fit. Examples include experience, expertise, learning style, and accessibility. If mentees and mentors are expected to self-select, guidance should help them decide how and where to find, select, and recruit an appropriate mentor. Pairing protocols include identifying who it is that does the pairing, what happens if a match doesn't work out, and a plan detailing the process of pairing from implementation to final pairing.

It's important that people understand how, when, and by whom matches will be made. Regardless of whether individuals choose their own mentoring partners or are assigned mentoring partners, pairing protocols should be established. Thoughtful pairing calls for a good learning fit. Factors to consider in deciding if there is a learning fit include but are not limited to expertise, experience, personality, accessibility, professional interest, proximity, educational background or affiliation, gender, personality, and compatibility.

One of the most sensitive and toughest mentoring practices is the actual "pairing dance" itself. Whether it is in real time or online, meeting potential mentor candidates can be a disquieting and uncomfortable process. Most organizations allow some degree of individual preference in the final selection process. Some organizations facilitate the process by arranging a networking event so that potential mentors and mentees get to meet many possible partners before making a final selection. The same objectives can be accomplished in electronic mentoring. One practice is to give participants the names of possible mentors and some questions to guide an e-mentoring conversation. In another version, participants pick mentor possibilities after reviewing online resumes; they then contact prospects and narrow down their selection before indicating a preference.

Some organizations adopt much more informal mentoring practices. Participants are encouraged to seek mentors to meet development goals. An HR manager or immediate supervisor may suggest some possible mentors or a mentoring partnership might naturally emerge during the course of business.

Some guidelines are helpful in assisting prospective mentoring partners in gauging their own learning fit:

- Consider whether a prospective mentor will challenge and encourage the mentee to constantly raise the bar for growth and development.

- Base your decision on whether there is a good learning fit for the learning needs and goals, not simply a convenient match.

- Determine whether the potential mentor has the expertise, experience, time, and willingness to help the mentee achieve stated learning goals.

Exercise 3.3, the Mentor Selection Worksheet, can be used as a tool to assist mentees in selecting a mentor. It can also be adapted for use by mentoring managers to facilitate mentoring partnership pairing. Frequently it is the mentor who sees a need, a knowledge gap, or future leadership potential in a peer or coworker and offers to mentor the person. Viewed from a mentor's perspective, these questions are also useful in determining if a potential mentee would be a good learning fit with them.

- *Assign accountability for managing, overseeing, and coordinating implementation.* One of the most challenging aspects of implementation preparation is building a workable and adequate mentoring implementation team to support the long-term viability and growth of organizational mentoring. Consider who should be responsible for program oversight, management, and coordination. Some organizations use a rotating committee structure to promote ownership and investment in the program. Others use this structure as a leadership development opportunity to reward and mentor their high performers. The implementation team may or may not involve the same individual(s) who started the mentoring initiative. Just as the initiative may look entirely different in implementation from what it was in rollout, so too will the coordinating and managing group. Configurations for oversight, support, management, and coordination vary with the size of the program.

EXERCISE 3.3

Mentor Selection Worksheet

Instructions: Mentees can use this worksheet to help determine which potential mentor best meets learning needs and mentoring partnership criteria. The worksheet can also be adapted for use by individuals who are tasked with making mentoring matches.

1. What are you seeking to learn, and why is it important for you?

   What?

   Why?

2. List your criteria.

   What is important to you in a *relationship?*

   What might be important to you in a *mentoring relationship?*

   What kind of mentor do you think you need?

3. Using your answers to question two, identify your top four criteria; record one in each cell at the top of a column. Then list potential mentors to see if they meet your criteria.

Write criteria here:	Criterion 1	Criterion 2	Criterion 3	Criterion 4
Potential mentor 1 Name:				
Potential mentor 2 Name:				
Potential mentor 3 Name:				
Potential mentor 4 Name:				
Potential mentor 5 Name:				

Some programs have one or several mentoring managers and an advisory board; others use a more decentralized approach and train people on site to assume all of these functions. Whoever assumes responsibility must be accountable to someone else. This someone else is usually the "owner" of the program, be it human resource development, training, diversity, or program development.

• *Prepare a marketing and communication strategy.* Individuals to be included and touched by the program (stakeholders) must understand the business reasons, the purpose, its intended outcomes, what is in it for them, and the pragmatics of the program. This is accomplished by marketing the program internally (to the target group) and perhaps throughout the organization or to specific others within or external to it. Using consistent messages to educate for understanding and inform those who need to know about the program (using a segmented marketing approach) ensures that the right people get the right messages at the right time.

• *Establish continuous feedback loops.* Unless the development and implementation process is iterative, it limits the shelf life of the effort. A mentoring culture is a work-in-progress. Those who plan a mentoring program must learn to ask for feedback, give it (when asked), receive it when it comes (especially when negative), accept it (not get defensive), and act on it (to make process improvements). Gathering input regularly serves many functions simultaneously. "Testing back" with key informants during the planning process promotes interest, fosters ownership, identifies potential obstacles, and strengthens mentoring efforts. It is not unusual for a mentoring program to look and feel quite different from the pilot as it matures. As feedback is gathered and considered, modifications should be considered, when appropriate, to strengthen and enhance the program. If participants see process improvements arising from their personal input, it makes them feel valued and creates value for the program.

Gathering feedback from multiple data sources is essential and should be part of the strategic effort of implementing a mentoring initiative. Information gleaned from reliable feedback sources allows an organization to respond promptly to changing conditions and circumstances and to continuously enhance the program.

• *Ensure visible support from the top.* Organizational responsibility for mentoring can be handed off, but it cannot be hands-off. Leaders must champion the effort and encourage other leaders to do the same by their personal example. They must talk about the value of mentoring for the future of the organization as well as its immediate payoff. This requires leaders to keep up-to-date and have current and accurate information about mentoring in the organization. They must find a way to show up when they can't physically be present, share their own mentoring stories, acknowledge mentoring successes, and make it clear enough so others see and feel that mentoring really matters. The revolving door of organizational leadership today makes the challenge of ensuring visible support from the top a formidable task. One CEO's commitment may not stem from the same set of assumptions as that of a predecessor. Visible support from the top—decision makers, leaders, those who hold perceived and real power, and those who hold the purse strings—must be nurtured.

• *Design education and training opportunities for the organization as a whole as well as for mentors, mentees, coaches, and key support personnel.* Mentoring education and training opportunities should include a continuum of multilevel learning experiences that meet a variety of learning and development needs. Rather than develop a one-time startup training program, program developers would do well to think about establishing ongoing learning opportunities to encourage people to take the next step in their mentoring skills, knowledge, and development.

Mentoring training and coaching should be required for key program personnel (trainers, mentoring coordinating committee members, and mentoring coaches). Program content should complement and mesh with existing organizational learning programs. For example, an organization may choose to train one or several leaders as mentoring coaches. These coaches could be available online or have "office hours" and be available to those who need coaching in particular mentoring skills. Some organizations offer commercial online resources to their employees so that they can beef up goal setting, time management, listening, and communication skills. Whatever the education, training, or information resource, it must be accessible, worthwhile, and not compromise relationship confidentiality. As mentoring matures in an organization, new education and training needs emerge. Consider how you might address them when they surface.

• *Set up a reward, recognition, and celebration plan.* Organizational practice varies when it comes to reward, recognition, and celebration. Some organizational cultures discourage individual recognition, reasoning that no one employee should be valued above another. Other cultures routinely provide monetary incentives, rewards, and public recognition. The need to celebrate is frequently minimized or relegated to the wish list (that is, deferred until there is time and money). Benign neglect of celebration represents a missed opportunity to promote individual, team, and organizational learning. Celebration should include regular and meaningful activity; meaningful celebration requires planning. Some companies hold an annual mentoring graduation celebration. At a minimum, organizations should build appropriate celebration markers into their mentoring calendar cycle.

Let's peek in on a celebration at Ideal Organization to see reward, recognition, and celebration in action. A once-a-year Ideal Mentoring Day is dedicated to celebrating mentoring excellence as well as personal and organizational mentoring milestones, and recognizing mentoring bridge builders (advocates and champions of mentoring). Ideal offers reward and recognition to departments and work teams that build bridges by creating innovative mentoring opportunities with demonstrable results.

As employees come to work on Mentoring Day, they cross over a make-shift "Bridge of Opportunity." Those who work remotely enter the Ideal Website through a portal depicting a virtual image of the bridge. Everyone looks forward to this day, which is filled with learning, networking, recognition, reward, and celebration. Employees pick and choose from a menu of activities. Some attend group mentoring sessions, or network with other mentors and mentees to share best practices. There is time set aside for mentoring conversations. Ideal's CEO shares his vision, his leadership, and some mentoring success stories he has gathered from conversations with employees. The day is festive, exciting, and definitely not to be missed.

Celebrating mentoring promotes organizational learning and heightens the sense of individual accomplishment and shared enterprise. It creates value for individuals as well as for their organization. It is a way to honor mentoring excellence and achievement and at the same time engage the heart, the mind, and the spirit.

- *Map out a contingency plan to address potential obstacles.* Once the initial draft of a mentoring implementation plan is complete, the time is ripe to consider potential obstacles. This requires humility and detachment, since probably everyone on the planning group is now invested in the implementation plan that has been developed. It is valuable to get feedback from the field to inform contingency planning. Walking through each participant's journey in the program (that is, an HR person, a mentor, a mentor coach) identifies potential obstacles and gaps and stimulates discussion of how to avoid and address them. Envisioning worst-case scenarios often brings up additional issues that may have been overlooked during the initial implementation planning.

- *Plan rollout and full implementation.* An ideal way to roll out a mentoring initiative is as a pilot, for use as a learning laboratory before it is fully implemented. To maximize the learning, specific details of the rollout should be spelled out well in advance. The plan should be concrete enough that everyone involved in the planning is clear about what rollout will look like in actual practice. Mentoring efforts are destined for failure if there is lack of clarity about the vision or confusion about the details. Since rollout and full implementation are likely to look dissimilar, a separate timeline for each is recommended. If the program is to be handed off to another team for implementation, a succession plan for transitioning the leadership responsibilities must be developed.

- *Gather and share stories and best practices.* Stories inspire. Best practices inform. One of the keys to selling, inspiring, and galvanizing participation is being able to relate to real-life mentoring experiences of peers, colleagues, and role models. Build in opportunities to gather stories and best practices. Group settings and networking forums enable participants to realize that others share their hopes, dreams, confusions, and concerns. They also set up a learning community where participants can learn best practices from each other. Gathering stories and best practices only goes so far. It is in the telling of stories and sharing of best practices that people open up to other possibilities. Organizations do well to incorporate stories and best practices into training new participants and to keep those already in the pipeline informed and energized.

Planning Implementation: Reflection on Practice

Planning successfully for mentoring implementation relies on the marriage of people and process. Sometimes people and process work in synchronous movement, that is, in the same time in relation to one another, and sometimes not. So long as the two move in *relationship* to one another, the planning work moves forward. Planning work is always part of something bigger than itself—a larger enterprise. Once that perspective is lost, so too is the meaning of the work.

What is the biggest obstacle you'll face in planning for mentoring implementation in your organization? It is time—or, more realistically, the perceived lack of it. It is what causes people to get in the way of their own process. When allocating time to plan mentoring implementation, be realistic in setting aside blocks of time. Planning on the run rarely works. Allocate time so that those who have to be in the room can be there (whether virtually or on-site). Don't rush the process. It takes time to create readiness, foster the right opportunities, and build in quality support. Each time a new initiative is created, you must cycle back through the process planning steps in order to achieve the right balance of people and process.

Planning is an indispensable process tool for engaging people in the shared enterprise of creating a viable mentoring culture. It is, after all, people and their commitment, not a piece of paper, that makes mentoring work. To grow a thriving mentoring culture, you have to take it one step at a time, focus your attention on balancing people and process, and continue to choose your actions consciously. Before you know it, you will be celebrating your own ideal success.

Part Two

Moving Forward

Mentoring at Work

CREATING A MENTORING CULTURE begins in earnest as an organization moves forward from taking stock to growing and nurturing a vibrant, supportive, and sustainable mentoring culture. Successful organizations work at bridging the transition between thought and action by first ensuring that a strong and dynamic infrastructure is solidly in place. Such an infrastructure promotes ownership, continuity, and momentum, all of which are prerequisites to supporting and accommodating a mentoring culture as it takes root, develops, and grows.

Infrastructure is the foundation on which a mentoring culture is built. The strength and focus of your infrastructure are critical; infrastructure is therefore presented as the first chapter of this part of the book. Infrastructure promotes sustainability by ensuring that mentoring ownership is well anchored within multiple layers of the organization. An organization with a mentoring-friendly infrastructure commits its leadership and time to mentoring over the long run; it also furnishes reliable, suitable, and sufficient financial, technological, human, and knowledge resources to support mentoring needs.

The Hallmarks of Mentoring

With this infrastructure at the base, the hallmarks that distinguish a mentoring culture can flourish. There are eight clusters of related mentoring practices, or hallmarks, that contribute to a vibrant and full mentoring culture. Each hallmark is differentiated from the others, yet they are interdependent. No one hallmark can work to its potential entirely by itself. Instead, the hallmarks build on and strengthen each other; together, they can produce synchronistic movement within the mentoring culture.

The eight hallmarks manifest themselves according to each organization's current mentoring practices. In a mentoring culture, all hallmarks are present, at least to some degree. The more consistently that the practices of each hallmark are present, the fuller, hardier, and more sustainable the mentoring culture is likely to be. It is important to keep the hallmarks—alignment, accountability, communication, value and visibility, demand, multiple mentoring opportunities, education and training, and safety nets—in mind while you grow and live the culture. My experience working with organizations as they create their mentoring culture suggests that the order in which these chapters are presented in this book fits logically with many organizations' needs. But the order is not sacrosanct. There is no one-size-fits-all sequence. The order in which you address the hallmarks should be linked to your organization and where the needs lie. You may find it best to start with the weakest area, or focus on a hallmark that might assure your organization some quick, visible successes.

Before moving forward, I invite you to read the brief descriptions of each hallmark here and then complete the Mentoring Culture Audit in Appendix One. The results of your audit should help you decide which hallmarks (each discussed in its own chapter) you want to focus on first.

Alignment helps prevent organizational mentoring from being perceived as an add-on to what is already in place and maintains its integrity. When mentoring is aligned, the business reasons to engage in mentoring are evident and tied directly to results, which are communicated regularly. As the organization's mentoring efforts become increasingly aligned, a ripple effect positively affects related systems and processes within the organization.

Accountability is seamless and routine in a mentoring culture. Roles and responsibilities for all the key players and mentoring goals are clarified at the beginning to manage expectations and encourage both self-accountability and organizational accountability.

Communication makes some mentoring efforts more successful than others. A mentoring culture has an effective strategic communication plan that it regularly implements and monitors. As a consequence, executives, managers, and coworkers all understand what mentoring is and know how to get involved in it. Periodic briefings promote awareness of the organization's mentoring commitment. Two-way communication channels reveal what is working and what isn't, ensuring a constant flow of information for making process improvements.

Value and visibility greatly increase the effect of mentoring. As the right people talk about mentoring in formal presentations, speeches, and informal meetings, the value is reinforced and momentum increases. Whether through e-mail, personal contact, role modeling, media, banners and posters, or conversation, ongoing advocacy persists in a mentoring culture. Reward, recognition, and celebration all offer opportunities to create value and visibility for mentoring efforts.

Demand for mentoring evolves over time and is stimulated by success. As more people enthusiastically participate in mentoring relationships, mentoring becomes normative. People voluntarily seek out mentoring relationships and use ongoing training, information, and resources. When mentoring partners complete learning goals, they continue to seek additional mentoring relationships and work on new goals. Mentors are mentees and mentees become mentors.

Multiple mentoring opportunities, including both formal and informal approaches, are available in a mentoring culture. The culture acknowledges, supports, and enhances multiple approaches and types of mentoring simultaneously, among them one-to-one, group, distance, and cross-cultural models. Self-directed learning is promoted and supported with mentoring resources (articles, books, references, and tools).

Education and training set the gold standard for mentoring practice and in this way foster management of mentoring expectations. Continuous mentoring education and training are strategically integrated into the organization's overall training and development agenda. Networking and support groups meet regularly to exchange best practices and promote peer learning. Opportunities for renewal education and advanced training are available for veteran mentors. Mentoring coaches, coordinators, and oversight groups continuously learn and keep themselves updated about mentoring best practices.

Safety nets support and strengthen the practice of mentoring within the organization; they help individuals and organizations deal more adeptly with any mentoring obstacles they encounter. If multiple safety nets, proactive and reactive, are put in place to address potential stumbling blocks or roadblocks, setbacks and negative consequences are minimized and mentoring efforts keep moving forward.

Remember that the hallmarks work together. The absence of one can potentially affect them all. For example, creating value and visibility would be impossible without communication; education and training without communication would be a long, slow, and possibly futile (or at least low-yield) effort; communication without alignment would create conflict.

Moving Mentoring Forward

Mentoring cultures, like all living organisms, are always in the process of becoming. Continuous and progressive improvement perpetuates movement. The more an organization works on establishing the hallmarks, the more deeply embedded they become. As the hallmarks integrate, organizations begin to act more synergistically and yet remain flexible enough to accommodate change as it occurs. The process of engaging with the hallmarks adds value and meaning to those in mentoring relationships or in planning, implementing, and leading as the mentoring continues to move forward.

As you take the next steps, remember that:

- Creating a mentoring culture is progressive.
- It takes time for the culture to develop, take hold, and mature.
- Continuity of people and effort are both critical.
- You must engage others.
- Just talking about or promoting best practices doesn't work; you must role-model them.

- You need to focus on mentoring excellence.

- Maintaining the big picture is vital.

- You have to keep working at it, keep up the momentum, and know that little things do make a difference.

The hallmarks facilitate successful movement from implementation to integration. As the organization's mentoring efforts move forward, they become increasingly evident and begin fitting together. As each effort is integrated, a system for mentoring emerges and more and more processes and programs benefit.

Chapter 4

Infrastructure

The rung of a ladder was never meant to rest upon, but only to hold
a man's foot long enough to enable him to put the other somewhat
higher.

—THOMAS HENRY HUXLEY, *LIFE AND LETTERS*
OF THOMAS HUXLEY

INFRASTRUCTURE BRINGS organizational mentoring to life. It is indispensable to a mentoring culture's continuity and success. But what exactly is
infrastructure? The term is used as shorthand and in numerous ways to
describe the components that enable a system to operate smoothly and
function properly. City planners work with the concept of infrastructure all
the time; components of a transportation system infrastructure are traffic
signal controls, roads, bridges, and tunnels. Our rapidly changing technological world has embraced the language of infrastructure, with its work-
stations, servers, routers, and networking. Use of the concept has become
so prevalent that the same terminology is part of everyday "organization-
speak," in the for-profit and nonprofit worlds alike.

According to Senge (Senge and others, 1994, p. 32), "Infrastructure is
the means through which an organization makes available resources to support people in their work." It facilitates effective functioning in an organization by supporting the structures that enable people get work done to
deliver service or product.

Although supporting growth and development of a culture, an organization, and the people within it, infrastructure also impedes growth and
development when it no longer serves a purpose or becomes an end in
itself. A flexible infrastructure optimizes use and deployment of organizational resources and is able to respond to needs as they change.

An infrastructure is required to implement mentoring coherently, com-
prehensively, and conscientiously. When and where an infrastructure
already exists, it becomes that much easier for organizational mentoring to
take hold. Trying to build a mentoring culture without an infrastructure is
slippery business. It takes more time to accomplish the work; the constant
backward-and-forward motion creates tension as the infrastructure and the

mentoring culture catch up with one another. Yet this is not all negative: a mentoring project sometimes becomes a catalyst for establishing an appropriate infrastructure, which in turn stimulates creation of a sustainable mentoring culture.

This chapter describes six infrastructure components that are particularly relevant to creating a mentoring culture. To ensure sustainability, these six components must be part of the infrastructure and work together to strengthen and stabilize the mentoring culture as it emerges.

Mentoring Infrastructure Components

The specific components of a mentoring culture's infrastructure depend on organizational practice, setting, and perspective. An infrastructure operates within a system and also within a structure. For instance, a transportation infrastructure may have separate structures for buses, trains, planes, and roads, each of which has its own infrastructure. A national nonprofit may have a particular chapter infrastructure, yet a local chapter might have its own committee infrastructure. In some cases, mentoring is implemented in silos or together with other learning and development platforms. A mentoring infrastructure entails commitment of financial, technological, human, and knowledge resources, as well as leadership and time. We examine the last two first, since they are often overlooked or taken for granted.

Leadership

One essential function of leadership is to engage in shaping the evolution of organizational culture (Schein, 1992) and building its infrastructure. Creating and building a mentoring culture requires ongoing participation and the commitment of executive leadership. Ultimately it is leadership's responsibility to build the right infrastructure to support organizational learning. When mentoring is felt, experienced, and perceived as a vested interest and commitment of leadership, the spirit of ownership permeates every level of the organization. Consider the contrast between two entities, NewCompany and OldSchool, as an illustration of how leadership can have a positive impact on mentoring.

Engaging in Leadership

Jack is the chief learning officer at NewCompany. As CLO, his responsibilities include developing an organizational learning culture. Specifically, his charge is "creating, implementing, and leveraging continuous learning opportunities, developing knowledge management systems, and maximizing intellectual capital." The very emergence of the role of CLO signals alignment with NewCompany's strategic learning priority.

NewCompany itself was born in a mentoring relationship, when Annabel and her mentor, Hal, became business partners and started the company. Their leadership commitment to mentoring was already solidly in place. Together, they recruited Jack, their CLO, whom they were sure would be able to create a learning organization to broaden their mentoring agenda as the company grew and developed. Because Jack's values and those of the company matched, he was the perfect role model for effective mentoring. He led by example and encouraged others to do the same. He was steadfast in his commitment and invited ownership and encouraged self-responsibility for all of NewCompany's employees.

In contrast, as OldSchool's example demonstrates, if leaders are not engaged in the mentoring culture then there is little chance of mentoring taking hold. At OldSchool, lack of clear career opportunities and strategic direction were depleting the number of talented midlevel managers. The brain drain and expense of recruiting and training new executives had taken its toll on the company's bottom line and was wreaking havoc on the human resources recruiting budget. At an executive committee meeting, Carol, OldSchool's HR director, outlined the problem and presented data to demonstrate the financial impact poor retention was having on the organization. As a solution, she proposed establishing a mentoring roundtable to retain and develop high-potential managers. Carol presented her idea but received a lukewarm reception. Her fellow leaders were concerned about the time people would need to take away from doing "real" work, and the possibility of raising unrealistic expectations about future promotion. Eventually, after some vigorous discussion, Carol received authorization to establish the roundtable.

At subsequent meetings, Carol presented regular updates and information about mentor and mentee participation. She was hoping that some of the leaders in the room would be willing to become roundtable mentors, but only one volunteered. As a consequence, additional mentors were pulled from other levels of the organization. She requested that executive leadership send out a letter to all current and potential mentors, to accomplish three purposes with one stroke of the pen. The letter would thank all OldSchool mentors for volunteering; it would restate the business case for mentoring as OldSchool's investment in human capital; and, because it would go out under the executive committee's signature, the letter would also demonstrate the committee's support for the program. The executive team vetoed the idea, with no discussion.

At the next meeting, Carol presented several other proposals to engage leaders with midlevel managers in the program. Seven pairs of glazed-over eyes confronted her. Without enthusiasm, endorsement, participation, or support from senior leadership, Carol felt the mentoring roundtable had little chance of making a significant impact in addressing the problem of retention among midlevel managers. She considered discontinuing the roundtable.

Beyond being personally engaged, leadership also needs to plan to support the mentoring culture, as Carol well understood. Realizing that the roundtable was going nowhere, and yet feeling strongly about the value of mentoring, she volunteered to take personal responsibility for mentoring all new high-potential managers. She knew doing so would be time-consuming, but she was so committed to mentoring and the company that she felt she should help decrease the rate of attrition. She saw it as a cost-cutting measure and a demonstrably constructive step. Members of the executive committee enthusiastically embraced her offer because they were glad to hand off the program to someone else.

After two years, Carol was OldSchool's one-stop shop for mentoring. She was effective—on a small scale—but utterly overworked. Ultimately, her other responsibilities prevented her from maintaining her mentoring efforts. She chose not to let senior management know that mentoring was becoming overwhelming for fear that it would reflect poorly on her leadership and her stance as an advocate for mentoring. Her executive committee colleagues had never owned mentoring and Carol neither took the time to communicate with them nor exercised the leadership needed to engage anyone else. Apparently, she never even thought about having someone else assume leadership.

Planning for Leadership Succession

Mentoring leadership cannot reside in one person. Nor should it, being too important and too time-consuming for responsibility to rest on only one set of shoulders. Leaders eventually move on, retire, or leave. In a mentoring culture, leadership replaces itself; part of the responsibility is to mentor future leaders and foster broad ownership so that the integrity and continuity of the mentoring culture is preserved. Many organizations understand this and rotate mentoring leadership so that there is always an incumbent, an emerging leader, and a veteran leader steering the mentoring agenda. Some organizations create a mentoring leadership cabinet made up of three to five leaders who rotate in and off the cabinet according to a prearranged schedule of service.

Leadership for mentoring must exist outside the mentoring program or initiative itself; leadership must commit to overtly supporting mentoring within the organization. Consider the contrast between Carol's circumstance and that of Garrison and his leadership group at another organization, who for five years functioned as the corporate spokespeople and champions for mentoring. They strategically deployed corporate resources to support organizational mentoring. Every member of Garrison's group felt a stake in seeing that mentoring received the kind of attention and support it needed. Garrison felt no qualms when it came time for him to retire. Leadership succession was carefully orchestrated to make sure his successor understood the importance of mentoring in principle and practice, and that support and leadership throughout the organization for mentoring was ensured.

Connecting Leaders to Learning and Mentoring

In a medium or large organization, mentoring leaders often sit outside the day-to-day operations of organizational mentoring. These are the individuals with the political muscle, organizational wherewithal, and clout to make things happen. In a small business, an administrator or coordinator may also hold the power and purse strings for ensuring the viability of mentoring within the organization.

But it isn't enough to have a stable of leaders committed to and advocating for mentoring; they need to continue their own learning so they are not undermining organizational mentoring, overtly or covertly. Organizational leaders must keep abreast of progress and current developments. Current knowledge, success stories, and data points should be part of the leader's communication toolkit. Periodic briefings to leadership help maintain the visibility and reinforce the value mentoring creates in an organization. They keep old knowledge from becoming a roadblock. To take full advantage of opportunities to enrich ongoing formal and informal mentoring and learning experiences, leadership must be active and present.

Jack carried the mantle at NewCompany by developing the mentoring agenda envisioned by its founders. Over time, five separate mentoring initiatives were implemented, attracting employee participation from all levels of the organization. Leadership engaged in mentoring and facilitated involvement for it throughout the organization. The "mentoring community" that emerged gathered twice a year to recognize and acknowledge mentoring participation, celebrate success, hear about program updates, share success stories, and highlight mentoring achievement. By keeping mentoring visible, leaders felt better prepared to carry mentorship forward in their districts and lead the charge. The fact that mentoring sat squarely on the agenda and high in the leaders' use of time was known throughout the company.

Time

As we've seen, creating and sustaining a mentoring culture requires time. It takes time to plan, implement, and see measurable results. It takes time for a mentoring culture to evolve. It takes time for relationships to develop and mature. Because time is such a scare resource, it is begrudgingly allocated, jealously guarded, and enviously resented. Therefore it is essential to clarify the business reasons for engaging in the time-consuming task of mentoring. Knowing and agreeing on these reasons can help balance and protect mentoring time against the demands of expediency, results, and immediate performance.

Mentoring partners must be able to make and keep time commitments. They need to be flexible enough to adjust to changing circumstances, clear about the time they do have, and savvy in managing their time well. For many individuals, the time commitment truly presents a challenge. Despite best intentions, they find themselves hard pressed to find time for mentoring. Although it is offered willingly, time is also considered the most valuable of commodities, one that busy people are hard pressed to find enough of. An organization can set parameters by

- Realistically assessing the amount of time mentoring will take, encouraging employees to allot enough time for mentoring, and setting appropriate guidelines (for example, "we anticipate you will meet a minimum of once a month with your mentoring partner. If you need to meet more often, that is up to you").

- Encouraging leaders to view the time employees spend on mentoring as important and not to devalue it. Many companies code and treat mentoring as if it were a revenue-producing activity since eventually mentoring increases productivity and the bottom line.

- Allowing time for mentoring even when it competes with project time commitments.

- Communicating clearly with supervisors regarding the time expectations for mentoring partners so they don't feel blindsided.

- Making time management training available to participants so they use the time they do have wisely.

The adage that time is money explains some of the resistance in regard to mentoring participation. The reality is that both time and money are limited resources, require commitment, and are interdependent.

Financial Resources

It takes financial resources and a long-term commitment to deploying those financial resources to create and support a mentoring culture. The biggest and most difficult obstacle is honoring a financial commitment once it has been made, particularly in an already economically challenged market. Any investment in human capital costs money and more. Time, labor, and productivity expended have an impact on the bottom line. If the corporate bottom line is affected, executive leadership is often tempted to let go of the line item.

The exact amount of an organization's financial commitment to mentoring is idiosyncratic to each organization. It should reflect the scope, goals, and complexity of the mentoring intent and purpose and be commensurate with the size and capacity of the organization. A mentoring budget is a telltale expression of commitment to a mentoring culture. The budget itself may not reflect the direct nonmonetary costs associated with mentoring.

Take, for example, another organization that has a thriving mentoring culture. It all started five years ago with a few small initiatives and a slim budget from just one division. As support grew through the organization, so did the budget. Ultimately, each division contributed money. Then, once the culture was established, the production costs, material costs, and dollars required to administer the mentoring initiatives leveled off. Now, from the time a new employee walks in the door throughout his career, the employee is engaged in mentoring partnerships with other staff members, with regional staff members, and in staff meetings. Roles and responsibilities, guidelines, and ground rules for mentoring relationships are part of the employee handbook. An open roundtable is held every Thursday morning for mentors who want to talk about mentoring, share success stories, and learn from each other's experiences. The employee newsletter showcases best practices and tips. Every retreat has a mentoring continuing education segment and opportunities to participate in group mentoring experiences.

In a mentoring culture, each department may have its own mentoring line items and some that are absorbed by a corporate administrative department. Where there is no mentoring culture, the real cost can indeed be unnecessarily high. In a highly competitive environment, for example, there might be no interdepartmental or corporate sharing of mentoring resources. Instead, each department creates its own mentoring program and fights for every mentoring dollar. No one knows from year to year if mentoring will be supported. In such circumstances, accessing or maintaining financial resources may look and sound like a Herculean task. Yet financial resources don't need to be substantial; they just have to be available. The administrative costs inherent in creating and supporting a mentoring culture should be carefully planned to ride out any financial fluctuations in the organization. Considering worst-case scenarios during the planning process and anticipating challenges ahead of time can be of enormous help.

Which financial infrastructure model best supports a mentoring culture? The one that works best for the organization. Some organizations put money into a common pot to launch organizational mentoring; then, as it takes hold and develops credibility, the responsibility for funding shifts to individual departments. Some organizations collaboratively share the financial responsibility; for example, the corporation may initiate mentoring and pay for launch events. Training and development, communications, and human resources may each have a budget line for mentoring. In some cases, the best chance for embedding mentoring into the culture comes from simply including an adequate travel budget so that mentoring partners can meet without incurring personal expense. Take the time to consider your organization's history of funding the launch and maintenance of culture change initiatives; use this information to plan how you will financially support mentoring in your organization. Be sure to consider what it takes to ensure the presence of adequate technology to support a mentoring culture.

Technology

Even a decade ago, we could not have imagined how significant, pervasive, and influential technology would become in how we conduct business, maintain relationships, communicate with employees, and educate our workforce. Technology includes so much more than fax, computer, video-conference, and telephone bridge lines. Internet and intranet present opportunities that represent only the tip of the iceberg; we have yet to fully explore what lies below the surface. Clearly, technology will continue to alter how we do business, extend our reach, and expand our capabilities.

Because it is so pervasive and instantaneous, technology requires more from the end user, not less. It shortens the speed for considering, reacting to, and making decisions, but we still need time for learning and processing information. Technology can also be invasive and add significant time pressures to the business day; witness mobile technology in the form of handheld computer devices and cellular telephones. Technology demands redefinition of workplace literacy. It necessitates building the workforce capability to access and use it. Inherent in the saying that you are only as good as your technology are both a promise and a threat. The promise is staying ahead of competitors, increasing efficiency and effectiveness. The threat is that technology needs to be accessible, affordable, and compatible; hardware must be maintained and up-to-date.

Today, technology (and all that it encompasses) plays a more important role than ever in creating a mentoring culture. It is no longer just about distance mentoring. As we discuss in subsequent chapters, technology in a mentoring culture can be a well-used information highway for gathering data and trends on mentoring; collecting best practices; conducting a mentoring relationship; delivering education and training; and having a house organ for communicating, disseminating, accessing, and storing information.

Access to technology is one thing. Knowing how to use it is quite another. It is frustrating when a mentoring partner lacks the ability to make technology work for the relationship. For example, hardware and software incompatibility between systems sometimes makes virtual communication impossible (when documents don't translate from one system to another or when a mentoring partner doesn't know how to use the technology). Technology is far from a mentoring panacea. In a mentoring culture, it is important to provide multiple options and make them work for the organization, rather than make the organization a slave to the technology.

Human Resources

In theory, the totality of individual workers within an organization makes up its human resources. The quintessential function of mentoring in any organization is to maximize these human resources, to raise up individual capacity through learning. Whenever capacity is leveraged, the whole organization benefits, with improved quality of organizational life, productivity, and business results. Since the infrastructure component of leadership has been addressed earlier in this chapter, this discussion focuses more generically on the array of human resources that support mentoring within an organization.

The importance of bringing the right people to the table to plan the mentoring work that goes on in the organization has already been emphasized. It is equally imperative that the right people be involved in implementing, managing, and monitoring the work. The decision regarding whom to include, select, name, and ask contributes to the ultimate success of a mentoring culture. It should not be taken lightly or left to chance.

Mentoring Management, Oversight, and Coordination

There must be a contact or point person within an organization to furnish general information, answer questions, and render support. The personnel needs to accomplish these functions vary according to the size of the organization. Whether online, over the phone, or face-to-face, a go-to person is essential. This can be a specific individual attached to another function, part of which could be electronically managed and buttressed by an HR professional. Those engaged in mentoring relationships, as well as in delivery and support of mentoring services, benefit from access to support, counsel, and information. Naming the contact or point person(s) is only half the battle; the person needs to be available and accessible.

Responsibility for implementation can be vested in a single individual or divested among groups of individuals at the same or different points in time. Conscious and careful selection, development, and utilization of human resource personnel are all critical. Who is selected and how the person is chosen affects the influence he or she will have in facilitating creation of a mentoring culture. Consider these questions:

- What human resources presently exist in the organization that can be used to manage, administer, and support mentoring?

- What additional internal and external human resources might be necessary?

- What competencies does this individual or group of individuals possess?

- What competencies should this individual or group of individuals develop?

Careful analysis of the answers to these questions enable you to avoid some of the pitfalls of organizational mentoring. For example, if little thought is given to the competencies required for servicing the mentoring agenda, or if coordinating or leading a mentoring initiative falls into someone's lap out of necessity, the need to expedite becomes the motivator, and the long-term viability of the program suffers. If professional development for key mentoring personnel is not a priority, sustaining mentoring becomes problematic. Those in the coordinating, managing, and administrative roles are frequently not encouraged to develop professionally in their mentoring role. When this happens, or a position becomes temporary "punishment" for poor performance or a default assignment because no position is available, mentoring becomes busy work instead of real mentoring. In these cases, the credibility of mentoring itself is suspect.

By contrast, in some organizations a seat on the mentoring oversight or management committee presents a clear opportunity for an individual to take personal leadership development to the next level. If those who lead and manage mentoring within their organization explicitly make their own growth and development a priority, they add value to the mentoring culture. They become role models for the very process they are supporting. They are part of a positive mentoring culture that supports the organization.

Exercise 4.1, Mentoring Practices: Management, Oversight, and Coordination, presents a matrix for determining your human resource needs with respect to organizational mentoring. You may decide to locate functions with one person or share responsibility among several individuals. In a larger organization, you may decide to have local teams as well as an organizational team.

Mentoring Practices: Management, Oversight, and Coordination

Instructions: Consider how each mentoring function listed in the left-hand column should be dealt with in your organization, and by whom. For example, advocacy, decision making, and monitoring might be handled by a governing board, whereas coordinating and managing might be attended to by a mentoring director.

Mentoring Function	Mentoring Structure	Individual(s) Responsible
Advocating		
Coaching mentoring partners		
Communicating information		
Coordinating		
Decision making		
Establishing policies and procedures		
Evaluating		
Facilitating matching		
Leading		
Managing		
Monitoring		
Overseeing operations		
Programming		
Training		
Troubleshooting		

With a mentoring culture and oversight in place, organizations need to determine the mentoring pool and how to best identify and match mentoring partners. Consider possible scenarios:

- Employees may be expected to find their own mentor. There is no vetting process for becoming part of the mentor pool; mentors simply post their intent and their profile on the corporate Website or bulletin board. Each application becomes an open posting so that others can determine for themselves whether this individual might be a potential mentoring partner.

- Mentors are assigned to interested employees. Interviews with each mentee and possible mentor candidates are required before a mentoring partner is assigned.

- Participation in mentoring is "highly recommended." Managers routinely recommend mentoring as a development opportunity option at annual employee review sessions and suggest potential mentors.

- High-potential employees are required to participate in two successive mentoring programs, one formal with an assigned mentor and one informal with a self-selected mentor, prior to applying for management positions.

The possibilities vary widely, and in all cases the task of identifying and matching participants is fraught with challenges. Many questions need to be addressed before an organization decides to establish eligibility guidelines and pairing practices. The answers depend on the specific mentoring initiative within an organization and must be internally consistent for each initiative.

The defining questions focus on the learners themselves. Who participates? Who is the target audience? Will this target audience expand over time? Will there be a pilot? If so, who will be included? Often an organization rolls out an initiative in a particular division or creates a pilot that is a cross-functional representation of the entire organization. Are there specific eligibility requirements? Is so, what are they? Is a recruitment process required? Do prospective participants need to submit an application? What is the process for creating and maintaining a list of mentors (known as the mentor pool) who are qualified and willing to serve? Exercise 4.2, Creating the Mentor Pool, lists a series of specific and rather thorny questions that must be addressed. Each question may raise yet others. Depending on the complexity of the organization, several conversations may be required to resolve these issues. The answers to these questions set the stage for specific mentoring practices.

EXERCISE 4.2

Creating the Mentor Pool

Instructions: Discuss the questions below as you consider the criteria for mentors.

1. What are the ideal personal characteristics and attributes of a mentor?

2. What are the positions of those who should serve as mentors? What positions should not? Why?

3. What strategies should be used to recruit potential mentors?

4. How will mentors be selected? Will everyone who wants to participate be selected? What happens if mentor candidates are not selected?

5. What does it mean to be part of the mentor pool? How important is it to let people know they are in the pool? Should the pool be replenished? If so, how? How often?

Note: When you use these criteria to select the mentor pool, it is important to establish ground rules to protect the individual confidentiality of potential candidates, much as you might when conducting a performance appraisal.

Identifying Competencies

James R. Fisher, Jr., developed a mentoring system consisting of four inter-related subsystems, one of which is his competency system. It includes three rubrics: general competencies, function competencies, and minimum requirements (Fisher, 1998). He advocates developing competency profiles and using them regularly. Exercise 4.3, the Mentoring Competency Template, adapts Fisher's competency sets specifically for personnel engaged in spearheading, managing, administering, or coordinating mentoring within an organization.

Exhibit 4.1 illustrates how the template based on Fisher's mentoring competencies can be used to evaluate individual competencies of potential candidates. In this instance, the competencies required were identified for the mentoring manager position. Each candidate's skills were then compared with the competency requirements for the position. The mentoring manager position was subsequently offered to Wesley because of his mentoring competency and functional competencies. His lack of leadership competency was outweighed by his previous successes as a decisive manager and communicator, along with his mentoring program experience. Although he was relatively new to the organization, Wesley already had a reputation of being a quick study. The group felt he possessed great leadership potential that could be developed once he was on board.

If the generic items listed under general competencies in Exercise 4.1 and Exhibit 4.1 (leadership, management, organizational know-how, mentoring know-how, communications, and decision making) are not applicable to your specific setting, adapt the exercise as necessary, using the three competency sets to guide you in identifying desired competencies or gaps and areas for development. The competency items can then be incorporated into a feedback tool to gather multirater input.

Knowledge Resources

Today's preoccupation with knowledge and knowledge resources is so pervasive that a customized knowledge vocabulary has emerged: "chief knowledge officer," "knowledge workers," "intellectual capital," "knowledge management." The simple fact is that we live in a world where competitor knowledge is critical to organizational viability (Wick and León, 1993). Without knowing more than other people, one finds it difficult to become a meaningful player in business today.

Organizations are in the knowledge-production-and-distribution business: accessing, gathering, storing, and delivering knowledge to their workforce and their customers. As Drucker says, "In a traditional workforce, the worker serves the system; in a knowledge workforce, the system must serve

EXERCISE 4.3

Mentoring Competency Template

Instructions: In this exercise, Fisher's three categories of required competencies are used as an analysis framework. The specific items listed under the general competencies, functional competencies, and minimum requirements categories are not inclusive and may not be specific to your situation. Use the template to change, add, or delete items, or use it as it is. Begin by identifying the individual. Check off the required competencies for each position.

Position	General Competencies						Functional Competencies			Minimum Requirements			
	Leadership	Management	Organizational know-how	Mentoring know-how	Communications	Decision making	Marketing	Production	Finance	Education	Experience	Accessibility	Availability
Mentoring manager													
Organizational leader													
Mentoring coach													
Mentoring trainer													
HR manager													
Supervisor													
Department manager													
Learning manager													

Adapted with permission from James R. Fisher, Jr., Ph.D., The Delta Group Florida. Fisher Competency Profiles © are part of the Fisher Paradigm ™©. Fisher Paradigm ™© is a system to leverage intellectual capital to realize the power of workers and to create a high-performance company.

EXHIBIT 4.1

Mentoring Competency Template in Use

This exhibit illustrates how the mentoring competency template can be used to evaluate the individual competencies of potential candidates. In this instance, the competencies required were identified for the mentoring manager position and compared with the existing competencies of each individual candidate for the position.

Position	Competencies and Requirements												
	General Competencies						Functional Competencies			Minimum Requirements			
	Leadership	Management	Organizational know-how	Mentoring know-how	Communications	Decision making	Marketing	Production	Finance	Education	Experience	Accessibility	Availability
Ideal mentoring manager	X	X	X	X	X	X	X	X	X	MBA	5+ yrs.	X	X
Sally G.	X		X		X	X			X	Ph.D.	10+ yrs.	X	
Ryan	X	X	X	X		X			X	MBA	1 yr.	X	X
Wesley		X		X	X	X	X	X	X	B.A.	5 yrs.	X	X

the worker" (2002, p. 7). Yet, despite the increased knowledge dependency, this component of an organization's infrastructure is often taken for granted.

Knowledge management enables an organization to simultaneously enrich its processes and practices. Knowledge resources are the springboard for the learning and development agenda and the mentoring that goes on within it. According to Arie de Geus, who worked for Royal Dutch/Shell for thirty-eight years and is widely credited with originating the concept of the learning organization, "the critical resource is now people and the knowledge they carry" (Colvin, 1997). The mentoring partnership itself offers a prime example of how carried knowledge is transmitted in an organization.

Some people bring knowledge into the organization with them. For example, from his first day on the job it was clear that Rick was a high performer. There wasn't anything he couldn't program a computer to do. In addition to being likeable, Rick was a born teacher and open to sharing his knowledge. The company's president, Roger, asked Rick to share with him some of the technical knowledge he (Roger) was lacking. In return, the president offered to help Rick achieve some of his development goals. The reciprocal mentoring relationship ("reverse mentoring") they developed offered each an opportunity to share personal knowledge resources with the other. As a result, they were able to ratchet up one another's efficiency and skill sets.

Many individuals hold the keys to organizational memory within their personal warehouse. They have been a part of the organization for so long that they "remember when." These people also possess rich stories and artifacts that shed brilliant light on the values driving a company. As this "tribal knowledge" is unlocked and shared, it becomes a powerful motivator and tool for understanding what has been passed down from generation to generation and why certain rituals, customs, and behaviors exist. Other individuals are the data collectors and manage the knowledge about demographics and trends in the organization. Some are the number crunchers and hold the keys to the warehouse and the bank. Trainers warehouse content and skill knowledge and deliver the platform for corporate learning. Store managers hold the knowledge to manage customer relationships.

The need to know depends on where someone sits within an organization and her job function and the assigned task at a particular moment. Part of knowledge management is being able to make judgments about the timeliness, utility, and appropriateness of that knowledge. The extent to which knowledge is shared depends on many factors, not the least of which is the amount of trust within the organization.

Mentoring involves managing several kinds of knowledge:

- Mentoring know-how and process (how and where to find a mentor, how to establish and maintain a good mentoring relationship, what to expect from a mentoring relationship)

- Specific expertise and experience (new product development, supply chain management, mergers and acquisitions, change management)

- Organizational knowledge (how work gets done, where to find the power brokers, how to succeed in the organization)

- Principles of learning (how to maximize and use resources, sequencing the learning, learning styles, emotional intelligence, and so on)

- Organizational mentoring knowledge (where to find and access resources, who would make the best mentor, when the program begins, how to sign up)

- Best practices (what makes for a good mentoring relationship, how to assign mentoring pairs, appropriate celebrations at the conclusion of a mentoring relationship)

- Subject or content knowledge (marketing, communications, change management, learning organizations)

Successful organizations don't warehouse knowledge; they share it. They also develop the capacity to consume it and transform knowledge in powerful ways that work to their advantage. Managing knowledge in a mentoring culture requires that knowledge be shared thoroughly and effectively, that opportunities for exchange of ideas and information be maximized, and that people step up to their responsibilities. A process for reviewing organizational effectiveness relative to these factors is in Exercise 4.4, the Mentoring Knowledge Management Checklist.

Infrastructure: Reflection on Practice

A mentoring culture requires an infrastructure to support it. Organizations possess leadership, time, financial, human, technical, and knowledge resources to some degree at a given time. Organizations that succeed in organizational mentoring use these resources wisely to develop mentoring practices that meet the needs of the organization and fit within the cultural framework. When combined with the right amount of readiness, opportunity, and support, mentoring practices transform mentoring in an organization into a mentoring culture.

Infrastructure does not exist in isolation and therefore is not static. Infrastructure evolves over time as an organization develops and matures; it changes in response to business conditions, needs, and opportunities. For example, a new acquisition can bolster a weak infrastructure, or a competitive threat may force emergence of new infrastructure components.

Without the presence of organizational learning, infrastructure can bestow a false sense of security. If an organization has an inflexible infrastructure, it frequently overlooks the value of process. Without process, relationships become vulnerable. Too little infrastructure raises the ante on competition for limited resources and sets off a chain of events that increase jealousy, impede collaboration, block cooperation, and erode relationships. To assess the strengths and weaknesses of the infrastructure that supports mentoring in your organization, review and complete Exercise 4.5, the Infrastructure Checklist.

Like the rungs of the ladder Huxley described in this chapter's epigraph, infrastructure components enable an organization to leverage organizational learning through mentoring. Accessing the various components elevates the mentoring work and enables individuals and organizations to reach the next developmental rung. The synergy resulting from combining infrastructure components and solid mentoring practices can have long-lasting, far-reaching effects. This synergy allows flexibility, creates organizational ownership, promotes clarity, and strengthens itself through feedback. These factors contribute to mentoring vitality and sustainability. Alignment, the hallmark addressed in the next chapter, helps ensure success and sustainability.

Mentoring Knowledge Management Checklist

Instructions: Review the sixteen items below and rank the effectiveness of your organization in regard to each item on a scale of 1 to 5 (5 = very effective, 1 = ineffective). Identify areas for process improvement in the column on the far right.

	Rating	Improvement Action Steps
1. Knowledge is shared, accessible, and used.		
2. Opportunities for sharing best practices are created.		
3. Expertise is well used.		
4. Self-directed learning is encouraged and supported.		
5. Critical reflection on practice is an expectation.		
6. Regular dialogue takes place to promote open and continuous exchange of ideas and information.		
7. Lessons learned are regularly shared.		
8. Knowledge is presented in multiple ways, sensitive to varying learning styles.		
9. Knowledge is disseminated in timely fashion.		
10. Multiple modalities and venues are used to transmit knowledge.		
11. Knowledge retrieval is facilitated.		
12. Individuals accept the responsibility for their own learning.		
13. Communities of practice meet regularly.		
14. Knowledge is filtered to make sure that it is from trusted sources.		
15. The amount and type of knowledge being disseminated is appropriate for the purpose and audience.		
16. Multiple ways of accessing data are made available.		

Infrastructure Checklist

Instructions: Assess the strengths and weaknesses of each infrastructure component in your organization. Some items may not be relevant to your organization. However, review them all and put a check mark by those that need improvement. Once you've completed the list, develop an action plan to strengthen your infrastructure.

Infrastructure Component	Key Tasks
1. Leadership	☐ Leaders have a vested interest in mentoring.
	☐ A spirit of mentoring ownership permeates the organization.
	☐ Leadership for mentoring is shared.
	☐ Leaders participate in mentoring events.
	☐ Leaders role-model by serving as mentors themselves.
	☐ Leaders keep up-to-date and informed about mentoring.
	☐ A mentoring leadership succession plan is in place.
2. Time	☐ Mentoring time is honored and encouraged.
	☐ Realistic time expectations are set.
	☐ Mentoring partners make sufficient time for mentoring.
	☐ Time is set aside at meetings to talk about mentoring.
3. Financial resources	☐ There is a long-term financial commitment to mentoring.
	☐ The mentoring budget line is protected.
	☐ The budget adequately reflects the scope, goals, and intent and purpose.
4. Technology	☐ Technology is used to promote and support mentoring, when and where appropriate.
	☐ Technology is available for use and is readily accessible.
	☐ Mentoring participants know how to use the technology available.
	☐ The hardware and software are in working order.
	☐ Technology is used to communicate and disseminate mentoring information.
	☐ Multiple technologies are available to facilitate distance mentoring (i.e., video-conferencing, bridge lines, etc.).
	☐ Technology support is available.
5. Human resources	☐ Competencies for required management and coordination are defined and published.
	☐ Person(s) has responsibility for mentoring management, oversight, and coordination.
	☐ People know how and where to contact the person(s) responsible.
	☐ Support people are available and accessible.
	☐ Those who facilitate learning through mentoring stay up-to-date and develop their skills in the role.

Infrastructure Component	Key Tasks
6. Knowledge resources	☐ Knowledge is shared, accessible, and used.
	☐ There are multiple opportunities for sharing best practices.
	☐ Information is stored and regularly disseminated.
	☐ Individuals share knowledge and expertise.
	☐ Information and knowledge resources are reviewed to ensure quality.
	☐ Critical reflection on mentoring practice is encouraged, and lessons learned are disseminated.
	☐ People have conversations about mentoring.
	☐ Mentoring networking opportunities exist.
	☐ Information is presented in multiple ways to address the range of learning styles.

Chapter 5
Alignment

If you cry "Forward!" you must without fail make plain in what direction to go. Don't you see that if, without doing so, you call out the word to both a monk and a revolutionary, they will go in directions precisely opposite?

—ANTON PAVLOVICH CHEKHOV

SAY THE WORD ALIGNMENT and many images come to mind. There is the image of balancing automobile tires so that the angle of the car's wheels is adjusted to make them perpendicular to the ground and parallel to each other. Alignment increases the life of the tires so they don't wear unevenly and ensures that the car tracks correctly when it is being driven.

There is the image of adjusting the gears in a clock so that they are in the proper relative position for the mechanism to function properly for precision timing and reliability.

There is the image of fitting eyeglasses, positioning them so that the frame is properly balanced and the lenses sit correctly on a person's face such that the eye is centered in the middle of the lens. This alignment ensures that glasses can be used to their maximum advantage and helps avoid irksome double images.

There is the larger choreographic image of the precise timing and sequencing that allows planes to take off and land safely. Leadership in the control tower permits seamless orchestration, and nonnegotiable ground rules promote consistency of practice and independent judgment within specific parameters.

Whether it is an automobile's tires, a clock's gear mechanism, eyeglasses, or airplanes, each instance requires maintaining, balancing, and meshing multiple components in order to operate reliably, seamlessly, and efficiently. In a mentoring culture, multiple components must work together in exactly the same way. Alignment is the hallmark of a mentoring culture that makes it possible for this to happen.

This chapter explores generic concepts underlying these familiar images of alignment and demonstrates how they apply to the internal alignment of an organization and a mentoring culture. First, we take a broad look at the concept of alignment and the challenges encountered in practice. Next, we deal with the specific characteristics of alignment. Finally, we turn to people, the six process components of mentoring, and the dynamic interplay among and between them.

Concepts and Challenges

Alignment is, by its nature, a continuous process; it must be constantly maintained even after it has been well established. Consider the example of tire alignment. You can have your tires aligned at the garage, yet over time the alignment may slip. Sometimes there are signals; your steering wheel might shake, or you might see erosion of the tread on the outside or inside of your tire. If you know what to look for and are paying attention, you might be aware of those signals. If not, you might depend on someone or something to remind you that a realignment is necessary. Alignment takes time and a big-picture perspective. Often, maintaining alignment requires many people. Witness the airport scenario in which multiple alignments must take place interdependently. Less-than-perfect alignment can have negative results ranging from annoying to disastrous.

Alignment has strategic value. It helps an organization live core values, maintain integrity, and promote ongoing effectiveness. It makes it easier to stay in sync while moving forward. It promotes a sense of balance and interdependence of functions, while creating the momentum needed for ensuring organizational vitality, viability, and vibrancy. Organizational alignment links to cultural congruence (explored earlier, in Chapter Two) but is narrower in focus. When we speak about alignment in this chapter, the focus is on achieving consistency of mentoring practices within an organization's culture. It builds on the assumption that a cultural fit exists between mentoring and what is going on in the rest of the organization.

The cost of nonalignment or misalignment is dear. Nonalignment occurs when no attempt has been made to bring about alignment. It is not a result of conscious effort. Misalignment means that some parts may work well or somewhat well. If something is out of alignment it may not necessarily have an impact on everything, but it can indeed knock a whole system out of whack. Misalignment creates compartmentalization, mistrust, and ineffectiveness.

Consider what happens as a CEO comes back from a conference, fired up about a competitor's mentoring program and how it has changed everything at that company. Solely on the basis of the CEO's enthusiasm and debriefing of the competition's program, the leadership team agrees to install a mentoring program. But without determining whether the CEO's vision fits with everyone else's, the mentoring program is doomed at the outset. The senior marketing VP charged with the responsibility of getting a mentoring program up and running within the year finds his meager reserves for the year severely taxed. The level of expectation is raised beyond the organization's delivery capacity. Skepticism creeps in. Some view the program as just another "flavor of the month" management fad. Others recognize that the program isn't tied to anything larger than the CEO's desire to adopt the competitor's modus operandi, and that it works at cross-purposes with employee development initiatives already in place. Many employees develop a wait-and-see attitude, and the program never gains any traction.

In sum, "alignment will make it much easier for your management team to move in the direction you intend. Without alignment, every bit of forward motion will be a struggle" (Bradford, 2002, p. 8).

Characteristics of Alignment

Organizational alignment is manifested in how work is structured and the clear-cut way in which individuals align their values, actions, and interactions with the values, vision, and strategic direction of the organization. When alignment is present, it transcends time and place and permeates the very fiber of the organization. Because it is organic, alignment needs to live in a state of perpetual motion. That is, organizations are never fully aligned but always working toward it. There is always a dynamic tension at play between what is and the desired state. It is not a state of being but an ideal for which to strive. Alignment is a perpetual process of balancing. It is a discipline that requires constancy and tending; like any discipline, it needs to be managed.

Alignment should be intentional, pervasive, seamless, subtle, and ongoing; it should not be forced. It does not equate to sameness or evenness. These are not factory parts that have to be made to specification and line up exactly, though they do need to fit together according to some pattern, acceptable standard, or design. There should be a standard for tolerable variation. What constitutes alignment varies with the organization (and within one). For example, an umbrella nonprofit organization might have a strategic initiative focusing on employee development. In addition to its established policies and timelines, it offers a menu of implementation options to each member organization. Each one can select from the menu and is encouraged to customize implementation within the requisite parameters.

Alignment in a mentoring culture necessitates consistency of practice among seven interdependent components. People and processes are the sine qua non of mentoring alignment within an organization. I have developed a Mentoring Alignment Tool (MAT) framed on these two major elements. It facilitates understanding the dynamic components of mentoring alignment, helps people assess where their organization is in the mentoring alignment process, and builds organizational mentoring that is in alignment with the organization and its goals. The process components are values, vision, understanding, strategy, structure, and communication. If the people or one or more of these process components are missing, this may indicate that mentoring is out of alignment. Completing the tool may also help reveal missing alignment components. If one of the negative impacts or results is apparent, using the tool can help pinpoint the source.

To illustrate the MAT in action, consider the situation at BigSeasons, where management has spent an inordinate amount of time preparing to roll out their mentoring program. They hire a communications consulting firm, prepare high-gloss promotional materials, and give the rollout lots of visibility. They truly feel they have developed unique and well thought-out mentoring schemata for their organization. From the outside and from the inside, "Mentoring at BigSeasons" looks and feels right. The Mentoring Development Team has taken great care to align the key components and feels enormously satisfied and enthusiastic. They have successfully created interest and energy for mentoring at BigSeasons.

Then, several things appear to happen simultaneously. The corporate vice president who initiated mentoring is given a plum assignment in Asia that occupies all of his time and that of his key support staff. Despite good intentions, he can't eke out time for Mentoring at BigSeasons on his already overbooked calendar. The preparation carries the program for a three-month honeymoon period, until it becomes apparent that the corporate VP's former protégé, one of the four regional mentoring managers, seems to be going through the motions and is short on the delivery end of his responsibilities. One colleague describes him as "totally indifferent" and "focused on only what he considers to be high-leverage activity." The VP's passivity takes a toll on his managers, resulting in lack of follow-through, ownership, and commitment within his regional organization. Those within the organization begin to write the program off because of the perceived inactivity and lack of follow-through.

Exhibit. 5.1 illustrates what BigSeasons's MAT might look like when completed. It indicates that three components are out of alignment: people, understanding, and communication. If BigSeasons is to recoup its momentum, these are the three components on which it must refocus its energies to restore wholeness to the mentoring initiative.

EXHIBIT 5.1

Mentoring Alignment Tool Completed for BigSeasons

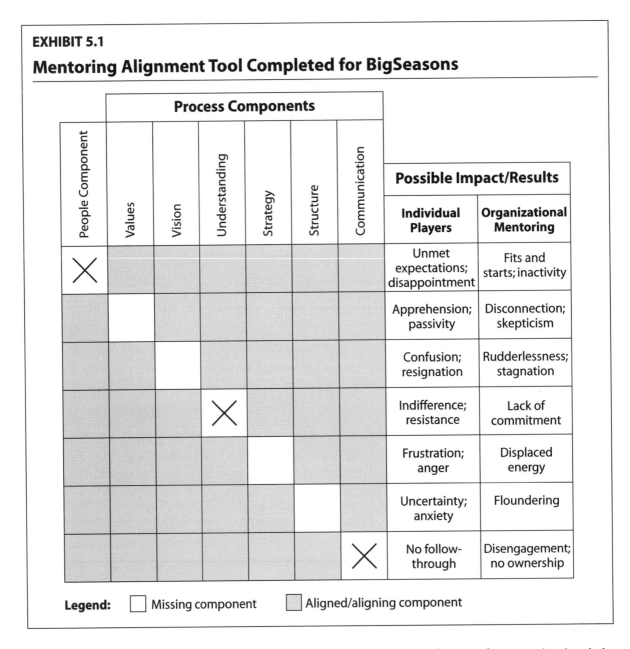

Process Components							Possible Impact/Results	
People Component	Values	Vision	Understanding	Strategy	Structure	Communication	Individual Players	Organizational Mentoring
✗							Unmet expectations; disappointment	Fits and starts; inactivity
	□						Apprehension; passivity	Disconnection; skepticism
		□					Confusion; resignation	Rudderlessness; stagnation
			✗				Indifference; resistance	Lack of commitment
				□			Frustration; anger	Displaced energy
					□		Uncertainty; anxiety	Floundering
						✗	No follow-through	Disengagement; no ownership

Legend: □ Missing component   ▨ Aligned/aligning component

If all the components are present to some degree, the organization is in (at least partial) alignment. When specific components are missing, individuals feel the impact and mentoring implementation is affected on the organizational level. Here, broken down, are some of the results you might see.

- If the people component is absent, individual expectations aren't met; the result is at least some degree of disappointment. If the right people are not in place and in appropriate roles, the organization experiences the mentoring effort in fits and starts of activity, if at all, because there is no one driving, nurturing, or tending the process.

- If values or principles are missing, individuals become apprehensive or passive. A feeling of disconnection (people just talk the talk) and skepticism grows because of the lack of reality and concern about organizational adhesion.

- Even with the right people in place and values authentically articulated and lived, if there is no vision for mentoring then individuals grow confused, pessimistic, and resigned to the status quo. With no roadmap to follow, there is little sense of where mentoring fits into the organization's future. It is not surprising that mentoring efforts without vision very quickly become rudderless, stall out, or stagnate.

- Without understanding the need and goals of mentoring and why it is important, it is difficult to rally internal support. Individuals become indifferent and resistant, and they often push back. This is when "we've tried this before" is heard. Individuals within an organization tend to go into tolerate mode, adding to a growing lack of organizational commitment.

- If strategy is missing, widespread feelings of frustration, and often anger, are experienced. People don't know in which direction to turn or what to do next, how to get from here to there. Energy is displaced and people end up putting in lots of hours for the wrong reasons.

- If structure is missing and all the other elements are present, uncertainty and anxiety abound and people act out because they feel that mentoring is a waste of time. Mentoring programs and initiatives without structure often flounder.

- Even if all the components except communication are in place, the result is lack of follow-through. Without follow-through, it is hard to get people engaged and develop ownership within the organization.

The Mentoring Alignment Tool serves several alignment functions. As a diagnostic tool, it promotes clarity of current reality—what is going on in an organization in regard to mentoring. It also identifies mentoring process components that are either missing or minimally functioning in an organization. Using the MAT in planning amounts to a heads-up as to what results might be anticipated if one or more components are not aligned. You can approach completing the MAT (Exercise 5.1, the Mentoring Alignment Tool) in several ways. You might start by locating what impact or results you are seeing now in your organization. Or start by determining what components are missing or in need of strengthening.

Mentoring Alignment Tool

This matrix illustrates the potential negative impact when one or more mentoring alignment components are missing. It may also help reveal missing alignment components if one or more of the negative descriptors apply.

Instructions: This tool can be used in a variety of ways, depending upon the organization's needs.

1. Consider the "Possible Impact or Results." The first column in this section describes how individuals are being affected by lack of mentoring alignment and the consequences being experienced in the organization. Locate the descriptors currently affecting individuals or the results being experienced, and see which processes may be involved.
2. The second column under "Possible Impact or Results" pertains to organizational mentoring in a similar way.
3. To determine which components might be missing or need to be strengthened, locate the related components.
4. Prioritize these components and build an alignment action plan.

Process Components

People Component	Values	Vision	Understanding	Strategy	Structure	Communication	Possible Impact/Results — Individual Players	Possible Impact/Results — Organizational Mentoring
☐							Unmet expectations; disappointment	Fits and starts; inactivity
	☐						Apprehension; passivity	Disconnection; skepticism
		☐					Confusion; resignation	Rudderlessness; stagnation
			☐				Indifference; resistance	Lack of commitment
				☐			Frustration; anger	Displaced energy
					☐		Uncertainty; anxiety	Floundering
						☐	No follow-through	Disengagement; no ownership

Legend: ☐ Missing component   ▨ Aligned/aligning component

Two examples may help clarify use of the tool. First, if you are experiencing resistance to rolling out or implementing mentoring and can't understand where it's coming from, the intention of your mentoring program may not be well understood; people might have very contrasting assumptions about the purpose or whom it is meant to serve. If this resistance is not addressed, it can result in a lack of commitment to your mentoring efforts.

Second, perhaps you've identified "lack of commitment" to mentoring. The cell to the immediate left, "indifference, resistance," offers an explanation for the behavior of some key players and a diagnosis that "understanding" was lacking.

We next turn our attention to the people component of mentoring alignment before discussing the specific process components that help people stay in alignment with mentoring and with each other.

People: Powering Mentoring

It is essential to harness mentoring horsepower and ensure leadership continuity if mentoring is to align within an organization. We have seen the importance of enrolling the right people in the planning effort. In this section, we expand and deepen our understanding of the variety of roles to be played and the individuals involved in those roles, as well as the leadership transition necessary to create and sustain a mentoring culture within an organization.

Conventional wisdom holds that involving key stakeholders at every phase of the process ensures that mentoring is aligned within an organization. Although the wisdom makes good sense, it does not demand enough. If people are not aligned in thought and deed, they often end up working at cross-purposes to one another and sometimes land far from their intended target or outcome. Alignment of people in a mentoring effort must take place continuously and on multiple levels.

Finding the Right People

When assigning mentoring to a particular workgroup or development team, it is imperative that the group include potential stakeholders, political advocates, people who have personal mentoring, interest, expertise, or skill, and individuals who have the time and are willing to make the commitment to the mentoring enterprise. To be successful, the right people must be involved, and they must be able to fill the right role function.

Doing this is no small task, as Elena, the CEO of a midsized energy firm, found out after she charged Brian, the firm's director of training, with the task of developing and implementing an organizational mentoring initiative for emerging leaders. Brian was highly enthusiastic about mentoring. Because of his personal charisma, he readily rallied support from training workgroup colleagues who volunteered to help him roll out a mentoring program. Brian's mentoring workgroup was made up of people very much like himself: supercharged creative thinkers, champions, and influencers. The group spent long hours in lively planning meetings in which the level of discussion was energizing and entirely satisfying. The Emerging Leaders Mentoring Program rollout generated excitement and anticipation. But when the initial mentoring cohort was selected, many managers were disappointed. Some were angry, others spiteful, and still others just plain resentful—all because "their" emerging leaders were not included as program participants. Brian's workgroup was not happy with the pushback they received on their pet project and felt that those not involved simply didn't get it.

Although they accomplished their objective of developing a mentoring initiative that pleased the CEO, what the workgroup created met the needs of only a few people. A major reason is that the group was too inbred and similar. Those included in a mentoring planning or implementation process have a distinct need to know—why they have been invited in and what role(s) they are expected to play. The planning group needs to include the voices of the publics that the mentoring process will ultimately embrace.

Creating and sustaining a mentoring culture requires that people play a variety of roles. The reality is that one person may serve more than one role, or several people may be required to fulfill the same role function. How can you identify specific people to fill particular roles and gauge existing gaps you currently have with regard to mentoring? How can you make sure that you don't overload any one individual with too many roles at one time?

Exercise 5.2, the Role Function Identification and Gap Analysis, is a tool that can help you manage this process. The role categories listed are those most frequently needed in an organizational mentoring effort. Some of the role functions are similar; for example, administrator and coordinator could be construed as one and the same. The distinction is that the administrator can be a day-to-day point person who answers questions, sends out information, and connects people with resources while the coordinator speaks more to the general functioning of the system and its parts. A coordinator may or may not be the "owner." One might expect the owner to champion the program, but the reverse is not always true. A resister is an organizational leader or manager who is skeptical about a mentoring initiative or program. It is important to identify key resisters, and listen to and understand their concerns and issues. If issues and concerns are not addressed or attended to, resisters can stonewall a process or sabotage the initiative altogether. Including resisters often promotes understanding, fosters ownership, and establishes the eventual goodwill and support required later on to grow the culture.

Explore and define what the role functions mean for you and how they can be useful to you in analyzing the people power you need to drive a mentoring culture. Review the list of roles to determine which are most relevant to your organization. Consider:

- Who needs to be involved to get buy-in, to implement, support, and grow mentoring within your organization?
- Who has the experience or expertise?
- Who might be able to carve out ample time to make a meaningful contribution in the role, and at what time in the process?

In completing the form, list the names of people who serve those functions already or prospects you would like to bring on board. Finally, decide how you plan to recruit the people you have identified. Remember that roles are required at different times, and not everyone needs to be on board at once.

Defining key players' roles and responsibilities is critical to accountability in a mentoring relationship, as we'll see in the next chapter. It also helps maintain alignment. If, for example, mentors are unclear about their roles, they consciously or unconsciously create a designer role for themselves, which may or may not be in concert with the intent of the mentoring effort—or perhaps at odds with what a program is trying to achieve.

Even with understanding what roles need to be filled, if you fail to include the right people, or if they join for the wrong reasons, you may miss the mark on alignment. Be alert to the fact that emotional baggage, a leadership void, attitude and behavior, and lack of time can all contribute to misalignment.

Ensuring Leadership Continuity

Harnessing horsepower for mentoring also makes demands on organizational leadership. It requires personal commitment to learning and growth in the role. It means nurturing other leaders so that they too can grow and develop in their respective roles. In short, it necessitates building capacity in others so that they are prepared and ready to steward mentoring within the organization. As described in the previous chapter, a supportive infrastructure ensures that systems are in place for leadership succession.

The reality is that mentoring coordinators, coaches, and supervisors change. Life intervenes. People change positions, move, get sick. External

Role Function Identification and Gap Analysis

Instructions: The list in the first column represents common mentoring roles that should be filled by people involved in developing, implementing, and maintaining organizational mentoring. Fulfillment of these roles could be satisfied by one or several people and be played out at different points in time. List additional roles that may be relevant to specific organizational needs. The second column offers a space to check off all those roles that are (or were) represented or that may need to be satisfied in the future. List the names of people who already serve those functions or prospects you may want to bring on board at some point in columns three and four. The last column is the "strategy column," where you can note how and when to bring people into mentoring to fill in various role gaps.

Role Function	✓	Name 1	Name 2	How and When to Recruit
Administrator				
Champion				
Communicator				
Coordinator				
Creative thinker				
Decision maker				
Enabler				
Evaluator				
Facilitator				
Implementer				
Influencer				
Leader				
Manager				
"Owner"				
Potential participant				
Power broker				
Purse strings/funder				
Resister				
Supporter				
Trainer				

factors influence the organization. Change is inevitable, and ensuring a strong base of support is essential to long-term mentoring sustainability. Buy-in, ownership, and personal meaning must be available to others. Being a mentoring leader requires replacing oneself, mentoring the next in command, planning for leadership succession, and letting go. The importance of succession planning cannot be overestimated.

Mentoring coordinators, administrators, and leaders must develop themselves and others to ensure continuity of mentoring within the organization. They must self-manage, delegate, and negotiate for resources they need. They must, above all, make a personal commitment to self-improvement in the role. This applies doubly for a small organization, where mentoring is often a one-stop shop.

Exercise 5.3, the Mentoring Leadership Development Plan, can be used as a personal development plan or as a tool for leadership succession planning. The seven target development areas listed are the most common; you could focus on all seven areas listed or only a few. Or modify the areas to suit your purposes.

Suppose you are completing your term as institutional mentoring manager and want to use this development plan as a way to prepare your successor. There are some tried-and-true strategies for enhancing performance in the role. One is to fill in the target areas in the first column with what you wish you had known when you assumed the role and what you'd like your successor to know. Ask your successor to complete the same column on a separate form. Collate the findings and prioritize the areas. To plan the learning activities, sit together with the successor or an HR manager and identify learning activities (including processes, resources, and people who can mentor or coach the incumbent. Depending on the situation, you may want to add others to the learning activity planning discussion.

In a second strategy, an executive director brings together the past and future mentoring leaders and facilitates the discussion. If so, three completed forms should be collated. Make the time frame reasonable, sequential, and logical and remember that some of the learning can be staged prior to assuming the responsibility as well as once in the job.

Process Components of Alignment

Process is where people and intent are ultimately tested. Failed mentoring efforts are often lacking many of the process components described here. Values, vision, understanding, structure, strategy, and communication are the process components of alignment. Their absence weakens the alignment toehold that is already in place. By the same token, "it is highly unlikely that

EXERCISE 5.3

Mentoring Leadership Development Plan

Instructions: The column on the left lists seven areas you may want to target for your own development or for your mentoring leadership successor. Under each target area, identify specific areas for development. In the middle column, describe the learning activities—including resources, processes, and activities—that support the target development areas in column one. In the last column on the right, list the time frame for completing the learning activities.

Target Development Area	Learning Activity (Process, Resources, Persons)	Time Frame
1. Corporate and "organizational" knowledge		
2. Interpersonal skills		
3. Leadership skills		
4. Mentoring best practices		
5. Project management		
6. Relationship-building skills (i.e., networking, feedback)		
7. Transition planning and management		

any organization could be perfectly aligned and totally one-dimensional" (Honold and Silverman, 2002, p. 93). Being aware of and continuously working at minimizing your weakest process components is required to keep your mentoring efforts in alignment.

Values

Values are the qualities, concepts, ideals, or principles that guide how we act and what we do. They directly relate to organizational behavior (Senge and others, 1994; Schein, 1999; Kouzes and Posner, 2002). If organizational values are shared, productivity and performance outcomes improve. In contrast, if individual and group values compete with organizational values, the result is misalignment. If an organization does not value learning and relationship, mentoring rarely becomes embedded. A mentoring program must embody the values that drive its practices, internally and externally. Alignment of values helps mentoring stay on course. As Kouzes and Posner have stated, "Without core beliefs and with only shifting positions, would-be leaders are judged as inconsistent and derided for being 'political' in their behavior" (2002, p. 48). If a mentoring program espouses one set of values and the mentoring that goes on under this umbrella embraces a differing set of values, people become passive, mistrusting, and apprehensive. With values out of sync and lacking internal consistency, the credibility of the mentoring activity is undermined. The feeling of disconnect and skepticism that ensues invites sabotage.

In institutional life, there are many things that get in the way of walking the talk (practicing what is preached). Role and market demands add untold stress and time pressure; needs and "shoulds" can easily be confounded. Consider, for example, what occurred with the local office of a national real estate company. Well known for its innovative and pace-setting sales practices, the company (which we'll call National Real Estate) created a mentoring program that was disconnected from its corporate values. Every new associate was automatically assigned a mentor and was required to meet with him or her weekly, as well as to shadow the mentor for three months. If by the end of six months the new associate had not closed any deals, 25 percent of the mentor's monthly salary would be deducted. If either a mentor or mentee fail to show up for a meeting, a $250 fee was imposed on the "guilty" partner. Yet the company continues to espouse internal collaboration and cooperation, flexibility, mutuality, trust, and interdependence as the answer to external competition.

It was no surprise, then, that more than healthy skepticism and lots of individual apprehension were voiced about what "came down from corporate." All of a sudden, mentors and mentees alike were reluctant to share information and leads. Mentoring in theory was far different from what it was in practice. Mentors "volunteered" reluctantly, and retention of new hires landed at an all-time low.

Extreme as this example may appear, it does reflect what actually happens when mentoring occurs in a values vacuum. In mounting any mentoring initiative, it is important to get in touch with the values that lie beneath the development and implementation of the process. The clearer an organization is about which values drive its mentoring practice and how mentoring creates value for the organization, the easier it is to achieve alignment. Those engaged in planning and implementing organizational mentoring need to use these values to inform their decisions and actions. The first step is to identify the values influencing and affecting mentoring work that goes on in an organization; "The answers to the question of values will come only when you're willing to take a journey through your inner territory" (Kouzes and Posner, 2002, p. 52).

Exercise 5.4, Values Identification and Alignment, presents a roadmap for that journey. Begin by listing the core values underlying the mentoring that goes on within your organization. For example, one of the most frequently espoused values is that employees should be self-directed learners. After values have been identified, they should be committed to paper, "posted," shared, and regularly referred to so that others are aware of how they lead to development of the mentoring process and programmatic decisions. Assess the degree to which your actions and your espoused values are in alignment. Finally, consider what process improvements you want, need, and should put in place to increase your alignment rating.

John Gardner said that "the problem is not to find better values, but to be faithful to those we profess" (1963, p. 53). Faithfulness is an alignment behavior well worth perfecting. Identifying values has to do with professed values (what the values are that inform what we do). A strong audit process helps individuals, groups, and organizations recommit regularly to core values, and this in turn keeps them "faithful," ultimately contributing to strengthening corporate culture.

Vision

Without vision, mentoring efforts remain merely programs, surviving but not thriving, hitting temporary targets but not moving toward potential (De Pree, 2003). Kotter makes the case for vision and the need to be anticipatory: "Unless many individuals line up and move together in the same direction, people will tend to fall all over one another" (1990, p. 5). Vision is a tool for helping individuals, groups, departments, organizations, and systems line up in the same direction. A lack of vision often contributes to

EXERCISE 5.4

Values Identification and Alignment

Instructions: List the espoused values underlying your mentoring efforts. Identify how each value is demonstrated in terms of what you say and how you express it (actions). It would be ideal to get feedback from others on how the value is demonstrated. Then rate (either independently or with others) the degree to which you think there is alignment between the first two columns. Use the results to generate actionable items in the final column.

Espoused Value	How This Value Is Demonstrated (What We Say and Do)	Rating 1–5 (1 = Low; 5 = High)	What We Need to Do More of in the Future

the feeling of confusion and hopelessness experienced by participants in organizational mentoring. It can also result in stagnation of mentoring efforts.

Vision requires mastery. It tests the mettle of leaders, who must push themselves to think beyond the pragmatic and the everyday, to imagine the possible. Kouzes and Posner (2002) talk about inspiring a shared vision. If vision remains the hope, dream, and picture of one or two individuals, it does not move others to action. It must be inspiring and shared in order to galvanize and get people headed in the same direction.

Imagine an employee with an interesting and innovative vision about what mentoring should be and how it should look in the organization. If this person is inspired (by someone actively and accurately communicating the overall vision and scope of mentoring) and if the vision is allowed to be shared (so that the mentoring development team then holds the same vision), the employee's innovative and creative thinking can be focused, the energy harnessed, and those ideas can be heard (and possibly acted on). But if the employee's vision competes with that of the CEO, for example, the employee is likely to experience confusion and lack of hope.

Creating a shared vision is a critical part of planning the work. As part of envisioning a mentoring culture, imagine that mentoring is about to roll out in your organization. The planning phase is complete, and word of mouth has generated a tremendous amount of excitement. Given this scenario, respond to these questions with as much specificity as possible:

- What is about to happen?

- How is it going to roll out?

- When will this rollout begin?

- Who is involved?

- What are they doing?

In asking these questions, review the shared vision as you begin to plan for roll out. Also engage the group in a second visioning process with the development group to make sure that there is clarity about the rollout. A bit further down the line, the scenario looks like this. Mentoring is flourishing, and you now have a fully integrated mentoring process embedded in your organization. Your expectations for mentoring have been exceeded. By everyone's account, mentoring has been hugely successful. Describe what is going on now:

- Who is involved?

- What are they doing?

- How does the process work?
- What impact is mentoring making in your organization?
- What changes are you seeing as a result?

A mentoring team, potential participants, interested stakeholders, or a group can use these questions to jump-start an envisioning process. This can be done initially by individuals or collectively in a group setting once the context has been set. The point is to create an inclusive vision, get buy-in, and achieve shared ownership of the vision.

Once individuals complete their own vision, then the process of sharing the vision begins. Whether responses are collated into a written document or done in real time with a group, it is important to establish a big picture of possibilities before identifying common themes or threads. Testing out the vision and getting feedback imparts energy and creates value for mentoring at all levels of the organization. The goal is to generate support. People will not be supportive if they don't understand what is expected, or if there is a disconnect between expectations and reality. Yearout, Miles, and Koonce (2001) suggest that what is needed is a "vision with legs" (p. 32). A mentoring vision with legs motivates and excites people. It frames the mentoring effort in the future and defines its intent. It is a bold, strong, compelling word picture of possibility.

Kouzes and Posner (2002) offer multiple strategies for creating common ground. Creating common ground is a process that takes time and patience. The energy that comes from sharing visions and ultimately creating a unified vision drives the mentoring activity that follows. It is not enough to listen and gather feedback. The feedback needs to find its way back into the planning process, giving life to the ultimate design and implementation of organizational mentoring.

Understanding

If shared understanding is the basis for decision making and implementation, the results are impressive. People know where they are headed and can be clear about their roles in helping the organization get there. They can better manage their own expectations and those of others. Without the spirit of shared ownership, commitment, and enterprise that shared understanding brings, people often become resistant and apathetic. They act out their frustration through gossip, sabotage, negativism, and indifference, undermining decision making and implementation.

Creating shared understanding is an important step in creating alignment. I recall a client who called me in to his organization to "fix a broken mentoring program." In fact, the so-called program never got off the ground because everyone sitting around the table had their own idea of what mentoring was and whom it was meant to serve.

Through a series of interviews with forty-four organizational leaders, my colleagues and I found that once people fully understood a problem, situation, or task they were able to make better decisions (Hall, Greenberg, and Zachary, 1987). With good decisions, implementation was more effective because it was aligned with their understanding and decision making. We also learned that understanding had to be nurtured and recreated. We learned that it couldn't and shouldn't be taken for granted, and that every time new players came into the picture they had to be brought up to speed and given the same information and understanding as others who were involved in the project or task. In that way, they were then ready to make sound decisions.

Shared understanding is the basis for sound decision making and implementation. Figure 5.1 presents processes needed to move from understanding to decision making, and finally to implementation. Some expectations may be met serendipitously if the shared-understanding stage is skipped, but most will not. If you've ever wondered why a group could not come to a decision, it may have been because there was never full understanding of the issue. If you did make a decision without understanding, you might have been challenged by implementation. Each person (as well as the group) has to see the whole puzzle and how pieces fit together, and understand how and why decisions are made and what needs to happen. Promoting shared understanding and awareness is an effective way to level the playing field and minimize politics. It must be nurtured, continuously recreated, and not taken for granted.

Understanding doesn't always come about as the result of a meeting. A lot depends on how people take in and process information. Some are information people and need to have time and data to review in advance of a focused conversation. Some jump right in and know how to ask questions to bring about immediate understanding. Recognition of these differing approaches offers clues about how to facilitate understanding.

Alignment conversation is another way of promoting understanding; it is particularly helpful in creating a climate of readiness for mentoring within an organization. One of my clients had a history of "mentoring" within the organization. A division had a buddy program focusing on new-hire orientation. Another division mentored all new department managers, and yet another coached high-potentials. Each program used the word mentor to describe the more experienced learning partner. Each of the so-called

FIGURE 5.1

The SDI Alignment Model

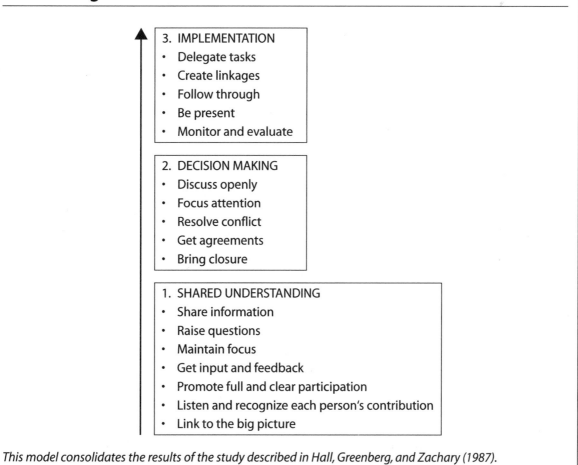

3. IMPLEMENTATION
- Delegate tasks
- Create linkages
- Follow through
- Be present
- Monitor and evaluate

2. DECISION MAKING
- Discuss openly
- Focus attention
- Resolve conflict
- Get agreements
- Bring closure

1. SHARED UNDERSTANDING
- Share information
- Raise questions
- Maintain focus
- Get input and feedback
- Promote full and clear participation
- Listen and recognize each person's contribution
- Link to the big picture

This model consolidates the results of the study described in Hall, Greenberg, and Zachary (1987).

mentors performed different functions, even though the same label was used. Employees were confused, particularly those who moved from division to division and were engaged in a "mentoringlike" experience. They brought their assumptions from one division to the other and made some false starts on the basis of those assumptions. It was difficult to make a commitment to a relationship that was a moving target.

Alignment conversation about mentoring is important so that contrasting assumptions about mentoring can be revealed. Exhibit 5.2 presents a menu of topics for this conversation. You may find that in trying to create shared understanding, one thing you accomplish is helping people embrace a new perception. It may take several conversations to do so, but without conversation and without productively involving people in the process the old paradigm of mentoring will not change.

EXHIBIT 5.2

Shared Understanding Conversation Guide

To-Do List	Topics	Conversation Considerations
Establish rapport	Purposes of this conversation: Informational Role recruitment Expertise Connections Advice	Take time to connect and get to know each other.
Talk about current mentoring effort	Why mentoring? Why now? Where mentoring fits into the big picture	Determine if individual is clear about where and how mentoring fits.
Talk about mentoring	What we mean by mentoring in this instance	Check in with person's experience with mentoring and models that he or she is familiar with.
Clarify roles	Why you are needed Roles and responsibilities Committee, team, and functional operations Other players involved	Find out if there are other areas of experience or expertise that might be useful to tap into. It may be that your alignment conversation is informational only. In this case, clarify the roles of those who will be involved.
Determine needs and expectations	Other information needed for clarity	Give the individual time to relate reactions to information you have shared and any concerns; find out areas that still need clarification.
Determine mentoring expectation	Timetable Deliverables	Be clear and explicit about the time required for completion of tasks and what you ask this individual to deliver on.

Strategy

Mentoring stands little chance of making an impact if the effort is scatter-shot and there is no coherent roadmap for moving forward together. Strategy provides the roadmap for avoiding expenditure of wasted time and energy and frustration. Values, vision, and understanding are prerequisites to formulating a sound organizational mentoring strategy.

Strategy begins with the end in mind. To achieve desired results, mentoring must be tied to sound business reasons—reasons that are applicable to any organization, whether for-profit, nonprofit, educational, religious, or other.

In this sense, business reasons define the purpose and the scope of organizational mentoring. They answer the questions "Why bother?" and "What for?" They are the desired outcomes, the ends; mentoring is the means for achieving those ends. Without concrete linkage to that purpose, the importance of mentoring is diminished, casting doubt on its sustainability. There is little justification for dedicating the required time, people, and resources to the effort.

Attracting, retaining, and orienting employees are fairly common business reasons for organizational mentoring (see Kaplan-Leiserson, 2003). Employee and career development are sometimes subsumed under those reasons. Mentoring is frequently part of an organization's leadership development mandate. Developing bench strength, increasing leadership in the pipeline, fast-tracking, and preparing the next generation of leaders are also popular reasons for organizational mentoring. Some organizations choose mentoring as a vehicle to promote diversity. Some use mentoring as a vehicle for planning for retirement. Others promote mentoring to build a better workplace, whether this means more cohesive, more connected, friendlier, or caring. Mentoring is a way of retaining and transferring intellectual capital, and of developing knowledge workers by transferring technical, organizational, business, and corporate knowledge. For still other organizations, mentoring is the means for increased employee competency, self-confidence, and commitment. If there is one theme that consistently reverberates throughout the process of creating a mentoring culture, it is goal setting. In addition to framing the accountability agenda, goals help pinpoint the strategy and form a critical link between business reasons and strategy. Goals align the focus of people with the work to be done.

Few organizations think in terms of strategic planning for mentoring. Strategic planning is a continuous process of organizational learning that puts life into the values, vision, and understanding that inform it. It prepares and strengthens organizational capacity to implement mentoring with clarity of purpose, resolve, and direction. In developing and implementing a mentoring strategy, involve as many points of view as possible in creating a strategy; be open to learning and updating your strategy as you engage in mentoring; identify the core competencies you need to build to strengthen organizational mentoring; continuously analyze and predict stakeholder behavior; and make sure every facet of mentoring supports your organization's values, vision, and understanding.

A means of checking the internal consistency of strategies of each component and consistency against the six other alignment components is found in Exercise 5.5, the Organizational Mentoring Strategy Map. If you find yourself using this exercise with a group, assign teams for each strategy; have them complete their strategy independently and then come to consensus. The teams should also review their outcomes and decide if their

Organizational Mentoring Strategy Map

Instructions: First, define your mentoring goal. Then take these steps:

1. List one mentoring strategy under each number in row one.
2. Fill in the blanks under each strategy.
3. When the map is complete, analyze results; look for common themes, and note blank spaces or duplication.
4. Determine what further goals and actions are needed to align your strategies with each other and with each of the six components in the first column.
5. Discuss results and how they affect implementation of the strategies, individually and collectively.

Mentoring goal:

Strategy (Write Strategies Here)	#1	#2	#3	#4	#5	#6
People involved in carrying out strategy						
Value(s) it relates to mentoring strategy						

Strategy (Write Strategies Here)	#1	#2	#3	#4	#5	#6
Vision that supports mentoring strategy						
Shared understanding that informs strategy						
Structure required to support strategy						
Communication needed to implement strategy						

strategy is internally consistent. Once the entire map is completed by the group, open up the floor for a full discussion of implications of findings. Finally, come up with action goals to close the gaps or come to a fuller alignment.

Whether you use this exercise individually or in a group, once your map is complete analyze the results, noting common themes, blank spaces, and duplication. Discuss implications of results and how those results affect implementation of the strategies individually and collectively. If you find that you are counting on exactly the same people to be implementing all the strategies, consider whether doing so is realistic and whether you should get other people involved. By the same token, you may decide that you have too many people involved or the wrong people assigned to a specific implementation task. The strategy map should yield a big-picture perspective as well as a roadmap to help you stay in alignment.

Structure

One of the six psychological hungers identified by Eric Berne (1996) is the hunger for structure, which in turn helps us create order. Structural alignment reflects how organizational mentoring is organized and operationalized—that is, the visible frameworks set in place to develop, implement, and evaluate mentoring efforts. Structure must be internally consistent with strategy in order to achieve proper alignment. If it is not, mentoring requires added diligence.

In many organizations, structure doesn't mesh with the culture. In fact, the mere mention of the word structure invites pushback. There is wisdom in balancing knowledge about culture and using this knowledge to align it for consistency with each of the remaining components: people, values, vision, understanding, strategy, and communication. Without structure, mentoring initiatives create anxiety and uncertainty because there are no guideposts to follow. Without structure (or structured nonstructure), maintaining mentoring alignment is a challenge.

In the ideal world, structure follows strategy. However, the reality is that most mentoring programs create their own structures before a comprehensive organizational mentoring strategy is put in place. There may, for example, be mentoring programs in each of an organization's highly competitive units. If each unit is trying to best the other in competing for the same corporate resources, the programs do not stand much chance. Great care and due consideration should be given to structural alignment so that it is functional and well suited to the organizational culture.

A structural trap is a condition in which "one part of the system requires people to act in one way, while another part of the organization requires them to do something that contradicts this" (Isaacs, 1999, p. 205). Silos create structural traps by inhibiting the flow of information throughout an organization. The organization is effective vertically within a department or a division, yet it lacks efficiency and flexibility in activities that requires cross-departmental cooperation (Bradford, 2002).

There are many kinds of structural traps. For example, a performance appraisal system may be out of sync with current institutional priorities. The result is that employees are rewarded for behaviors that don't create value. One subtle cultural trap is language, because of the stigma and loaded nature of certain words.

Considerable thought should be given to the words selected when designing and implementing a mentoring program. Labels and names carry with them a range of meaning, explicit as well as implicit. The names for partners should culturally fit the organization and the purposes of the relationship. That is, the purposes of the mentor-mentee relationship should be identified first and then the words used to designate the relationship, not the other way around (which is what is most usually done). The names used to describe the nonmentor partner in a mentoring relationship include protégé, mentee, mentoree, intern, learning leader, shadow, buddy, apprentice, peer mentor, colearner, and others. The challenge, as Sayles puts it, "is to find the language and descriptions that mirror the new realities and not the old hierarchies" (1990, p. 11).

In addition to the often hidden meaning, there is also a layer of historical or contextual meaning. Test your market to get a sense of some of the visceral reactions to the names you select. Exercise 5.6, a Sample Vocabulary Alignment Evaluation, presents a way to determine the cultural fit of some popular titles for people being mentored. Use the exercise as it is or adapt it. You may also choose to make it a prototype in determining the cultural fit of the title you choose for the person doing the mentoring.

Language can also be a signal for change. For example, if you visit an organization and everyone is telling you the same thing about mentoring, it indicates a high degree of alignment. If everyone has been telling you the same thing for many years, this indicates that it is time to gather some data to see if recalibration is called for or if everyone still means the same thing by what they are saying.

Communication

Communication is the oil that greases the gears of successful alignment. Clear and consistent communication is essential to achieving a return on an organization's mentoring investment. Inconsistent and ineffective communication touches people on many levels and in different ways. Lack of

Sample Vocabulary Alignment Evaluation

Instructions: What images come to mind as you look at each of these words? Do these same images come to mind for other people in your organization? How do the images mesh with your cultural tradition? Would the name be a good fit with your culture?

Title for Person Being Mentored	Image Evoked for Me	Image Evoked for Others	Organizational Traditions	How Would It Fit with Our Organizational Culture?
Mentee				
Protégée				
Protégé				
Buddy				
Emerging leader				
Big brother or sister				
Learning leader				
Intern				
Preceptee				
Mentoree				

communication can knock the legs out from under organizational mentoring. It is challenging enough to effectively follow-through when there is communication, let alone without it. Waiting until all the pieces of a mentoring process are picture perfect before communicating coming attractions is risky business. By that time, it may be too late to get the buy-in and ownership needed to align organizational mentoring. As we've seen, feedback is vital to creating a mentoring culture and an essential part of the communication process.

Information flows through organizations every day. It is mediated by power and influence, to be sure, but also by who is listening and when. When old information conflicts with current reality, it is a sure indicator that communication is out of alignment. If people fail to take responsibility for staying current, they won't be able to align their actions with current organizational realities.

Alignment: Reflection on Practice

Alignment is a process of movement that demands agility. It is fraught with challenges that affect the functionality and effectiveness of organizational mentoring. The work of alignment promotes consistency of practice, cultural fit, and coordination. It is demanding but well worth the effort because:

- Mentoring thrives when there is alignment.

- It helps maintain mentoring integrity.

- It promotes exchange of knowledge and information that can result in successful business results.

- The gains realized from alignment of effort exceed what any single organization or team can do on its own.

- As an organization becomes increasingly more aligned, ownership and the organizational learning expand.

- It produces internal cohesion that spurs an organization to be far greater than the sum of its parts.

- It has a ripple effect, touching and affecting related systems and processes.

If one or more of the seven alignment components are missing then it is difficult to achieve the momentum needed to move with agility, intentionality, and coherence. In fact, the missing component is usually the root cause for lack of alignment. Alignment practices you may need to adopt for each of the components are recapped here:

People

- Identify role functions.
- Analyze gaps.
- Put a mentoring leadership development plan in place for current and future leaders.

Values

- Identify espoused values.
- Analyze behaviors that demonstrate values.
- Analyze and fill gaps.

Vision

- Create a shared vision of full implementation (the ideal).
- Create a shared vision of the initial rollout.
- Get feedback on the vision.

Understanding

- Continuously work at creating understanding, especially among new players.
- Be aware of how people take in and process information.
- Hold periodic alignment conversations with stakeholders, individually and as groups.

Strategy

- Identify, gain consensus on, and publish business reasons.
- Articulate goals.
- Map strategy.

Structure

- Conduct a structural analysis of the mentoring you offer to all of your target groups.
- Establish and use a consistent and meaningful mentoring vocabulary.

Communication

- Consistently and effectively communicate.
- Make sure information is up to date.

- Continuously link progress and results to business strategy.
- Seek feedback.

Mentoring can, and often does, become the catalyst for organizational alignment and a model for success for the organization as a whole, perhaps more long-lasting than the mentoring culture it helps create. Mastery of alignment in mentoring transcends the arena, and the process of alignment itself becomes self-perpetuating. As we'll see in the following chapter, alignment and accountability work together to support a mentoring culture.

Chapter 6
Accountability

Greatness is not where we stand, but in what direction we are moving.
We must sail sometimes with the wind and sometimes against it
—but sail we must, and not drift, nor lie at anchor.

—OLIVER WENDELL HOLMES

ACCOUNTABILITY IS SERIOUS BUSINESS today. Shareholders exact increasing accountability. Funders and internal stakeholders require more and more information and data. Organizations and institutions look internally and ask more of themselves and of each other than in years past (Zachary, 2003a). As the demand for accountability increases, new practices and processes are required.

The Association, a nonprofit entity that offers patient education for member families, began operation five years ago with five employees; it now has fifty employees and will soon hire twelve more. Many of the newer employees lack understanding of the Association's mission, values, and goals. As one founder commented, "They understand the words, but they don't understand what they really mean to us. We're concerned that in the effort to serve our clients well, our employees may have lost sight of what our core business really is. We all need to be on the same page." With this comment, the idea for a mentoring program was born. All employees were urged to find mentoring partners; they were to either be a mentor or find one.

The founders assumed, erroneously, that everyone would participate. Certainly, people could have. Unfortunately, nobody did, because everyone assumed that someone else would step forward first. One of the major reasons for the lack of mentoring success at the Association was lack of accountability.

Accountability requires shared intention, shared responsibility and ownership, and shared commitment to action and consistency of practice. Without them, it is easy to miss the mark. Communication, education, and training are central to ensuring accountability; but they can go only so far when it comes to ensuring positive action and results. Accountability also involves the processes of (1) setting goals, (2) clarifying expectations,

(3) defining roles and responsibilities, (4) monitoring progress and measuring results, (5) gathering feedback, and (6) formulating action goals. Each is discussed in turn after we first broadly address the concept of accountability.

The Concept of Accountability

Accountability has become the key driver for organizational learning, performance, design, and behavior; as such, it has a multiplier effect. Without shared accountability, it is nigh unto impossible for an organization to effectively achieve its vision and create the positive energy necessary to get desired results. This requires a broader and deeper approach to accountability. For mentoring in the organization to be on a steady, productive course, each of the accountability processes should be clear, owned, multilayered, proactive, achievable, and self-perpetuating. Let's examine these core criteria.

• *Clear.* Accountability requires clarity at the forefront. Clarity is the key to meeting expectations and fulfilling roles and responsibilities; it encourages self-direction and helps avert false starts and potential problems. Indeed, as Lencioni has said, "The enemy of accountability is ambiguity" (2002, p. 214). To hold someone accountable, what is required of them must be made clear.

• *Owned.* Personal and organizational accountability go hand in hand. Shared ownership for accountability creates a supportive climate that promotes productivity and energizes sustainability. Ownership does not come cheaply, however; rigor is required (McCall, 1994).

• *Multilayered.* Accountability cascades through the many layers of an organization. Individuals accept self-accountability where and when appropriate, teams embrace accountability, and the organization as a whole supports and creates value for accountability by consciously fostering it throughout the organization.

• *Proactive.* Accountability paves the way for the future. It is not about what was but what will or what can be: "The real value and benefit of accountability stems from a person or an organization's ability to influence events and outcomes before they happen" (Connors, Smith, and Hickman, 1994, p. 64).

• *Achievable.* Accountability becomes just a lofty ideal if it is not achievable. Achievability requires a solid grounding in reality, ensuring that adequate human and financial resources are available and an action plan is in place.

• *Self-perpetuating.* The goal is ultimately self-perpetuating accountability that is formally structured and that becomes part of the underlying culture of the organization. The cultural expectation is that setting goals, clarifying expectations, defining roles and responsibilities, monitoring progress and measuring results, gathering feedback, formulating action goals, and integrating process improvements are part of how business gets done in the organization. Change does not alter commitment to the process.

Accountability is the ultimate capacity-building tool. Because it enhances performance, it has tremendous leverage and can produce long-lasting results. Attention to accountability processes and criteria can help an organization as it develops its mentoring program, yet it is people (supported by the structure) who actually make it happen. In addition, both individual and partnership accountability should be part and parcel of the mentoring relationship. In reality, self-accountability is the heart of facilitating self-directed learning. By setting expectations and creating mechanisms for assisting mentoring partners to be accountable, mutual responsibility is enhanced. In a mentoring culture, a premium is placed on mutual responsibility and accountability takes place on many levels. Together, these processes and criteria form an accountability matrix (see Exercise 6.1, Accountability Matrix) that you can use to increase your organization's accountability.

Setting Goals

Goals significantly increase the chance of creating and sustaining a mentoring culture within an organization. Without them, mentoring initiatives and relationships are prone to drift and often become entirely rudderless. If there is nothing to keep mentoring on course, and no sense of direction, it becomes all but impossible to make real headway. Goals set the parameters that circumscribe the mentoring effort. They frame and define the focus of the work to be done, eliminate ambiguity, constitute a framework for gauging progress and measuring success, ground the learning, and set a context for mentoring. They increase motivation because they harness and focus energy and action.

The process for setting goals needs to be accomplished on several planes, depending on the penetration of the effort desired and the complexity of the organizational structure. The initial goal setting must be implemented on the macro level. In some organizations, this activity focuses on the entire business entity or perhaps on certain segments (for example, to acculturate and orient new employees). Another level of goal-setting activity takes place between the mentoring partners. Each mentoring partnership within

EXERCISE 6.1

Accountability Matrix

Instructions: As you establish each of the six text accountability processes listed in the left column, use the indicators to determine if you have met the criteria for accountability success.

	Indicators of Accountability Success					
Accountability Process	**Clear?**	**Owned?**	**Multilayered?**	**Proactive?**	**Achievable?**	**Self-Perpetuating?**
1. Setting goals						
2. Clarifying expectations						
3. Defining roles and responsibilities						
4. Monitoring progress and measuring results						
5. Gathering feedback						
6. Formulating action goals						

an organization defines its own learning goals. In practice, this happens when statements of broad intention are crafted into actionable goals and strategies. There must be alignment between the organizational goals for mentoring and individual mentoring goals in a mentoring culture.

Organizational goal setting can be implemented through a series of conversations or as an extended goal-setting session. To be effective, these conversations must cover the three parts of what can be called a goal triptych: components, statement, and audit. Together, they have a greater effect than the parts individually because they are connected to one another.

Setting goals that are clear, owned, multilayered, proactive, achievable, and self-perpetuating takes time. There are layers of goals within goals; that is, in developing a goal you must be sure it fits under the umbrella of the larger organization's goals. Exercise 6.2, an Organizational Framework for Setting Goals for Mentoring, is designed to help transform your mentoring idea and intention into a SMART organizational goal (one that is specific, measurable, action-oriented, realistic, and timely). This exercise can be completed as a discussion guide for a group as a whole, separately by individuals before they meet together, or as a needs assessment by stakeholders and groups within the organization. The collected input serves as the basis for coalescing around a goal or series of goals that a group can agree to in principle.

Exercise 6.2 covers the first two parts of the goal triptych; with it, you can develop a high-level statement about what mentoring will enable you to do and what the bottom line is. For example, BigBookcase chose mentoring as one of several vehicles to develop the next generation of corporate leaders. Their draft goal statement reflected this intent: "The goal of our mentoring program is to develop eight to ten emerging leaders to fill the gap created by our current leadership, most of whom will be retiring over the next five years. Senior leadership is committed to growing its emerging leaders into agile, knowledgeable, and smart leaders and to creating a strong cadre of leaders who will have the capacity, knowledge and wisdom to move BigBookcase from good to great."

Exercise 6.3, the Goal Audit Checklist, reflects the third part of the mentoring goal triptych. It is an accountability tool for making sure that your evolving goal statement is on target. The audit can be used in a number of ways. Each person on the team can complete it individually and results can be tabulated, followed by discussion. Or an entire team might discuss each item. Or the draft goal statement can go out into the organization with a request for feedback using the goal audit exercise form. Once the audits are tabulated, you share results and revise the draft goal statement accordingly. The exercise may also be adapted by asking respondents to use a Likert scale and rank the extent to which each component requirement is met.

EXERCISE 6.2

Organizational Framework for Setting Goals for Mentoring

Instructions: Record your answers to each set of questions. Debrief the answers to each question and come to consensus.

Organizational need	What organizational needs and challenges is your organization facing right now that might be met by mentoring?
Intended audience	Whose interests and needs will be served by mentoring? How might participants benefit?
Organizational benefit	Why is mentoring important for the organization?
Learning outcomes	What cognitive, affective, and behavioral changes might you expect to see as a result of mentoring?
Compelling reason	Why are we developing a mentoring process or program? What is the one compelling reason?
Bottom line	What will we be able to do better or smarter as a result?
Draft goal statement	Now, from the information you have gathered in this exercise, prepare a draft goal statement. Be sure to set a time to revise your statement before you solicit feedback on it.

Goal Audit Checklist

Instructions: Review the draft goal statement (prepared in Exercise 6.2) and record your responses in the spaces below.

SMART Goal Component	Yes	No	What Needs to Be Changed, Added, or Deleted?
Specific: 1. Is what we want to accomplish clear? 2. Are our goals specific and concrete?			
Measurable: 1. Can the goals we have identified be measured? 2. Will we be able to measure our success?			
Action-oriented: 1. Are the goals future-oriented? 2. Are the immediate results we anticipate apparent? 3. Are the long-term results articulated?			
Realistic: 1. Is what we are attempting to accomplish through mentoring achievable? 2. Can we accomplish our goals ourselves, or will we need to rely on collaborators and other resources?			
Timely: 1. Is this the right time to get started? 2. Is the time we have allocated for creating this initiative adequate?			

One caveat: goals are helpful only to the extent that they meet learning needs. As needs change over time, goals must be revisited and adapted periodically. Published goals clarify intent and thus help manage expectations. They affirm commitment to achieve the goals and therefore create momentum. "Publication" comes in many forms, among them announcements, news stories, speeches, and brochures. When initiatives are well under way, keeping the goals visible maintains the focus and facilitates ongoing accountability.

Clarifying Expectations

Once goals have been set, it is tempting to assume that everyone is on the same page. Yet individuals, teams, and organizations that move too quickly from goal to task without first clarifying expectations usually find themselves disappointed in the ultimate outcome, be it performance or results. It is unrealistic to hope for accountability unless our expectations about others' intentions and behaviors are clarified. Too often we dance around setting expectations for myriad reasons, perhaps thinking that discussing them will have a negative impact on others, undermine trust, create suspicion about intention, or appear to be too structured an approach.

The possible negatives are outweighed by the fact that clarifying expectations promotes individual, team, and organizational accountability and focuses individual and collective energy and effort. The very act of articulating expectations promotes self-accountability. If individuals know what is required, they can self-manage better and feel a sense of ownership in meeting desired results or performance objectives. It's a delicate balance. The reality, as Lencioni says, is that "a little structure goes a long way toward helping people take action that they might not otherwise be inclined to do" (2002, p. 21). One must also avoid the temptation to go overboard and create too much structure.

Agreed expectations are important but not sufficient to guarantee sustainable accountability. Expectations must be individually and collectively owned. There are six process steps for promoting shared accountability, whether in a mentoring relationship, a mentoring coordinating group, or mentoring advisory committee:

1. Identify expectations

2. Agree on expectations

3. Agree on an audit process

4. Develop a timeline

5. Implement the audit

6. Adopt process improvements

Steps one through four can take as little as ten minutes or perhaps an hour. Steps five and six flow back and forth between each other. If these last two steps are ignored, the entire effort is negated.

The critical nature of clarifying expectations is well illustrated by confidentiality concerns. Confidentiality expectations present a challenge on many levels for those engaged in mentoring. In addition to whatever confidentiality assurances are put in place in a mentoring relationship, there are other considerations from a systems perspective. For example, HR managers frequently report difficulty in balancing the need to be supportive without compromising partnership confidentiality. Although there is a need to know how the relationship is going, they fear being intrusive. As a result, mentors and mentees may feel there is either too little or too much support. One way to minimize this angst is to manage expectations ahead of time. When your mentoring team comes together initially, discuss what confidentiality means to you as a team and what it might mean in the context of mentoring within your organization. Exercise 6.4, Managing Expectations About Confidentiality, outlines some of the questions to address in managing individual and organizational expectations.

Defining Roles and Responsibilities

When roles and responsibilities remain unclear, multiple untested assumptions often supplant them. The resultant ambiguity leads to unintended consequences:

- Individuals do the minimum required.

- There is an attempt to get work done using a scattershot approach, and others have to pick up the slack.

- Long hours and extra work are exacted that are not essential to obtaining the result.

- Resentment and frustration block productivity.

- Work gets completed, but not as efficiently and effectively as it would otherwise.

- The lines of accountability are blurred.

In contrast, clear definition of roles and responsibilities promotes autonomy, ownership, and self-accountability. If individuals are confident about what is in their control and what is not, they step forward to accept responsibility with full knowledge of what is expected from them. Roles and responsibilities acted on with a sense of ownership inspire and energize commitment. It is only when people feel like owners and have choices to make that they can "truly exercise personal responsibility" (Kouzes and Posner, 2002,

Managing Expectations About Confidentiality

Instructions: Clarifying expectations about confidentiality is essential. With your mentoring team or group, discuss responses to these questions.

1. What might confidentiality mean within the context of a mentoring relationship?

2. What safeguards need to be put in place to honor the confidentiality of mentoring relationships within our organization?

3. What are the boundaries of confidentiality that cannot be crossed, from a systems or organizational perspective? Do we need to communicate them? If so, how?

4. If confidentiality is compromised, what is our game plan? How will we implement it? What steps are involved? Who will manage the process?

p. 231). Defining roles and responsibilities identifies specific benchmarks for performance, creates boundaries around the work to be done, and, accordingly, fosters self-accountability.

Everyone engaged in mentoring needs to understand roles and responsibilities and the expectations of other players. Understanding cannot be achieved unless care is taken to articulate, develop, and share descriptions of the respective roles and responsibilities of all the players. Each organization must first identify its own key players. In one organization, it may involve a mentor and mentee and perhaps a manager. Or it could involve many persons, each with a degree of relationship and responsibility.

Figure 6.1 identifies the key players and the "silent partners" (all the individuals who might be involved or affected directly or indirectly in mentoring) within one organization. Before defining the roles and responsibilities for each player, the organization's mentoring task force brainstormed their player list. They then filled in the inner circle (those most engaged) and the outer circle (those stakeholders affected but not as engaged). The complexity of their organizational structure was reflected in the diagram. The organization's descriptions of roles and responsibilities for mentors and mentees is presented in Exhibit 6.1.

FIGURE 6.1

Players' Circle: An Example

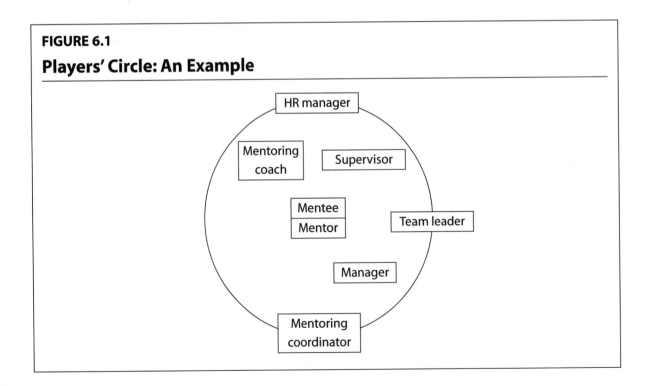

EXHIBIT 6.1

Mentor and Mentee: Sample Roles and Responsibilities

Mentor	Mentee
Initiate contact with mentee	*Commit to participate as an active learner in the relationship*
Build rapport	
Connect three times per month with mentee, at least twice face-to-face	*Connect three times per month with mentor, at least twice face-to-face*
Create at least one new learning opportunity every quarter that links directly to organizational business goals and to mentee's responsibilities	*Be a risk taker*
	Ask for help when needed
Provide general guidance and support	*Take responsibility for completing program requirements*
Help resolve major difficulties completing program requirements	*Experiment and try new ideas*
	Follow through on assignments
Give professional career-related advice	

Exercise 6.5, Players' Roles and Responsibilities, offers a sample format for itemizing roles and responsibilities for key players (mentoring partners, managers, coaches, support group). As part of this process, you should consider these questions:

- What does mutual accountability mean?

- What will regular interaction look like?

- What should the duration of the relationship be?

- Should there be minimum and maximum time frames? If so, what should they be?

- Should we encourage flexibility regarding time frames?

- How many mentors or mentees should a person be engaged with at one time?

- Who has the responsibility to make the initial contact?

- Should training and education programming for mentors, mentees, and supervisors be required, or voluntary?

Once you have answered these questions and defined specific player roles and responsibilities, the next steps are to seek feedback, refine, and eventually communicate your results. Several ways to communicate results encourage accountability. The first and probably most obvious approach is

Players' Roles and Responsibilities

Instructions: The column on the left lists some of the players involved in accountability. Expand the list as needed to include appropriate senior leadership and organizational managers. Once you have customized your list, itemize the roles and responsibilities for each player.

Player	Roles and Responsibilities
Mentor	
Mentee	
Supervisor	
Human resource manager	
Department manager	
Mentoring coordinator	
Mentoring coach	

to use what you have found to be the most effective format in your organization to post job openings. The second approach is to incorporate roles and responsibilities into whatever branded mentoring materials are developed. Defining roles and responsibilities furnishes a mechanism to clearly assign accountability to those answerable for carrying out the mentoring strategy at all levels of the organization. Setting goals, clarifying expectations, and defining roles and responsibilities provides a frame or standard for monitoring progress and measuring results.

Monitoring Progress and Measuring Results

Monitoring progress and measuring results go hand in hand. Monitoring progress allows us to understand "movement," what is happening in situ as learning unfolds; measuring results generates data points to compare against a standard and each other. Both can be a source of formative and summative data to spur process improvement and development. Together they are an essential accountability process for individuals, mentoring partners, and organizations that want to build their capacity to grow and improve.

Monitoring Progress

Progress should be monitored on the individual, partnership, management or oversight, and organizational levels. Monitoring personally on a daily basis is a powerful, and even dynamic, tool for promoting learning insights and self-accountability.

Self-Accountability

Journaling can be effective for both mentors and mentees in helping to clarify thinking, capture the richness of learning experiences, sort out feelings, and analyze the content of what is occurring. It also yields a written record and keeps the individuals and relationships focused and on track. On this point, one mentor reflected, "The journal is much more about them than me. I use it as a tool to remind me. Reading the notes from the last meeting prompts me for the next meeting." A log or journal can also be informative to those who coach, coordinate, or manage mentoring in an organization. It can be used to record queries, conversations, and reflections. Reviewing it regularly often reveals clues about how to strengthen mentoring support or points to learning needs and suggest teachable moments.

Ongoing monitoring and evaluation should be embedded in the mentoring relationship routine. I always remind mentoring partners to check in with each other regularly about the learning process, learning progress, and the relationship—and not to wait until something goes wrong. In this way, they share accountability and make it easier to keep a mentoring relationship on track. Monitoring does not need to be a cumbersome process, but it should be regular, whether once a month or every quarter.

As an example of a multipronged approach in action, supporting partnership accountability, consider the Partners for the Future mentoring program of the Greater Phoenix Chamber of Commerce. It started by giving mentoring partners a feedback form (see Exhibit 6.2), which was formatted in a stand-alone style and combined with content from the Mentoring Partnership Reflection in *The Mentor's Guide* (Zachary, 2000, pp. 126–127). Program participants were asked to complete this feedback form monthly and share their results quarterly with the program coordinator. If participants chose not to use the exact form, they could instead use it as a model to follow.

The chamber's mentoring program coordinator also e-mailed a goal feedback form to program mentees, in which participants are asked for information about their goals for each six-month period of the program. In addition, the coordinator periodically met with each mentee to monitor progress. At the quarterly luncheon meeting for all mentors and mentees, program participants networked and shared best practices for accomplishing their mentoring goals. In addition to promoting and supporting regular partnership feedback, the goal form afforded the mentoring coordinator data that allowed her to monitor progress, extend additional support to individual participants, and offer point-of-need mentoring education sessions when warranted. The existence of these forms forced accountability conversations that mentoring partners might not otherwise have had.

Participant Check-In

It is advisable to set up a check-in schedule to ensure that program participants are contacted regularly and to assign responsibility for making contact. Brief touch-base conversations can help participants stay on course. Some organizations e-mail mentoring program participants a set of three or four questions every quarter, both as a reminder for the participants and to monitor progress. For example, several questions might stimulate some reflection on learning and refocus a relationship:

- What goals are you and your mentoring partner working on right now?
- What have you learned so far?
- What are some of the ways you are applying what you are learning?
- What challenges have you faced in your mentoring partnership, and how have you overcome them?

EXHIBIT 6.2

Sample Feedback Form for Mentoring Partners

Mentoring relationships develop and grow over time. Partners for the Future provides this form as a tool to help you work at continuously improving the quality of your learning and your mentoring experience.

Instructions: Complete this feedback form after each mentoring session. Then use it as a starting point for the next session. There are two options for using this form:

1. Mentor and mentee complete the form independently at the close of each mentoring session and then discuss their individual responses with each other.
2. Together, mentoring partners discuss each item and complete the form.

Relationship

1. Words or phrases to describe the quality of our mentoring interaction:

2. What went particularly well for us:

3. Our greatest challenge:

4. We need to work at improving:

5. Action strategies to improve the quality of our mentoring interaction:

Meeting

1. Our mentoring session was held on:

2. We worked on these learning objectives:

3. Our progress in achieving these objectives:

4. Conditions that promoted learning:

5. We need to work at improving:

6. Objectives for the next meeting:

Learnings

1. One thing I am learning about myself:

2. One thing I am learning about my mentoring partner:

3. One thing I am learning about our mentoring relationship:

4. Personal insights and learnings:

Source: Partners for the Future Mentoring Program, Greater Phoenix Chamber of Commerce (2000).

Other organizations hold regular videoconferences, conference calls, or networking meetings to monitor progress—and to motivate others to monitor their progress.

Measuring Results

We all know that what gets measured gets done. Measurement is a long-term commitment that requires adequate preparation and is all too often put on the back burner. Yet failure to continuously measure results detracts from the value initially created and limits an organization's ability to achieve sustainable mentoring results. Granted, measurement can be intimidating; images of dollar signs, bean counters, formulas, and statistics materialize at the mere mention of the word. Questions arise. How rigorous do we have to be? How much measurement is enough? Who will own this function in the organization?

Success factors become extremely important for deciding what to measure. Together with the goals, they frame the measurement and evaluation process. There are many ways to go about measuring success: questionnaires, performance assessments, focus groups, and using key informants, to name a few. Some organizations are survey-averse. To get accurate data, you need to know your organization and what works in the culture. Also be sure to think first about data already available to you. Before you collect new data, know what you are going to do with it—and have adequate criteria to evaluate the data you do collect.

Monitoring and measuring progress can create value for an organization if it is done deliberately and is carefully planned and continuously embraced. Spending adequate time in planning reaps dividends for years to come. Exercise 6.6, the Evaluation and Measurement Worksheet, can be used to guide the preliminary data-gathering conversation about these important issues.

Evaluation can be the springboard to capacity building when a multileveled approach is implemented. The best way to ensure that results are measured is to plan the evaluation process with the same intentionality as the mentoring initiative. Evaluation must be well thought out to ensure its value. The methods of measurement, data collection procedures (both qualitative and quantitative), data analysis treatments, and dissemination of results should be detailed as part of the planning process. It is important not to lose sight of the fact that the purpose, process, and product of mentoring center on learning. As part of the measurement process, you must:

- Consider the yardsticks or benchmarks to be used for each category.

- Determine which persons, places, or resources can provide the answers to your questions.

EXERCISE 6.6

Evaluation and Measurement Worksheet

Instructions: Before you explore the methods and instruments presented in the remainder of the chapter, answer as many of these questions as you can.

1. What are your criteria for measuring success?

2. How will you go about measuring success?

3. What baseline data do you already have?

4. What additional data will you need to measure success?

5. How will you go about obtaining these data?

6. What will you do with the data collected?

7. Who will be responsible for gathering, analyzing, and interpreting the data?

8. How will results be distributed?

- Know what you are going to do with the data before it is collected.

- Collect the data that enable you to answer your questions. (Consider who will be accountable for collecting those data.)

- Designate someone to be accountable for monitoring progress and measuring results. In many organizations, there is a function or a person already in place that can make this happen effectively and efficiently.

- Analyze the data and interpret the results and what they mean in light of the questions you identified.

- Be clear about who needs to know your results—and when.

- Share your results and make appropriate process improvements to managing mentoring within your organization.

Considering these points helps you identify what you may need in building your measurement yardstick.

Interviews

One way to capture some participant learning is to collect longitudinal data. Conducting interviews over time creates tremendous value when it comes to accountability. The reasons are many. First, the very act of conducting interviews promotes self-accountability because it forces self-reflection. Second, by studying interview data over time, you can see how mentoring journeys develop and change. Third, the patterns and themes that emerge from analysis of the interviews often suggest benchmarks and milestones for monitoring progress. Exercise 6.7, Matching Questions and People, is an opportunity for you to decide whom you want to interview and the kinds of questions to ask in the interviews. Also develop a timetable for when the interviews are to be conducted and by whom. In addition to interviews that take place during the program cycle, consider conducting follow-up interviews six to twelve months after the conclusion of a mentoring relationship, since some of the most dramatic results from mentoring appear well after the conclusion of a relationship. Exit interviews, gathered from individuals who leave a mentoring program voluntarily or serendipitously, are helpful in identifying process improvements. They can fill the gap of a missing closure experience and produce incidental learning and insight.

Baseline Data

Many organizations overlook the opportunity to use currently available data as a baseline for measuring results; instead they end up reinventing the wheel. Comparing baseline data with new data gathered at strategic intervals can produce useful information. For example, in a mentoring

EXERCISE 6.7

Matching Questions and People

Instructions: First, in the subcolumns under Populations to Be Interviewed identify the groups of individuals you want to interview or survey. You may want to add extra columns. Next, look at each question category and decide which of them apply to the populations you've identified. Then determine what questions you might want to ask each group.

Question Categories	Populations to Be Interviewed		
Challenges and successes			
Changes in self			
Changes observed in others			
Commitment			
Concerns			
Contact and connection			
Critical milestones			
Insights and learning			
Journaling			
Learning (content of new learning)			
Learning process			
Learning progress			
Mentoring conversations and meetings			
Observations			
Program			
Recommendations			
Resources (human, financial, information)			
Stumbling blocks			
Support from others			

program focusing on accelerating the development of emerging leaders, one could use particular data:

- Number of emerging leaders engaged in mentoring relationships
- Promotion rate
- Feedback from multiple raters
- Promotion level
- Number of external hires
- Competency assessment results

At IKEA, mentoring is the key strategy for meeting future leadership and diversity needs. IKEA's North American program, entitled Partners for Growth, facilitates individual learning and promotes personal and professional growth by cultivating organizational leadership, supporting career development across the board, increasing and supporting diversity through the organization, and strengthening the IKEA culture. IKEA uses a matrix to collect data and demographic information for each participant in the program: sex, age, diversity, and information about current job, location, and participation in the program. Each of its measures of success is tracked so that both preprogram (baseline) figures and postprogram figures can be compared. IKEA was also interested in how mentoring affected location turnover rate. The company wanted to be sure it was meeting its own criteria for success. For example, one of the success factors is that mentees request to become a mentor. Another success factor is successful completion of the entire mentoring program cycle. The matrix also contains tracking and anecdotal information about the program itself.

Benchmarking

Benchmarking is a process tool for comparing and measuring organizational processes against gold-standard industry-specific practices. Organizational results and performance are measured against those that are consistently best-in-class. Its ultimate purpose is raising the bar and improving the level of organizational performance: "By finding, analyzing and adopting the proven best practices of best-in-class organizations—focusing on work processes rather than numbers, asking 'how' rather than 'how much'—benchmarkers can revolutionize their own business functions and reach peak performance levels quickly" (Cheney, 1998, p. 1). Once gaps are identified, new processes and approaches are strategically planned, integrated into the organization, and continuously monitored to gauge success.

Benchmarking can be carried out within an organization as well as externally. When done internally, it is used to compare the units under one organizational umbrella or to compare an organization's performance against itself over time. When done externally, it is used to compare performance against best practices of other organizations. The benchmarking process can become a complicated, labor-intensive, and costly endeavor, but it need not be. Many successful models for benchmarking and resources are available to measure mentoring efforts against those that are best in class. For example, you might take these steps:

- Determine which exemplary practice or process you want to benchmark.
- Select processes against which to benchmark.
- Identify best-in-class practices or organizations.
- Collect and analyze benchmarking information.
- Conduct gap analysis.
- Make an action plan to close the gap.
- Share results.
- Monitor progress.
- Continuously update benchmarks and integrate process improvements.
- Recalibrate benchmarks.

Although the number of steps varies with the benchmarking model, all include the same core processes. It is important to select a model that is doable for you and your organization. The gains are worth it, especially the added bonus of pushing thinking to a whole new level of possibility.

Gathering Feedback

Feedback encourages accountability in subtle and not-so-subtle ways. It fosters ownership, nurtures commitment, and creates ongoing value for mentoring participants, mentoring programs, and organizations as a whole. The feedback process itself builds relationships, opens lines of communication, encourages participation, drums out resistance, engages people, and creates continuing interest and awareness. Information, insights, and learning gathered through the feedback process have tangible and immediate application. In addition, regular feedback fosters a culture of continuous improvement and is the backbone of a learning organization. Gathering feedback can be a means to an end (for instance, a data-gathering tool for monitoring progress and measuring results) or can stand alone as an intrinsic part of the accountability process.

In some organizations, feedback is associated only with critiquing performance. Negative feedback can foster accountability in the short run, but feedback misses the promise of its potential unless it is ongoing and constructive. Gathering feedback helps people hold each other accountable long before it's too late to resolve the situation.

To reap the full benefit, feedback must be embraced proactively. It is not just about amassing data but being able to use the data so that they can be harvested for improvement and change. Gathering feedback is a two-pronged process: learning from feedback and feeding back what is learned so that the return on the investment is clear and commitment is consolidated.

Care must be taken to encourage candid feedback. This can happen as informally as asking an open-ended question ("How are we doing?"). The idea is not to wait until something goes amiss but to ask the question regularly. An example may bring home the point. Phyllis's mentor, Greg, is concerned that he may have overwhelmed her with information at their last mentoring meeting. At their next meeting, a conversation ensues:

Greg: Phyllis, I was concerned after our last session that in my enthusiasm I may have done too much of the talking and gone overboard in providing you with information. I want this to be a good learning experience for you. I have lots I want to share, but I don't want to overwhelm you. I guess what I'm asking is for some feedback as to your reaction. Tell me what you thought. Was it helpful? Did it work for you? Was it too much?

Phyllis: Well, Greg, I'm so glad you asked. I was planning to give you some feedback myself, but I didn't want you to think that I didn't appreciate your time and what you were trying to do. I thought I'd taken it all in, and what I hadn't I thought I'd captured in my notebook. When all was said and done, I was a pretty confused camper.

Greg: Sometimes I confuse even myself! Seriously, what do you think might have worked better for you and your style of learning?

Phyllis: I am an experiential learner. I need to get some basics, try it on myself, and then process it. That always raises good questions for me and gives me a better context for learning. I felt a little at sea last time. I didn't understand some of the terms; some went right over my head.

Greg: Are you game for trying another approach then?

Phyllis: I want to learn as much as I can from you. So, yes!

Greg: What questions have you brought with you today? Maybe we can start there.

Phyllis: That sounds like a great way to begin.

Without this conversation, Greg might have continued talking past Phyllis, and she might never have achieved her learning goals. She was afraid to offend him since she was so grateful for his time and wisdom. He demonstrated his caring by opening himself up for feedback and being sensitive to her needs as a learner. His approach gave her the permission and space to be authentic. As a result of their conversation, two things happened. Phyllis was able to ask for what she needed when she needed it, and feedback on learning from the previous session became a regular item on their mentoring session agenda.

The Feedback Cycle

The model feedback cycle that I first presented in *The Mentor's Guide* (Zachary, 2002) and have revised since was developed to frame mentoring feedback conversations. It has also been successfully used when planning, implementing, and coordinating groups seek feedback from within the organization. The continuous nature of the feedback allows you to enter at any point (see Figure 6.2).

An example illustrates one way in which the feedback cycle can be used. After one company's mentoring task force held its first meeting, it decided to gather feedback about its emerging plan from key stakeholders within the organization. Task force members individually met with key stakeholders and asked for reaction to the general approach of the mentoring fast-track program they were developing. They wanted to know if it made sense in light of the business case, if they had targeted the right group, if they thought the program would generate enough interest. In addition, they wanted to get input about the overall concept of the mentoring program, obstacles the program might face, and issues and concerns people might have.

Task force members agreed to listen to all feedback and not to push back when they heard something they disagreed with (which, in fact, did happen). By listening, they learned that the program didn't meet the needs of the target group. The task force then went back to the drawing board to reframe their ideas. Once the reframing was complete, they again went out into the field to gather more feedback. The information they gathered was invaluable in helping them decide to delay the program until there was more readiness and receptivity within the organization.

As the task force learned, the purpose of gathering feedback must be clear. There must be ownership of the feedback and responsibility for acting on it. It must be multilayered, gathered from multiple individuals or groups, and proactive with an eye toward improvement in the future. Effort must be made to be sure that the request for feedback is targeted and specific. Last but not least, feedback must be ongoing and invite further feedback.

FIGURE 6.2

The Feedback Cycle

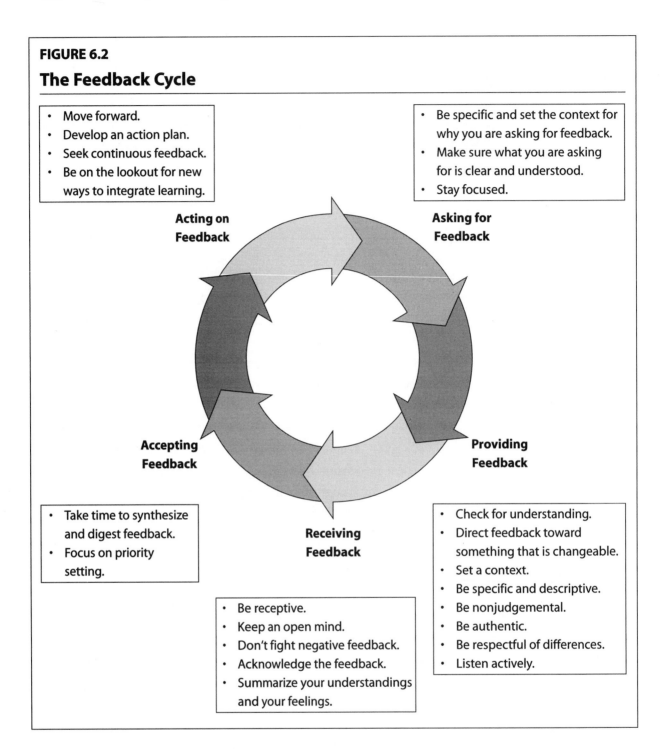

- Move forward.
- Develop an action plan.
- Seek continuous feedback.
- Be on the lookout for new ways to integrate learning.

- Be specific and set the context for why you are asking for feedback.
- Make sure what you are asking for is clear and understood.
- Stay focused.

Acting on Feedback

Asking for Feedback

Accepting Feedback

Providing Feedback

Receiving Feedback

- Take time to synthesize and digest feedback.
- Focus on priority setting.

- Check for understanding.
- Direct feedback toward something that is changeable.
- Set a context.
- Be specific and descriptive.
- Be nonjudgemental.
- Be authentic.
- Be respectful of differences.
- Listen actively.

- Be receptive.
- Keep an open mind.
- Don't fight negative feedback.
- Acknowledge the feedback.
- Summarize your understandings and your feelings.

Feedback Loops

Since mentoring is a work in progress, feedback is essential. A feedback loop describes a strategic approach to gathering feedback consistently from key constituents and interested stakeholders. It is a mechanism for thinking about and gathering feedback systemically. Feedback loops promote accountability for mentoring planners and implementers, key organizational informants and participants, and organizational leaders. Never underestimate the value of gathering feedback while a mentoring initiative or process is being planned and implemented. Reliable feedback ensures that mentoring customer needs are met and that rollout and implementation is successful.

Feedback loops that are accessed during rollout and implementation promote accountability of planning and coordinating groups and identify areas for process improvement. Exercise 6.8, Establishing Planning and Implementation Feedback Loops, offers a conversation guide for thinking about how to apply the concept of feedback loops in your organization.

Formulating Action Goals

Failure to act on lessons learned is a major stumbling block to successfully establishing a mentoring culture. It compromises the raison d'être of mentoring and becomes a barrier to integrating process improvements. For mentoring advocates sitting on a mentoring planning, implementation, or coordinating group, their sense of ownership, enthusiasm, and investment is high. The rose-colored glasses they collectively don often prevent them from asking for, openly receiving, accepting, and acting on feedback. This is natural enough. After planning and implementing a program, who wants to hear that we've missed the mark? But we must hear it, or our efforts will surely be doomed to failure.

What we "hear" confirms some or all of our thinking and assures us that perhaps we are on the right path after all. Or it lets us know that there are gaps in our thinking, that we've made faulty assumptions, or that we need to take into account special circumstances, individual attitudes, and concerns. The next step, one that is frequently overlooked because of time constraints, is to reflect critically on what we learn so that we can take action by formulating appropriate action goals and integrate process improvement. Accountability demands no less.

Accountability is the portal to process improvement. It opens the doors to action by requiring that goals be set, expectations clarified, roles and responsibilities defined, progress monitored, results measured, and feedback continuously gathered. The key to its success lies in the ever-present dynamic interaction of multiple indicators: clarity, ownership, multilayeredness, proactivity, achievability, and self-perpetuation. Without accountability, doors remain shut (and often locked) to individual and organizational learning.

Accountability: Reflection on Practice

There is great wisdom in Oliver Wendell Holmes's words that opened this chapter. Without accountability, it is easy to drift aimlessly or find oneself mired in the shallows. Accountability helps a mentoring culture sail forward and evolve. Accountability based on the six processes discussed

EXERCISE 6.8

Establishing Planning and Implementation Feedback Loops

Instructions: Have your mentoring team discuss these questions during the planning stages.

1. What feedback loops do we need to set up in order to get quality feedback on our ideas, emerging plan, and final product?

2. What reliable feedback loops already exist in our organization? Who do we *want* to include? Who do we *need* to include? Who will we include?

3. How will we go about seeking feedback? What is our strategy? What is our timeline?

4. How will we report what we learn from the field?

Then, after the program has been implemented, discuss these questions:

1. What feedback loops have we previously tapped into?

2. Draw a map showing your feedback loops. Notice where they are connected to one another and where they are not. What gaps exist?

3. What is working well? What could work better? What are some of the best practices that have emerged for gathering feedback?

4. What three things can we do to improve our feedback process?

5. What new strategies might we try?

6. What is our timeline?

here (setting goals, clarifying expectations, defining roles and responsibilities, monitoring process and measuring results, gathering feedback, and formulating action goals) promotes the integrity of the mentoring culture. The accountability processes are multifaceted and involve the dynamic interplay of the indicators of accountability success. Each accountability process must be clear, owned, multilayered, proactive, achievable, and self-perpetuating in order to promote integrity of each of the accountability processes, thereby ensuring internal consistency. Review this list of accountability practices, both as a check on the status of your accountability process and to develop a list of what remains to be done.

Setting Goals

- Identify organizational need, learning outcomes, business results, criteria for success, SMART goals, benefits, and audience.

- Develop a statement of goals.

- Get feedback.

- Make appropriate revisions.

Clarifying Expectations

- Identify and agree on expectations.

- Establish boundaries.

- Agree on the audit process and timeline.

- Implement the audit.

- Adopt process improvements.

Defining Roles and Responsibilities

- Identify players and their roles and responsibilities.

- Clearly articulate and communicate roles and responsibilities.

Monitoring Progress and Measuring Results

- Review goals and success factors.

- Define what you want to measure.

- Agree on questions to be answered.

- Ascertain what data are available and what data need to be collected.

- Identify data analysis procedures.

- Identify a point person.

- Develop a dissemination plan for findings.

Gathering Feedback

- Agree on a regular feedback mechanism.
- Identify methods and procedures.
- Establish feedback loops.
- Publish findings.
- Act on feedback received.

Formulating Action Goals

- Critically reflect on findings.
- Establish SMART goals.
- Integrate process improvements.
- Begin the process again.

The work involved in accountability makes it possible for us to gauge progress, make process improvements, and move forward. Communication, the subject of the next chapter, enables us to actually do the work.

Chapter 7

Communication

Tell me and I'll forget; show me and I may remember; involve me and I'll understand.

—CHINESE PROVERB

COMMUNICATION IS FUNDAMENTAL to achieving organizational effectiveness and business results. It drives transmission of knowledge and information as well as organizational learning. Its impact is experienced on many levels (individual, relationship, group, and organizational). The effects of communication are far-reaching; it increases trust, strengthens relationships, and helps align organizations. It is critical to creating and supporting a mentoring culture. Without it, there is no mentoring vitality, much less sustainability. Communication creates value, visibility, and demand for mentoring. It is also the catalyst for developing mentoring readiness, generating learning opportunities, and providing mentoring support within an organization.

In this chapter, we look first at some of the challenges that communication presents in actual mentoring practice. We then focus on specific criteria for effective mentoring communication. We use process models, a communications-strategy matrix, and a multiphase model to identify the specific components of communication necessary for creating a mentoring culture. Throughout this chapter, the focus is on using communication as a strategic tool for mentoring knowledge management.

Challenges of Communication

Communication is frequently overlooked. We assume that communication is omnipresent and therefore take it for granted. Yet making this assumption can wreak havoc by setting up barriers, shutting down channels of communication, adding confusion, creating false expectations, and compromising trust.

These were some of the problems that Jim, the director of institutional advancement at Rho College, faced when he decided that mentoring would be the perfect antidote to weakening alumni relationships. With the input of key staff members from his office and the Alumni Affairs office, he developed a mentoring program and then personally recruited ten mentors and mentees to kick off the pilot group. Just as he was compiling the volumes of material he had amassed, Jim was called away by Rho's president to work on a high-priority assignment that took him out of the office four days a week. Rather than put the project on hold, Jim gave all the mentoring resource material and the responsibility for developing a mentoring orientation manual to his direct reports. His staff tried to get further clarification from him, but he repeatedly responded, "I have every confidence in you. Just get it done!"

Everyone knew that Jim was a stickler for detail and that the mentoring program was his pet project. They also knew that he liked attention to his projects to be comprehensive and detailed. In his absence, the staff actively engaged in completing the project. It took them several months to assemble the manual. Once it was completed, Jim reviewed the manual, gave it his blessing, and sent it off to all the mentors and mentees who had agreed to participate. He eagerly anticipated that their enthusiasm would match or exceed his. Such was not the case.

Mentors and mentees were overwhelmed with the orientation materials they received. Although they were happy to finally receive some material, its painstaking detail and sheer quantity intimidated them. Most, if not all, of the mentors took one look at the formidable size of the manual, perused its table of contents, and immediately put it on the shelf. Mentees, on the other hand, were calling the alumni office to ask for clarity, saying that the material was "way too confusing." They didn't know what to read (since there was so much), or when; further, they weren't sure what they were supposed to do with what they did read.

Jim called his staff to task for not being more sensitive to the differing information needs of mentors and mentees. He quickly assigned them to another project while he set about revising the manual himself. When he originally signed off on the manual, staff clearly felt they had met his expectations. They were caught completely off guard when Jim took the project away so abruptly.

This example offers several illustrations of leadership in general and communication in particular. We see the results of what happens when people and process—both important elements of communication—are neglected. We see the adverse effects created by well-meaning but insensitive leadership communication and communication without due consideration of those on the receiving end. The bulk of the manual sent the unintended message that mentoring was expected to be a highly structured process and a lot of work. Another message was that information was more important than the learning needs of the intended audience. Jim was guilty of sending mixed messages to his own staff and setting unrealistic expectations by not taking the time to meet their learning needs. We will return to this example to illustrate potential improvements to communication efforts.

Communication Criteria

Most successful organizations establish criteria for communication, adopt them as standard operating procedures, and hold themselves accountable for adhering to them. Criteria, include, but are not limited to the following:

- Communication maximizes organizational resources. It leverages existing infrastructure components. The questions "What works best?" and "How can we use a particular resource to our strategic advantage in our communication?" are routine and at the forefront of any initiative.

- Communication is strategic. It is proactive and starts with the end result clearly defined. A strategic, sequenced communications plan is developed.

- Communication is consistent and focused. To borrow a media expression, "communication stays on message." Mixed messages make people uncomfortable and can send them into a tailspin.

- Communication is aligned with the culture. The vocabulary, language, and medium that are used fit the culture. Signage, internal press releases, and company intranet all reflect that cultural fit.

- Communication is targeted to meet receivers' learning needs. Individuals cognitively take in and process information in their own ways. They have different learning needs and capacities. Effective communication attends to this variation.

- Communication is honest, clear, and trustworthy. It is not just a set of attention-getting words in an e-mail or on a piece of paper. It is genuine, authentic, and accurate.

- Communication takes full advantage of every available opportunity. Business-as-usual venues become an opportunity to communicate and engage in meaningful conversation. Being clear about what needs to be said and consistently reinforcing the message opens up opportunities.

- Communication is sensitive to multiculturalism and diversity. It is inclusive and respectful of difference.

- Communication is regular and on time. It has a rhythm that creates momentum. If communication is episodic, the potential momentum is lost.

- Communication is two-way. Feedback and dialogue are part of the culture. Feedback is invited and integrated into continuous quality improvement of organizational communication.

Exercise 7.1, the Communication Criteria Checklist, helps you determine whether or not your organization meets these criteria and identify potential obstacles that may block communication efforts. This exercise can be approached in several ways. It can be used as a tool to evaluate the effectiveness of organizational communication or mentoring communication. In either case, evaluate your results, prioritize those items you want to address, and determine what action needs to be taken. For example, perhaps there is no current and timely vehicle for organizationwide updates other than e-mail. A strategy might therefore be to create a monthly mentoring newsletter for those participating in mentoring activity.

Benefits of Communication

Communication enables the various parts of the organizational infrastructure to operate efficiently and synergistically. The communication link among and between the parts of an organization allows the infrastructure to become more than just the sum of its parts. Four underlying concepts are vital to communication in a mentoring culture: communication drives learning, transforms resistance, builds trusting relationships, and eases transition. We touch on each of them in turn.

Communication Drives Learning

Organizational learning depends on an organization's ability to communicate effectively. The better the communication, the more organizational learning takes place. Learning, and thus communication, is an organizational imperative. Applying principles of adult learning to communication opens up additional possibilities for meaningful connection, information, and interaction. In addition, reframing communication as learning yields insights and strategies for reaching people more effectively. For example, understanding that people take in and process information in varying ways suggests the use of a multipronged approach. One simple strategy that takes differentiation into account is called the seven-by-seven rule of thumb, meaning that the same message should be communicated in seven ways—for example, (1) a blast e-mail announcement; (2) a feature story in the organizational newsletter; (3) specific and concrete talking points for managers

EXERCISE 7.1

Communication Criteria Checklist

Instructions: Review each criterion and determine if communication in your organization meets it. Seek input from others to validate your personal or team assessment. Then prioritize those items that might get in the way of your communication efforts. Brainstorm strategies to overcome each priority item you identify.

Criteria	Yes	No
Communication maximizes organizational resources.		
Communication is strategic.		
Communication is consistent and focused.		
Communication is aligned with the culture.		
Communication is targeted to meet receivers' learning needs.		
Communication is honest, clear, and trustworthy.		
Communication takes full advantage of every available opportunity.		
Communication is sensitive to multiculturalism and diversity.		
Communication is regular and on time.		
Communication is two-way.		

to communicate to direct reports; (4) a mentoring brochure with pictures and diagrams and the specifics of the mentoring initiative; (5) a white paper describing the background, rationale, and overview for mentoring; (6) a message from the CEO linking mentoring to business results; and (7) frequently asked questions (FAQs) addressing anticipated or previous questions posted on the Web and on company bulletin boards.

In addition to reinforcing the message, using this approach permits multiple touch points to hook the learner. Basing a communication strategy on how people are likely to process it also offers a promising approach. If the purpose is to reach some concrete thinkers, preparing a concept paper might not be the best approach to reach them. On the other hand, if you are communicating with individuals who need to understand the larger picture, just offering details without the rationale is less than satisfactory and might even end up making them suspect your motives. Remember that information and communication overload can make it difficult to learn. Too much too soon can be intimidating and inhibit learning. The opposite is also true: communication that is "too little, too late" hampers learning.

Communication Transforms Resistance

It is not uncommon to experience resistance to mentoring (and particularly formal mentoring) at almost any level of an organization. A mind-set rooted in past experience leads people to think, "We've done it before and it won't work. We can't afford it. We don't need to take time away from real business with this soft stuff." The task for communication then becomes an educative challenge, breaking down resistance by helping individuals bring their assumptions into consciousness, reflect on them, and transform those assumptions that are no longer valid.

Galpin's resistance pyramid, based on Nieder and Zimmerman's resistance hierarchy, is well worth considering. In his model (shown in Figure 7.1), satisfaction at each level of resistance reduces resistance at the next level (Galpin, 1996). Resistance can be overcome by providing people with knowledge and skills so they are more willing to change. The boxes on the left suggest what can be done to overcome resistance at each level. Accomplishing these tasks will help people move up the resistance pyramid and lessen their resistance to change. Much as in Maslow's hierarchy of needs, people become less resistant as needs are met at the lower level. For example, by directing mentoring communication at informing employees of opportunities for involvement in a mentoring initiative, you open up people to learning about mentoring and acquiring requisite mentoring skills. Once they learn more about mentoring and gain new skills, they feel more confident and willing to participate.

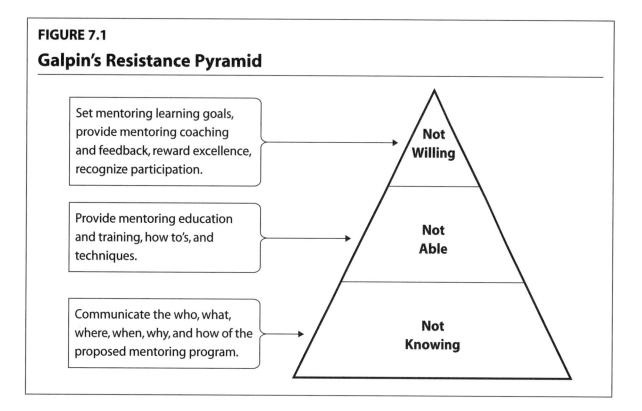

FIGURE 7.1

Galpin's Resistance Pyramid

Set mentoring learning goals, provide mentoring coaching and feedback, reward excellence, recognize participation. → **Not Willing**

Provide mentoring education and training, how to's, and techniques. → **Not Able**

Communicate the who, what, where, when, why, and how of the proposed mentoring program. → **Not Knowing**

Resistance is a reality factor that should not be easily dismissed. Inviting and working with resistance requires time and avoids false steps later on. The challenge is to convert resistance into commitment (Scott and Jaffe, 1995). Even before the sources of resistance become apparent, a typical first reaction is denial, perhaps given voice as "Maybe mentoring will pass, like the last corporate initiative." Information is the best remedy for denial. People need to know what the expectations are and what is going to happen. Once they are past denial, they often exhibit resistance through acting out, anger, anxiety, and pushback. They also have a need to live their resistance, at least for a while. This is when it is important to give them time to digest information and refrain from pushing for commitment too soon.

An organization that doesn't pay attention to resistance may eventually pay a dear price for its inattentiveness. Inattention or avoidance may slow, impede, compromise, or block a potentially successful implementation effort. Carefully listening to and evaluating the sources of resistance helps an organization proactively avoid obstacles that impede mentoring efforts. Inviting resistance out into the open diffuses it and surfaces invaluable information that is useful for strengthening the implementation effort.

Communication Builds Trusting Relationships

Communication is the basis on which relationships are built. Relationships, whether in mentoring partnerships, among a coordinating team, or between and among mentoring collaborators, are vital to the mentoring enterprise.

Relationships take time to develop and often need to be built from the ground up. Communication can build trust and relationships, as an illustration from a group of employees shows.

Five stalwart employees have been competitors for years. Each quarter they compare their numbers against each other and compete for the company's coveted sales award. They have never been in the same room with one another, even though they attend many company functions at the same time. When they are selected to serve on a task force charged with developing a companywide series of mentoring initiatives and mandated to sit down at the same table, they balk and squawk but eventually resign themselves to it. The first few meetings do not go well. Everyone holds their cards close to the vest and reveals as little about operations as he or she can get away with.

It is only after the CEO comes into the room during their third meeting and talks openly about her vision of the company that they are able to shift the focus away from themselves and toward building relationships with each other. They grow curious about each other as human beings, and the more they learn the easier it is to build trust and galvanize the team. Their journey from competitors to collaborators affects them personally and influences how they work with others. As they begin to trust more, others respond in kind.

The turnaround comes as a result of the CEO's agility at clearly communicating her vision, thus empowering the task force to work toward fulfillment of the vision. Their common understanding of the vision engages them in a sense of shared enterprise. They are then able to set up goals, tasks, and timelines to accomplish their work.

Communication Eases Transition

Organizational transition often signals a cultural shift. It is communication that keeps people feeling included in and connected to the organization during this period of time. A carefully planned communication strategy can get people on board with a mentoring initiative. For example, suppose a CEO is very excited about the new corporationwide mentoring strategy about to be launched. He knows well that it represents a significant cultural shift from how business was conducted under the aegis of the former CEO. Instead of making "the grand announcement" (as his predecessor did), he begins preparing his people for the transition by visiting each plant and engaging them in conversation about his vision and the role of organizational learning in ensuring success. The executive team follows his lead and begins talking about the advantages of mentoring, citing statistics and best practices in similar businesses. Shortly thereafter, open mentoring information sessions are offered throughout the company to answer questions and explain the benefits of mentoring to the several segments of the "internal mentoring market."

The success of this program is testament to the fact that developing a strategy to signal intention, manage expectations, and lead people through the transition promotes awareness, understanding, acceptance, commitment, action, and integration.

Components of Communication

Combining two process models offers a structured approach for formulating mentoring communication strategy. The first model, Galpin's Communications Strategy Matrix (1996), includes six specific components for crafting a comprehensive communications strategy. The second model, steps of change, is a useful way of focusing on the specific purposes of communication. The progression in six phases of awareness, understanding, acceptance, commitment, action, and integration is commonly used throughout the literature with little or no attribution and is closely allied to educational, psychological, and sociological theory and various sources. I have selected Trudell's six-step change model (1997) as a frame of reference.

We touched on the topic of stakeholders briefly in Chapter Three. Here we cast a wider and deeper net as we analyze the processes, strategies, and practicalities for reaching them effectively.

Who Are the Stakeholders?

The mentoring communication process must include thorough stakeholder analysis. Stakeholders are those people who have a need to know about mentoring or are likely to be affected by it, individuals who have an interest in or make decisions about mentoring. Potential stakeholders might also include funders, senior management, trainers, mentors and mentees, supervisors, store managers, direct managers, HR specialists, new employees, and so on.

Once the stakeholders have been identified, the next task is to focus on the objectives for communicating with the stakeholders. These objectives—awareness, understanding, acceptance (buy-in), and commitment—become the four phases that guide development of a communication strategy.

Awareness focuses on furnishing basic information and "coming attractions." Typically an announcement links mentoring with business reasons, values, and strategic direction; gives generic information about the process; and demonstrates senior management's involvement, support, and commitment.

Understanding lays the groundwork for creating organizational readiness and support for mentoring; it builds on awareness and takes it to the next level. In this phase, management demonstrates commitment and reaffirms the strategic rationale. This phase establishes the big picture, explains the benefits to employees, and outlines the roadmap indicating where mentoring is going and when.

The next phase is acceptance, or buy-in. Here the big picture becomes more detailed and training is undertaken. The follow-up phase of communication that occurs once mentoring is launched entails reaffirming management support, values, strategic focuses, gathering feedback, and making process improvements. It is impossible to maintain commitment to a mentoring culture if people within the organization lack awareness and understanding and there is no buy-in.

Once commitment is affirmed, individuals take action to implement that commitment. Finally, mentoring becomes seamlessly integrated (integration) into how they conduct their business.

To return to the Rho College example from the beginning of this chapter, remember that Jim did not focus on building awareness, understanding, and acceptance before asking for mentor and mentee commitment. His intention was to get acceptance and hope that the orientation manual would fill in the void. Although he has made people aware of the program, he never really gets them to the understanding phase. Unfortunately, skipping this phase precludes ultimate buy-in (acceptance).

What Is Our Purpose in Communicating?

Without understanding why we do things, it is difficult to rally support and commitment—and impossible to maintain alignment. There are two levels of purpose analysis involved here: the organizational, and the purpose or benefit as seen through the eyes of the stakeholder. The worksheet in Exercise 7.2, Identifying Mentoring Communication Objectives for Each Stakeholder, addresses organizational purpose. With it, you can identify mentoring communication purposes and validate your stakeholder list. In completing this exercise, you may find that people (or groups) you thought were stakeholders are not because there is no purpose for including them. In this event, you can delete them from your list of stakeholders and perhaps save some time, energy, and expense.

When a mentoring initiative is announced, one of the first things people want to know is, "What's in it for me?" They are right to ask. Mentoring should have a business benefit for every group of potential stakeholders.

EXERCISE 7.2

Identifying Mentoring Communication Objectives for Each Stakeholder

Instructions: In column one, list the stakeholders—the people within and external to your organization who need to know about mentoring within your organization. Try to segment your internal market and identify whom you think you need to influence. For each stakeholder you have listed, identify the purpose of your communication. For each purpose you identify, describe the learning or behavior objectives of the communication. For example, if the purpose is to increase awareness, what do you want to increase awareness of, and why?

Stakeholder	Purpose of Communication			
	Awareness	**Understanding**	**Acceptance or Buy-in**	**Commitment**
	What specifically does each stakeholder need to become more aware of?	What do you want your stakeholder to understand?	What do you want your stakeholder to buy into (e.g., the idea, a program, participation)?	What kind of commitment (e.g., time, tender, talent) do you want your stakeholder to make?

Creating a Mentoring Culture by Lois J. Zachary

Exercise 7.3, Stakeholder Benefits, addresses these issues from the stakeholders' perspective. The answer to "What's in it for me?" explains why an organization, department, group, and individuals choose to spend time and energy on mentoring. The stakeholders listed are fairly common but may not be representative of your organization. Tailor the exercise to your own situation. Gathering input from stakeholders is helpful in promoting mentoring in your organization. Appealing to what's in it for them helps stimulate interest, generate excitement, and build support.

What Are the Key Messages?

Key messages are the content part of the communication sent to each stakeholder, aimed at specific communication objectives. For example, if the purpose of communicating with HR managers is "awareness," a memo might contain a news item such as this one: "In response to the many requests we have recently received to assist new managers in finding mentors, we are in the process of developing a formal manager orientation mentoring initiative that we expect to roll out as a pilot early this fall."

Exhibit 7.1, Sample Key Messages, presents snippets of key messages itemized on a Mentoring Communication Strategy Matrix. These are but a few examples; note that different messages are required at each phase in creating a mentoring culture.

EXHIBIT 7.1

Sample Key Messages

Stakeholders	Objectives	Key Messages
Managers	Understanding	· All managers have a responsibility to participate. · All managers have a responsibility to advocate for organizational mentoring. · All managers have a responsibility to actively support mentoring initiatives.
Participants	Understanding, acceptance	· The development of organizational mentoring programs (OMPs) has incorporated continuous feedback from organizational partners. · This OMP pilot is one of several mentoring initiatives going on at once. · We anticipate that the pilot will be modified and improved as time goes on. · We are depending on your input.
Mentors	Acceptance	· If learning goals have not been completed by the end of the program year, it is your option to continue for longer than the one-year program period.

EXERCISE 7.3

Stakeholder Benefits

Instructions: Identifying stakeholder interest is an important part of any communication strategy. For each category below, identify the benefits (purpose and outcomes) that stakeholders *might derive* from creating a mentoring culture in your organization. Seek input from your team and interested stakeholders to validate your responses. Responses should answer the questions, "Why would this stakeholder be interested in mentoring?" and "How might they benefit?"

Stakeholder	Benefits to Stakeholders
The organization as a whole	
Your organization, division, or department	
Mentors	
Mentees	
Other	

Auditing key messages, both before and after they're sent, is good business practice. Once a message is released, it is difficult to retract. It is much like writing an e-mail message and hitting Send too soon. To prevent problems, take time up front to evaluate the message itself and determine if it meets a number of requirements:

- Is it clear?

- Is it timely?

- Is it consistent (externally and internally)?

- Is it proactive?

- Is it honest?

- Is it linked to the big-picture strategy?

- Which venues and vehicles will we use?

Nowhere does the familiar saying that the medium is the message ring louder and truer than when it comes to the venues and vehicles used for communication. A venue is the space or place facilitating the learning, and the context and environment in which stakeholders receive key communication messages. A vehicle is the specific means or method used in the venue.

Deciding how to communicate a message is just as important as the message itself. "How?" is a process question, by its very nature frequently an afterthought. A proactive and deliberate strategy avoids missed opportunities and facilitates maximum visibility. How a message is communicated merits a deliberative process that begins with conversation about what works and doesn't work in the organization. Think about how communication takes place in your organization, and answer two questions: When communication goes exceptionally well in your organization, which venues (settings) and vehicles (means) are used? When communication goes poorly, which venues and vehicles have been used?

Answers to these questions have practical and immediate implications for creating a mentoring culture. Consider which venues and vehicles should be avoided and which are most advantageous, and plan your mentoring communications accordingly.

Venue

Again, a venue is a space or place in which learning occurs. The venue—sometimes called the learning environment, climate, setting, or milieu—plays a major role in determining whether or not meaningful learning takes place. If the venue is conducive to learning, it facilitates and accelerates the communication process; if it is not, it can block effective communication.

There are many possible communication venues. Imagination is the only limit. The goal is to use multiple venues that reach the internal and external stakeholders. Some mentoring communication venues with the most leverage and impact are listed, with examples, in Exhibit 7.2. Review this list to stimulate ideas of other venues you can make use of for communicating about mentoring within your organization or among organizational partners.

EXHIBIT 7.2

Examples of Mentoring Communication Venues and Vehicles

Venue (Space or Place)	Vehicles (Means and Methods)	Comments
Meetings and organized events	Dialogue sessions Networking sessions Lunch-and-learn sessions Panel discussions Speakers Mentoring roundtables Traveling road show through the organization Mentoring briefing and info sessions Awards dinners Celebration ceremonies	These are opportunities to: • Give the big-picture perspective • Bring people together to share and celebrate experiences • Stimulate discussion of hot topics • Disseminate information
Print and media	Newsletters Articles Press releases News flashes Desk drops Mentoring white paper Communications toolkit Branding Application forms Memorabilia Notebooks Journals CDs Banners Signage Mentoring FAQs Mentoring manuals Information packets Video	Use multiple vehicles simultaneously to: • Promote awareness • Spread the word • Increase understanding • Raise visibility • Announce events • Support mentoring Create a mentoring communication toolkit that bundles together appropriate materials and user-friendly guidelines. "FAQs" is shorthand for frequently asked questions. Collecting questions that are frequently asked and publishing the answers often clarifies confusion.

EXHIBIT 7.2 (continued)

Venue (Space or Place)	Vehicles (Means and Methods)	Comments
Electronic and telephonic communication	Intranet Website E-mail alerts Mentoring chat rooms Web cast Videoconference Telephone bridge line Closed-circuit television Call scripts	Develop a central address for mentoring communication Look for alternative ways to reach and expand your mentoring audience.
Physical or virtual resource location	Mentoring library Mentoring reference list Resource room or center Kiosk Bulletin board Mentoring manager or point person	Build up your collection of quality mentoring resources. Make sure your resources are accessible and well located.
Face-to face interaction	Touch-base conversations Word of mouth	Schedule planned conversations at critical points in the mentoring journey. Encourage informal mentoring communication.
Two-way feedback	Performance review Human resource intervention Customer service feedback Formal and informal	Establish formal feedback mechanisms. Encourage informal feedback.

Vehicle

In contrast to the generic environment of venue, vehicle focuses on the more specific means and methods. For example, when Jim recruits mentors from among the alumni at Rho College he has to focus on developing awareness of the program; understanding of roles, goals, and benefits; getting buy-in; and nurturing commitment. He uses the specific vehicle of an alumni meeting to recruit six mentors and makes personal phone calls to the remaining four. Were he to use multiple vehicles simultaneously and "stage" his communication, the mentors might be more receptive to the manual they subsequently receive.

Organizations use many mentoring vehicles for promoting awareness, understanding, buy-in, and commitment. Some are listed in Exhibit 7.2; a few more detailed examples follow to give some texture to those listed in the exhibit.

Lunch-and-Learn Session

A lunch-and-learn session, where the menu is food and mentoring, is an informal opportunity to promote awareness by stimulating interest, facilitate shared understanding about mentoring, and support those engaged in mentoring. Many organizations regularly hold such sessions, where mentoring becomes one topic in a menu of many.

Briefing or Information Session

The purpose of a briefing or information session is awareness. The session sets the climate and introduces the concept of mentoring, fitting it into the larger organizational picture. Usually the focus is on making the case for mentoring, why it is important, and what the benefits are to the individual, the organization, or the profession. Some CEOs make the case in person or on video. Individuals who have had successful mentoring relationships may present their stories, perhaps on a panel. It is helpful to include data and information about industry trends.

"Breakfast of Champions"

"If you want to achieve success in a new venture, you first have to have a champion" (Edwards-Winslow, 2002). Those who champion mentoring within an organization are critical to ensuring its success. Sometimes championing is done for the right reasons, but their knowledge and assumptions about what mentoring is and what it will eventually look and feel like within the organization might be neither accurate nor realistic. Keeping champions up to speed helps manage their expectations and at the same time better positions them to manage the expectations of others whom they influence.

"Breakfast of Champions" (General Mills's Wheaties motto) has come to stand for the periodic breakfast gatherings that organizations hold for their mentoring champions or advocates. This elite circle of influence comes together—by invitation only—to stay current and brainstorm venues and vehicles for their individual and collective mentoring advocacy within the organization.

Mentoring White Paper

When senior management takes the time to present a well-thought-out written document making the case for mentoring and linking it to business results, the document becomes a reference tool that lives well beyond its initial presentation. The white paper can be used to stimulate dialogue, discuss resistance, and invite feedback. It is a particularly useful tool for presenting the mentoring idea and the big concepts that support it. It promotes awareness and understanding.

Communications Toolkit

One means for ensuring consistency in communicating messages is preparation. Developing the right materials and well-designed instructions as to when and how to deliver key messages has a high yield. For example, in Jim's mentoring initiative aimed at promoting alumni-student relationships, if he (or someone he hires) develops a communications toolkit, he could hand it off to his direct reports knowing full well that they now have (1) an idea of what is being communicated and to whom, (2) more information about the "learners," and (3) a sense of where their charge of developing an orientation manual fits into the big picture.

A communications toolkit is essential in a large organization, where many people have to deliver key messages in differing forums. This is particularly important for leadership. Preparing leaders with reliable and consistent materials enhances and elevates communication efforts.

Branding

Branding is a vehicle for creating name recognition for a mentoring effort. Whether there are multiple initiatives under one umbrella or many mentoring initiatives, taking the time to brand mentoring visibly links it to strategic purpose and helps create demand. Branded signage, graphics, announcements, presentations, and Website work together to nurture commitment and embed mentoring within the organization. Branding must be well thought out and aligned. A logo or tag line that ends up being cutesy or that sticks out like a sore thumb is risky. It can backfire and result in a situation from which it is difficult to recover.

Mentoring FAQs

The questions asked at an information session or briefing, an open forum, or just in the hallway in response to a white paper or any other document are important. They can be the grist for developing a powerful communication message because they meet learners where they are. Use FAQs to structure and broadcast consistent and specific messages. The answers to FAQs can be useful in identifying items that should be included in a mentoring information packet, posted to a Website, or covered in a mentoring newsletter.

Mentoring Website

Technology offers many options for creating organizational readiness, creating varied learning opportunities, and supporting organizational mentoring. Many organizations are just now discovering the potential. A well-conceived, well-implemented, and well-maintained Website can make retrieval of mentoring information effortless. It can be a source for general information about a mentoring effort, a database of success stories, a menu of learning resources, and a place to post periodic news bulletins. Depending on resources and capability, a Website becomes the address for screening potential applicants, suggesting possible pairings, or even electronically making pairings. By offering links to other sites (internal and external), it offers access to learning opportunities and self-assessments that can help users find and close gaps in their own performance as mentors or mentees. Some Websites have a "Submit a question" or Help link; some also offer mentoring tips.

Mentoring Resource Center

Whether virtual or stand-alone, a mentoring resource center is a go-to place to access resources as needed. I have watched this concept unfold over the last decade. One company I worked with started out by using wall displays consisting of Lucite pockets. Throughout the company, they were prominently hung with signage including their branding. Every month the corporate mentoring coordinator would add to the materials available. As materials became dated, she removed them. Today, this same company uses those location resource centers as well as a central location filled with books, manuals, exercises, and training materials. In addition, they have mentoring information packets and newsletters available.

Another company I worked with decided to develop a virtual resource center. They continuously update their mentoring bibliography, post new training materials (including Microsoft PowerPoint slides), and offer supplementary material electronically to anyone who requests it. Both companies depend on a point person to maintain the integrity of the resource center.

Mentoring Roundtable

A mentoring roundtable is a facilitated conversation where people come to talk about mentoring. The event takes place once a month, or perhaps quarterly, on a schedule. A mentoring dialogue topic is posted, and people bring their curiosity, experience, and wisdom to the session, never knowing where the conversation will lead but fully confident of being engaged and learning something new.

Customer Service Feedback

Feedback plays an important role in ensuring effective communication. It is important to look for ways to tap into feedback. Getting feedback on communication messages, venues, vehicles, and effectiveness is the only thing that generates quality process improvement. Regularly sending out periodic surveys, conducting focus groups, and doing needs assessment should be factored into every communication strategy matrix.

The vehicles used depend on the level of communication needed and the audience to whom the communication is targeted.

What Is the Timing and Sequencing of Communication?

Each component in the communication strategy matrix builds on the previous one. Now, we focus on the timing and sequencing of communication: when and how often key messages should be communicated. Timing is a critical variable in the learning process. Ideally, when should be the "teachable moment," the time when there is the most readiness to learn? The mentoring cycle or programmatic implementation schedule identifies ideal milestones for connecting with stakeholders.

Communication touch points might be keyed to the predictable phases of mentoring: preparing, negotiating, enabling, and coming to closure. Specific milestones in each phase create readiness to learn? Communicating about coming to closure after the midpoint of the enabling cycle sends the message to begin planning for closure of mentoring relationships. The cycle might suggest some hot topics or communication messages. An e-mail message to mentors might ask "How are you offering support to your mentoring partner?" or say "Here are five tips for providing feedback to your mentoring partner." Communication might also be tied to program milestones, with publicity and reminders of specific events and dates. Letting people know when and how to expect communication also creates readiness.

When to communicate also needs to be considered in light of other things that are happening in the organization. If too much activity occurs simultaneously, or there are factors affecting the organization (a reorganization, a merger), people may not be as receptive to the key messages. Balancing contingencies such as these with consistency often requires innovative thinking.

Galpin (1996) points out that "messages are most effective when they are consistent and repetitive. Consistency helps establish the credibility of the messages. Repetition helps people see the importance of the messages and the importance of changes the messages are communicating" (p. 50). If communication is inconsistent, people put their own spin on what is happening. They may interpret a lull as "interest is dwindling"; mentoring isn't very important right now," or "I don't need to focus on mentoring as much."

Sequencing communication is critical. For example, if communication about Rho College's alumni mentoring program were sequenced properly, participants would prepare for receiving and using their orientation manuals. As it is, the brief cover memo that accompanies the manual is not up to the task.

Who Is Going to Be Accountable for Implementation?

Without ownership, sustainability is problematic. Accountability may be assigned, but ownership for accountability must be accepted and acted on to ensure results. As discussed at length in Chapter Six, ownership needs to be named and claimed. Jim has taken responsibility for initiating contact with prospective participants, but then he assigns others to developing the mentoring program at Rho College. With a plan in place, his direct reports might take on the responsibility for sending a welcome letter immediately following Jim's contact. If Jim does not abdicate his responsibility as a department leader and owner of the program, he could follow up with a breakfast meeting orienting participants to their role, distribute the manuals, and walk people through them. Exhibit 7.3 is a completed matrix using Rho College as an example.

Effective communication promotes readiness, generates opportunity, and provides support. Exercise 7.4, the Mentoring Communication Strategy Matrix, is adapted from Galpin's model (1996); it presents a blank matrix worksheet that can be used to develop a communication action plan. You will probably find occasion to complete and revise a communication strategy matrix whenever feedback and needs warrant, circumstances change, specific initiatives are mounted, or specific communication milestones are reached.

Communication: Reflection on Practice

In this chapter, we have focused on two approaches among many that can inform and strengthen a developing or established mentoring culture. The communication strategy matrix generates a level of readiness. The very act of making an implementation action plan sets the wheels in motion. In fact, the communication strategy is often part of the implementation action plan, so the two parts happen simultaneously in interaction with each other. The action plan requires specification of basic steps, the pragmatic key tasks, specific responsibilities, and timelines of how to get the "job" done. The role of leadership is essential in driving communication. The combination of strategy and action builds momentum that facilitates responsible implementation.

EXHIBIT 7.3

Rho College Alumni and Student Mentoring Program

Who Are the Stakeholders?	What Is Our Purpose in Communicating?	What Are the Key Messages?	Which Venues and Vehicles Will We Use?	What Is the Timing and Sequencing of Communication?	Who Is Going to Be Accountable for Implementation?
Alumni Office	Buy-in	Mentoring is a tool to strengthen alumni-college relationships.	· Presentation at monthly roundtable meeting · Program brochure	First meeting of new quarter	Jim, with president of college and key alumni
Mentors	· Awareness · understanding · Buy-in · Commitment	· This is what is happening. · This is where we are going. · This is what it means to you. · Continue the legacy. · Gain visibility. · Reconnect with former classmates. · Gain new skill. · Network. · Opportunity to give back.	· Promotional letter · Brochures · Announcement in alumni bulletin · Personal phone call · Follow-up letter	September–October	Jim and staff Include president and alumni at strategic points.
Mentees	· Awareness · understanding · Buy-in · Commitment	· We value the expertise and experience of our alumni. · They are doing remarkable things. · You have that potential. · Here's what it could mean to you. · You have to make a commitment if you want to participate. · Here's what you need to do if you are interested.	· use hallway to display banners. · Brochures · Applications	September–October	Jim, staff, student development office, president, and key alumni where appropriate

Who Are the Stakeholders?	What Is Our Purpose in Communicating?	What Are the Key Messages?	Which Venues and Vehicles Will We Use?	What Is the Timing and Sequencing of Communication?	Who Is Going to Be Accountable for Implementation?
Communication Office	Action	· This program is important to the college, and here's why. · Here's what we want to do and how we are going to do it. · We need branding, brochures, and posters.	Three meetings, one each month	August	Communications officer, president, and key alumni will share responsibility, with communication officer taking the lead role.

Here are some questions for reflection that help you build communication momentum in your own organization.

Criteria

- Does your organization meet the ten communication criteria laid out in this chapter?

- If not, which are missing?

- What must be done to bolster weak areas so that mentoring communication is more effective in your organization?

- Are there other communication criteria that should be adopted in order to make maximize your efforts?

Concepts

- How effectively does communication drive learning in your organization?

- What are the most effective ways your organization communicates to break down resistance?

- Does your organizational communication promote trust?

- Is communication used effectively when your organization faces transition?

- Does your organization embrace a disciplined approach to communication?

Stakeholders

- How knowledgeable is your team about organizational stakeholders?

- Is it successful and accurate in identifying stakeholders?

EXERCISE 7.4

Mentoring Communication Strategy Matrix

Instructions: Use this matrix as a handy planning, implementation, and evaluation tool for developing a comprehensive strategy for mentoring communication.

Who Are the *Stakeholders*?	What Is Our *Purpose* in Communicating?	What Are the *Key Messages*?	Which *Venues and Vehicles* Will We Use?	What Is the *Timing and Sequencing* of Communication?	Who Is Going to *Be Accountable* for Implementation?

- Is a stakeholder analysis conducted prior to embarking on a communication strategy?

Purpose

- Has the purpose for mentoring been adequately clarified?
- Can you clearly articulate your purpose so that you can communicate it to multiple audiences in a way that is meaningful to them?

Key Messages

- Is there clarity about the key messages that are to be communicated, and to whom?
- To what extent are the messages timely, consistent, proactive, honest, and tied to strategy?

Venues and Vehicles

- Which venues and vehicles are used most effectively in your culture?
- Which are overused? underused?
- Which venues and vehicles for communication are available?
- What venues and vehicles are not available but would be nice to have?

Timing and Sequencing

- Is a timeline in place for the internal communications plan?
- What milestones is the timeline keyed to? Is the timeline broadcast so others know what to expect in advance?

Accountability

- Is a reporting plan in place?
- Has a communications toolkit for mentoring been developed?

Clearly, communication facilitates creation of a mentoring culture. Whenever communication is elevated in a mentoring culture, it has a multiplier effect and enriches the entire culture, creating an organizational win-win. Do not underestimate the power of communication. It is the very core of who we are and what we do—individually, in relationship, in our organization, and in our global community. Communication is one of several contributing factors that enhance the value and visibility of mentoring, to which we turn in the next chapter.

Chapter 8

Value and Visibility

It makes a great difference to the force of any sentence whether there be a man behind it or no.

—RALPH WALDO EMERSON,
REPRESENTATIVE MEN (1850)

EMERSON'S QUOTE brings home the point that the potential impact of words by themselves is lessened if the humanity underlying the words is not apparent. Visibility connects us with the person behind the words. Human connection creates new meaning and adds value to the words. Similarly, in a mentoring culture those who walk the talk every day create value and visibility for organizational mentoring by connecting us to it through their example. For Emerson, it is clear that words and deeds must be connected. He speaks to this need again when he says, "What you are stands over you the while, and thunders so that I cannot hear what you say to the contrary" (from his Letters and Social Aims of 1875). As has been recognized through the ages, it's vital that words and deeds be connected.

Value and visibility rely on the personal practice of role modeling by senior leaders and the organization's practices of reward, recognition, and celebration. Together these practices help to create value and visibility.

Identifying the Value

Value is a hot topic in organizational life. It is a term that describes both an input and an output mechanism. Value propositions and value statements are input mechanisms that drive action strategies. "Values" is a critical component for maintaining organizational alignment. Value is also an output mechanism, the worth that comes from action. It is the latter on which we focus now.

To assist in evaluating how mentoring is creating value in your organization and to identify strategies for adding further value, review and complete Exercise 8.1, Strategically Adding Value. Use the exercise of completing the form to start conversation about how mentoring is adding value in your organization, and how that value might be increased. You can

Strategically Adding Value

Instructions: Use this form to evaluate how your mentoring efforts are adding value to your organization, and to craft an action plan to boost the capacity to add value.

1. How is mentoring adding value to your institution? (Examples: retention of key players, development of new talent, faster solutions to business problems)

2. Identify five contributions mentoring consistently makes that add value to your institution. (Example: ease of collaborative networking)

3. How and where might your mentoring efforts not be adding value? (Example: mentors feel overburdened)

4. Brainstorm six new ways to add value over the next six months that link to business goals and objectives.

5. Identify the actions that have the highest likelihood of success, and prioritize them.

6. Develop appropriate action goals and timelines.

Action	Strategy	Timeline

also use the exercise to help identify those actions with the highest likelihood of success and to establish action goals and timelines. Organizations that regularly monitor how mentoring creates value increase the momentum and sustainability of their mentoring efforts.

Showing Support Through Visibility

One of the primary challenges in creating and sustaining a mentoring culture is ensuring visible support from senior management. Because of their inherent positional power, leaders play a key role in promoting the visibility of mentoring and the growth and development of a mentoring culture.

Daniel I. Kaplan, president of Hertz Equipment Rental and executive vice president of Hertz Corporation, offers an illustration of visibility: "Nothing a leader can do or say escapes notice. Every action and response, even a chance remark, gives out some signal that will be picked up by someone and passed on to others" (Kaplan, 1997, p. 145). In short, leaders' remarks and actions send important signals. If leaders are not personally aligned with mentoring, then lack of commitment will soon be obvious.

Leaders naturally want to be associated with success. Unless they see the value in mentoring, they are not likely to lend their support; in such a case, both visibility and value are diminished. Since engaging top leadership in mentoring is a critical success factor in creating a mentoring culture, thoughtful strategic planning is the key. Exercise 8.2, Planning for Visible Support from Senior Management, can be used as an implementation guide. It lists some preliminary questions to be considered prior to creating an action plan for engaging senior management (champions, advocates, and other key players) in rollout and implementation.

Linking mentoring with broader organizational processes heightens visibility and weaves it into the fabric of the culture. If an organization spends sufficient time discussing the underlying dynamics of mentoring visibility, it can generate ideas that often have lasting impact. An organization should periodically analyze how the visibility of mentoring is being driven and how effective it is, and brainstorm ideas about how efforts to enhance visibility might be strengthened.

As part of this process, ask, "What concrete things is our organization doing to make its commitment to mentoring visible?" Examples might be descriptive brochures about mentoring in recruitment materials, a performance review process with learning goals that can be achieved through mentoring, delineation of required mentoring competencies for new leaders and managers, or inclusion of mentoring as part of the organization's value proposition.

Planning for Visible Support from Senior Management

Instructions : Complete these questions to develop a helpful implementation guideline.

1. What will support from top management look like? What will leaders be doing? How is their support being expressed? In answering these questions, you might draw lessons from past experiences in which senior leaders were visible. For each action, indicate whether it is part of development, rollout, or implementation.

Development	Rollout	Implementation

2. Who must be involved? Give generic role descriptions (e.g., human resources, top officers) here.

Identify and Name Specific Individuals	How Will They Be Involved? (e.g., Coach, HR Generalist)	What Will They Be Doing? (e.g., Coaching, Seeking Feedback, Meeting with Mentor and Mentee to Set Goals)

3. Which leaders currently champion mentoring? For each leader listed, give reasons for the person's involvement.

4. Who else within the organization has the potential to champion the mentoring? How can we recruit and motivate them? What is our game plan? What is the strategy (e.g., training, rewarding)?

Review your itemized list. Mark items that are working well with an asterisk; put a delta symbol by items that need improvement; and identify specific actions that might reinforce, strengthen, and ensure continued support for items that are working well. Then consider this question: "What things aren't we doing that we would like to be doing?" Items generated should then be added to the delta list. Develop a strategy and timeline for each item on your delta list.

Practices That Stimulate Value and Visibility

Role modeling, along with reward, recognition, and celebration, are specific practices for generating value and visibility within an organization. Each is described here.

Role Modeling by Leaders

Positive role models exert powerful influence. Their example extends a compelling invitation to learn their story, follow their example, travel alongside them. As Laurent Daloz says, the mentor's gift "is not the opportunity to become like them but the challenge to become more fully ourselves through them. They call forth the best we have. They invite us to transcend ourselves" (1999, pp. 224–225).

Joe Kanfer, president and CEO of GOJO (which manufactures and distributes PURELL Instant Hand Sanitizer), is a mentoring role model to his employees. Like the best of mentors, he has had (and continues to have) multiple mentors in his life—some from within his own business and others from the corporate and nonprofit world. What he values most about his mentors is what he learns as a result of observing them in action. For him, "mentoring comes best when it is real and in real time" (Zachary, 2003c).

Joe has been at the helm of GOJO since his midtwenties, when he took over the business from his uncle and mentor, Jerome "Jerry" Lippman, who founded GOJO in 1946. Jerry respected hard work and integrity and always took time to talk with Joe and others about his values. Today, Joe considers many of his direct reports to be his mentors, and many of them consider him their mentor. He hires idiosyncratic people who are "courageous enough to speak" and teach him things about himself, his style, and what they feel he needs to hear. Joe models behaviors he believes in and wants others to emulate that. His actions enable others to act. He inspires by example. Those he mentors buy in and inspire others. As these efforts multiply, they magnify the value and visibility of mentoring.

The actions of those who lead and support organizational mentoring need to reflect genuine commitment to mentoring. If what leaders do and say about mentoring is not aligned, credibility is suspect and sustainability is undermined. Leaders must therefore be actively and visibly engaged in the mentoring effort if it is to be successful. They must be advocates and be publicly supportive of mentoring. They must share their time, stories, and vision. They must conscientiously work at engaging their people.

The term role model is linked with mentors in many ways. It is an oft-cited characteristic of a "good mentor," a desirable mentor qualification, a tangible mentor behavior, and a frequently articulated mentor responsibility. Mentors who are role models demonstrate the possible in action, raise the bar for relationships and performance, and embody desirable characteristics. In this sense, they serve a psychosocial function (Kram, 1988, p. 32). According to Margo Murray, "Role models often exhibit success, exemplary behavior, achievement and style, ability to get things done, knowledge or organization policy and philosophy, apparent enjoyment of position and accomplishment" (2001, p. 14).

To maximize the opportunity to create value and visibility through role modeling, it helps to more fully understand all that role modeling entails. Despite its positive possibilities, the efficacy of the mentor as role model is a topic of much debate. Some believe that mentors do not have to be role models (Conway, 1998; Cohen, 2001). Kouzes and Posner (2002) speak to a downside for leaders: "An obsession with being seen as a role model can lead to being too focused on your own values and your way of doing things. It can cause you to discount others' views and be closed to feedback. It can push you into isolation for fear of losing privacy or being 'found out'; it can also cause you to be more concerned with style than substance" (p. 395).

Another liability of role modeling is the cloning phenomenon, the temptation to recreate oneself in another's image. For a mentor, serving as a role model may be an unconscious opportunity to lead another down the same primrose path. A mentee might become enamored with the persona of the mentor and lose his own individuality or uniqueness in the process of imitating the other. Both mentor and mentee must resist the temptation to become the other if the relationship is to result in growth and development of the partners.

Even so, despite these challenges the possibilities inherent in role modeling hold enormous appeal and potential. Creating a mentoring culture requires leaders who are committed to learning about themselves, their people, and the organization they serve—who unabashedly model learning and purposely infuse it into every aspect of what they do and how they do it. As poet David Whyte reminds us, "With a little more care, a little more courage, and, above all, a little more soul, our lives can be so easily discovered and celebrated in work, and not, as now, squandered and lost in its shadow" (1994, p. 298). Reward, recognition, and celebration create value by modeling care, courage, and soul.

The leaders at Ideal Organization (recall Chapter One) model caring by writing personalized notes to their mentees. They model courage by what they say and when they say it. Sometimes just the right words uttered at just the right moment are the best and most remembered treasure. Leaders role-model soul by paying attention and expressing appreciation appropriately. At Ideal, mentors are attentive to learner needs. There are resources available to help mentors select meaningful mementoes or books, items that relate specifically to the purpose or content of the mentoring, for those whom they mentor.

Reward, Recognition, and Celebration

The practices of reward, recognition, and celebration help create value and visibility for individual and organizational mentoring in numerous ways. They feed basic psychological human needs for satisfaction (Berne, 1996). They breathe spirit and passion into the lives of individuals and organizations (Bolman and Deal, 1995). They strengthen bonds and build connection among people. They create a more complete sense of purpose and shared enterprise (Bellah, 1986). They reduce the inherent sense of isolationism and siloism that comes from "bowling alone"; instead, they create community (Putnam, 2000). They promote learning and accountability (Zachary, 2000).

Reward, recognition, and celebration represent and shape a mentoring culture. According to Deal and Key, "What we choose to recognize and reward is witnessed as an expression of the ideals of a company's culture" (1998, p. 48). When acceptance of a new culture is displayed, by a group or an individual, it is important to reinforce and reward the desired new behavior (Simonsen, 1997) to keep people focused and motivated.

Yet despite the tremendous payoffs, reward, recognition, and celebration are not a high priority in organizations today. Too often, they are regarded as special events which are not built into organizational life. In a mentoring culture, however, reward, recognition, and celebration are relied on to help create value and visibility for mentoring.

Reward

When the topic of reward is placed squarely on the agenda, the discussion that follows usually reveals much about an organization's culture. In some organizations, the very idea of tangible reward for mentoring is irrelevant because "it's just part of the job." In organizations where the culture does not single out one individual over another, reward is antithetical. Many organizations believe that mentoring brings its own psychic reward (personal satisfaction, meaning, and contribution) and anything else is superfluous. Other organizations engage in a variety of reward practices and reap considerable benefit from doing so. Some say reward is a powerful motivator for promoting accountability because it sets a standard for excellence. Some sing its virtue as an alignment tool.

Even though the topic of reward is a hot button and sometimes sparks contention, it needs to be discussed openly early in the development process of a mentoring culture. Here are some questions to ask and consider:

- Do we have a policy for giving rewards?
- Do the rewards we have established fit the culture?
- Will the rewards be meaningful to recipients?
- How can we be consistent in how we reward mentoring?
- What small rewards will make a big difference?

Organizational practices run the gamut. Two examples of reward practices are financial incentives and support, along with appreciation.

Financial Incentives and Support

In addition to rewards, the organization can offer individual and team financial incentives that reflect time and effort spent on mentoring. Much as it may seem a leap to reward for time spent mentoring versus time spent generating revenue, the long-term result is usually justified. Some organizations offer an incentive based on time spent; others reward mentors according to the number of mentee relationships; still others make financial rewards on the basis of sustainable mentee productivity and accomplishment. In this case, it is frequently the mentor who is rewarded through a qualitative bonus structure or direct payment on a per-mentee or per-hour basis.

It is important to make sure that adequate learning opportunities are available to train, develop, and support mentors, mentees, and personnel engaged in supporting the mentoring effort. The costs of these opportunities are often subsidized. There are often additional travel costs associated even with in-house mentoring training, workshops, and development opportunities. Some organizations only subsidize startup costs to ensure participation, with the expectation that these costs will be covered by internal budgets once rollout is complete.

Learning in an organization depends to a large extent on the availability, adequacy, and accessibility of resources. Some organizations are able to make resources available in-house and at no direct cost to those who have a need for the information. Most are not able to do so and need to look for other ways. Some offer resources such as books and tapes at a discounted rate. Others establish resource entitlement packages where employees have a mentoring resource allowance for purchasing books or tuition for a leadership course (held, for example, at a prestigious university).

Appreciation

Human beings want and need to feel that they are appreciated. It is important to take the time to meet this desire, and to express appreciation. "The ritualistic 'thank you' is one of the world's most common expressive events" (Deal and Key, 1998, p. 48). A simple thank-you or expression of specific appreciation (for example, "I really admire the fact that you . . ." or "I really appreciated it when you . . .") is often all that is needed to validate the effort or contribution of a mentoring partner, a team of mentoring planners, mentoring champions, and those who support mentoring every day. In other cases, a more public expression of appreciation is required that describes and praises both the effort and the outcome.

Mentoring partners often quite naturally look for appropriate ways to express appreciation to each other. They may have difficulty in deciding what would be appropriate and how much it should cost. Organizations can help the process along by supporting it and suggesting guidelines.

Recognition

Recognition is another way of acknowledging the efforts of contributors, exemplary performance, and participation of coworkers. Mentoring recognition, like mentoring reward, runs the full gamut of practice and possibility. A mentoring culture involves the contribution of numerous people at many levels of an organization, not just mentors and mentees. It is important to be as inclusive as possible. For example, in a large organization it might be important to "think globally" and include recognition of the chief learning officer or chief executive in support of mentoring as well as mentoring coordinators and mentoring coaches in various divisions of the organization. It is equally important to "act locally" and recognize quality mentoring efforts and contributions within a department or division.

Recognition can be formal or informal, public or private. Recognition by a supervisor or direct report can prove immensely satisfying to some people. The unsung heroes of a mentoring effort are the members of the task force, development team, or advisory panel that labors to create the culture. Usually these group efforts are acknowledged once or twice at the beginning of an effort and then forgotten. Linking back to their efforts as the culture matures helps sustain organizational memory and nurture their continued investment and commitment.

Recognition for the organization's commitment to mentoring can take many forms. Picture, for example, what it's like at Ideal Organization, where mentoring is serious business. Traditionally, the month of May signals the beginning of a new mentoring cycle and the start of celebrations. Each day of the month, another employee is recognized for mentoring success. Employees who are not engaged in mentoring attend information sessions. Those who are engaged participate in networking sessions to share their experiences and learn about the best practices of their coworkers. New mentoring materials and information are prominently displayed. Nationally recognized mentoring experts present state-of-the-art practices at lunch-and-learn sessions during the month. The annual mentoring luncheon that culminates the monthlong festivities is hosted by Ideal's CEO, who discusses how mentoring is contributing to the achievement of business goals. Mentoring advisory panel members completing their term are recognized for past service to the organization, and new advisory panel members are introduced.

A program as elaborate as Ideal's doesn't fit every culture. Some organizations have developed mentoring awards in several categories, such as "mentoring excellence," "most innovative mentoring experience," and "best examples of mentoring at a distance." Awardees can be selected by soliciting names from participants or managers. The actual award itself may range from a handshake and a certificate to a substantial monetary reward or gift.

Mentoring can be included as an eligibility criterion for other awards (leadership excellence, most improved manager, exemplary leadership). Uniform mentoring rewards tied to specific criteria can be established and awarded on a corporate or divisional basis. In this case, eligibility criteria should be published and broadcast through the organization. Individual or team contributions to enhancing the mentoring culture might be rewarded by highlighting people's mentoring efforts and how they have made a difference in productivity, satisfaction, or retention.

Here are additional possibilities for mentoring recognition:

- Put mentoring on the agenda by way of one of the many forums available. For example, leadership breakfasts may not always deal especially with the topic of mentoring, but mentoring is still part of the "agenda." A mentoring update is included with meeting materials, offering some combination of participation data, recent successes, mentoring updates, and mentoring outcomes. Leaders bring mentees to the breakfast meeting with them.

- Identify storytelling opportunities. Routine meeting agendas (organization, unit, team) include a mentoring item. One mentoring pair shares their story; a participant, coach, or department head talks about how mentoring has transformed the organization. Mentors and mentees are invited to share their experiences at orientation sessions. Organizational champions tell their own story and are prepared to share other success stories.

- Include mentoring competency as a standard part of the performance development plan. Doing so increases recognition and acceptance of its importance and reminds employees of its importance as part of their own development and in developing others.

- Honor excellence. "Employee of the month" is a popular current phenomenon. In a mentoring culture, you might see criteria for the honor of "mentee (or mentor) of the month" or even a "mentoring champion of the month."

- Use recognizable visible artifacts such as pins, plaques, signs, and notepads judiciously. In some organizations, those engaged in mentoring wear buttons that indicate their status ("mentor in training," "looking for a mentor," or "Mentoring 2005 participant"). Be alert to ways to be inclusive in recognizing people.

- Showcase mentoring excellence wherever feasible and appropriate.

- Ensure that senior leaders look for opportunities to engage employees in conversation about mentoring.

When practiced well, recognition can consistently stimulate the value and visibility of mentoring. If your organization falls short on recognition, review the possibilities listed here. Also consider further ways to consciously look for the means to express appreciation and be inclusive in recognizing people.

Celebration

Celebration adds value and creates visibility for mentoring. It is an underrated, underused, and underplayed organizational practice. The widespread belief that celebration is synonymous with "party" diminishes its unique contribution in energizing, elevating, and expanding individual and organizational learning.

Celebration offers an occasion for marking mini-milestones, major ones, significant accomplishments, and the end of a cycle. For example, once a development team completes its mission, it is often disbanded and an implementation group or administrator steps in to shepherd mentoring through its next phase. Before this transition occurs, make the time to celebrate the contribution of each team member and the team's accomplishments. Celebration is natural closure and a transition to the next phase or stage. It drives commitment and sustains ownership throughout the organization.

Mentoring organizations help ensure successful celebration by:

- Engaging stakeholders in planning and implementing their own celebration. Planning and implementing celebration gives visibility to people and to the mentoring effort. It also creates an opportunity for new leadership to emerge.

- Identifying success criteria and plan on the basis of desired outcomes so that accountability is factored in from the very beginning.

- Making celebration meaningful. Celebrate organizational and individual learning and success. Engage people's hearts and heads.

- Encouraging mentoring partners and administrators to celebrate mini-milestones along the way rather than waiting until the end of a mentoring cycle.

- Facilitating celebration for mentoring partners.

- Aligning celebration with the organization's culture and values.

- Welcoming innovation.

- Gathering feedback on the celebration afterward.

Reliable input helps ensure that reward, recognition, and celebration add value for the intended recipients. Strategies for gathering necessary input might include conducting a survey or focus group, asking managers what they think their employees would value, brainstorming by committee, and validating responses by asking employees. Exercise 8.3, Creating Value Through Reward, Recognition, and Celebration, introduces a template for gathering and recording data from external best practices, needs-based practices, and effective organizational practice. You can then use the data gathered in Exercise 8.3 to generate discussion by means of Exercise 8.4, Debriefing the Data.

It takes care, courage, and soul (Whyte, 1994) to make sure that work is productive and meaningful. Organizations that are successful at implementing reward, recognition, and celebration for mentoring know this. They optimize organizational learning and foster continued ownership while engaging employees so as to create value for them and the organization. They are strategic and systematic in their planning. They build in multiple mechanisms for enabling reward, recognition, and celebration. Exhibit 8.1 presents a portion of a strategy implementation grid used to do just that. This company gives a mentor a bonus of $500 for each mentee that he or she partners with; the bonus is attached to the annual holiday bonus. It certifies its mentoring coaches and publicizes their achievement and certification. Exercise 8.5, the Strategy Implementation Grid, presents a blank form for you to complete.

EXERCISE 8.3

Creating Value Through Reward, Recognition, and Celebration

Instructions: Complete each of the boxes to inform your reward, recognition, and celebration strategy. First, gather best practices externally from the field. Next, solicit organizational input from potential stakeholders. Finally, conduct organizational reconnaissance to determine what is working particularly well in the organization right now that can be leveraged to enhance reward, recognition, and celebration. Use the information from these data sources to plan your strategy and begin the conversation suggested in Exercise 8.4.

	Rewards	**Recognition**	**Celebrations**
Best practices (external input)			
Organizational input (surveys, focus groups, conversations)			
Organizational best practices (what currently exists)			

EXERCISE 8.4

Debriefing the Data

Instructions: Use the data gathered in Exercise 8.3 to generate a strategic conversation about each of these questions. Try to avoid focusing on tactics; stay with the big ideas and concepts. Then use your answers to inform the development of your action plan.

1. How should mentoring be rewarded?

2. Should all participants be recognized and rewarded?

3. Should excellence and participation in mentoring be recognized? If so, how?

4. How should accomplishments be celebrated?

5. How should the program cycle be acknowledged and recognized?

6. What would make an appropriate celebration?

EXHIBIT 8.1

Sample Strategy Implementation Grid

Categories	Types	Recipients	The Process	Timing
Reward				
	Mentoring bonus	Mentors	$500 per mentee	December 24
Recognition				
	Certification	Mentoring coaches	Presentation and introduction at an annual management retreat	End of course and HR retreat

Value and Visibility: Reflection on Practice

Value and visibility are not easy to come by. They require work and reflection. Here are some questions to consider in raising the level of mentoring value and visibility in your organization:

- Where in the organization do role models for mentoring exist?

- How do our leaders serve as role models?

- In what specific ways do we encourage role modeling among our mentors?

- What is the level of mentoring visibility we want to achieve? Have we achieved it?

- What do we do consistently as an organization to raise the level of visibility for organizational mentoring?

- How do managers and senior leaders personally promote mentoring visibility?

- Is the value we think we are adding meaningful to our internal stakeholders?

- How do we determine our effectiveness in adding value?

- What strategy do we have in place to make sure we continuously add value?

Value and visibility are created when people feel mentoring is meaningful to them and connected to a larger purpose. As Emerson reminds us, visibility and value are increased when connections are made and meaning is created when humanity stands behind the words. Role modeling, reward, recognition, and celebration are high-leverage activities that create and sustain value and visibility; value and visibility in turn create organizational demand for mentoring. Demand, as we shall see in the next chapter, adds to the value and visibility of mentoring within the organization.

Strategy Implementation Grid

Instructions: For each category on the left, indicate how you will reward, recognize, or celebrate. Then identify the recipients, the process, and the timing.

Categories	Types	Recipients	Process	Timing
Reward				
Recognition				
Celebrations				

Chapter 9

Demand

There are two ways of exerting one's strength; one is pushing down, and the other is pulling up.

—BOOKER T. WASHINGTON

IF LEADERS PUSH mentoring down into the organization, people are not likely to want to participate in it. Pulling people up by motivating them to want to succeed makes it more likely people will see value and want to engage in it.

Demand is a fundamental business term referring to the need or desire for a product or service. If something adds or creates value, people will demand it. We have only to look at the burgeoning demand for cell phones. It's not just the changing look of cell phones that has people trading in their land lines (and old cell phones), but the improved functionality—the new tasks that we are now able to do with our cell phones, from using the cell as an alarm clock and appointment reminder to linking up to the Web. Some of these functions cross the line between service and technology, and both increase demand.

Creating Demand in a Mentoring Culture

In a mentoring culture, demand is expressed in a variety of ways. Each augments the value of mentoring within the organization, as an example illustrates. Great Community Bank was established to meet the diverse banking needs of small-to-medium-sized business owners. It is dedicated to helping entrepreneurs better manage their businesses by offering loans for cash flow and investment, along with customized individual financial consulting services. The bank partners in building community through its Business Mentoring Program, in which a team of managing consultants work together to mentor one or two small startup, high-potential businesses a year. The bank's mentoring first occurred from inside by going out to the wider community; eventually, mentoring occurred internally and its community presence expanded as well.

A bit reluctant at first, Martin, Rosa, and Patti, the bank's mentoring team, were soon amazed by the array of new possibilities that emerged at monthly meetings with their mentee. Their collective feedback inspired and infused the mentee with optimism and confidence. Watching their mentee's confidence and perspectives expand created value for them. As time went on, Martin, Rosa, and Patti became increasingly enthusiastic and proud of the work they were doing together and the results they were able to help their mentee achieve for her business.

Their group mentoring experience was unlike what each experienced daily at work. The depth of knowledge, expertise, and experience of their mentoring team colleagues pleasantly surprised Martin, Rosa, and Patti, who, previous to their mentoring roles, had rarely interacted at the bank. Their collective wisdom inspired all of them. Their palpable excitement about the experience and the impact they were making was hard to miss. Martin, who had a ten-year history at the bank, was renewed and reinvigorated by his participation. When Rosa contacted Martin and asked if he would be willing to mentor her, he readily agreed. Prior to this experience, Martin would never have considered putting aside time for mentoring because he was so busy. Since he had developed a personal relationship with Rosa through the mentoring program team experience, he was much more open to it and made the time.

Patti, who had never been involved in a mentoring team before, although she had mentored others previously, shared her enthusiasm for mentoring with her own manager, her coworkers, and her professional colleagues in the community. She looked for ways to use the group mentoring experience with her direct reports. As a consequence of their shared experience, Martin, Rosa, and Patti started meeting regularly for lunch to discuss how they could leverage their newly discovered synergy and collaboratively bring value to bank clients.

Because of Martin, Rosa, and Patti's enthusiasm, other managers volunteered to participate in mentoring teams; soon the bank had built the capacity to mentor four businesses a year. As a result, the bank gained a reputation as a real player in the community; this translated into an expanded customer base and a 30 percent increase in total deposits. Other companies in the community took notice and wanted to learn more about how the bank was achieving such desirable results. The local United Way wanted to adopt the bank's best practices and build the capacity of its constituent board leaders to take their organizations to the next level. The CEO's schedule grew crowded with requests from outside companies for presentations. He was eager to share his pride in what his people were accomplishing.

Internally, Patti's success with her own team trickled down through the organization, and other managers wanted to emulate her success. Like Rosa, other employees began to see mentoring as a professional growth opportunity. Informal mentoring relationships increased within the bank, as did the desire for more training and skill development to maximize the opportunity. Before long, mentoring was talked about in the boardroom as well as on the bank floor. The bank was well on its way to creating a mentoring culture.

Impact and Indications of Demand

It is easier to describe demand when you see it in actual practice than to define it a priori. The Great Community Bank example speaks to how demand is experienced when it is present and nurtured in an organization. I consider demand as one of the hallmarks of a mentoring culture because of the enormous power and effect it has in the organizational culture. The power of demand can be seen in a range of ways, described in the next sections.

The Multiplier Effect

Mentoring creates a buzz that, over time, spurs further demand. Interest in and expressed desire for mentoring become self-propagating. As the story of Great Community Bank illustrates, one mentor's enthusiasm for the process stimulated her to replicate the experience for her coworkers. Patti asked for assistance from the HR manager. As a direct result of this contact, the manager was moved to start her own managers' mentoring group.

Increased Motivation for Participation

People want to be engaged in mentoring. As they catch the energy, they look for ways to learn more about mentoring opportunities. They choose to participate in formal mentoring and seek mentoring relationships on their own. Mentors want to be mentees. Mentees want to be mentors. Many are engaged in several mentoring relationships simultaneously. Rosa's admiration for Martin, coupled with their mutual respect for one another and the excitement of working together, was enough to make them both receptive to engaging in their own mentoring relationship.

People are voluntarily vocal in their support and actively advocate for mentoring, not because they have to but because they want to. They readily share experiences and talk about mentoring and how it creates value for them and the organization. The bank's senior leadership was enthused about how mentoring seemed to be creating new relationships and strengthening team operations. The bridges the bank built internally as a result of the program began creating a culture of intrapreneurship. Soon everyone wanted to be on board.

Conversation and Dialogue About Mentoring

Informal conversations take place around the water cooler, in the boardroom, at meetings, and in the parking lot, where people talk enthusiastically and optimistically about mentoring. In time, fence sitters and resisters grow positive about mentoring. Conversation is more than chatter; it is serious business. People want to understand more about how to benefit from their mentoring experiences. Conversations between and among mentoring partners are meaningful and have considerable impact. Martin and Rosa, for example, talk about mentoring and their mentoring relationship, not just about what is being learned.

Demand and Credibility Work Together

Demand produces credibility, and vice versa. The right leaders authentically advocate for mentoring and become role models for mentoring. Their example inspires and motivates others to do the same. Both Rosa and Patti led by example, and their influence and success encouraged others to do the same.

Momentum

With demand present and well managed, mentoring stays visible and perpetuates continuity, even through tough times. Demand can turn on itself and have negative results, though, if expectations are unrealistic or unmanaged. The bank was unable to accommodate everyone who wanted to work with future community business leaders. However, the experience was so positive that it generated internal demand that resulted in creation of a self-organizing mentoring system within the institution that facilitated the growth of its coworkers. The energy of those engaged in mentoring drove further demand and produced a momentum of its own.

Application of New Insights and Learning

As people hear about others' experiences, the bar is raised for what is possible for them. Individuals seek more learning, information, and resources about how to increase their mentoring effectiveness and enhance their experiences. Demand stimulates curiosity and opens up perspectives. Witness Martin's new openness and sense of renewal.

Demand can have powerful and enduring impact, even greater than the sum of its parts. As mentoring and its benefits become known, demand increases. Demand takes on a power of its own and creates a desideratum. The net effect of demand widens the net.

What Factors Prevent Demand from Flourishing?

Given all the possible positive outcomes, why does it often seem so difficult to create demand in an organization? What gets in the way? A number of factors individually or together contribute to lack of demand for mentoring in an organization.

Credibility

When the bank rolled out the mentoring program initially, it did so amid considerable skepticism. No one volunteered when the program was first announced; they felt they could not afford the time. They didn't think there would be a direct personal business benefit. The program itself had little visibility, no precedent, and limited credibility. Although the bank's external customer service was excellent, there was no established structure and certainly no history to support its internal customers—the employees.

It takes people and process to create a mentoring culture. With either ignored, demand is adversely affected. It may be that the individuals, leaders, or participants lack credibility. Individuals may say (or think) things that reflect negatively on the people or process ("If this is another one of Bill's bright ideas, I'll pass on it" or "I'd never want to participate in a program if Bill and Mary are in it. I'm so much more experienced than either of them"). Sometimes it is the process that is not credible ("We tried mentoring several years ago and it was a waste of time. I won't get involved in another HR-sponsored project").

It is difficult to persuade others if you don't have credibility yourself. According to Conger (1998), one of the factors in establishing credibility is relationship. Relationships are built on trust. Without trust, credibility is impossible. If a person, team, or department that is promoting mentoring within the organization cannot be trusted, credibility is suspect at best.

Leader Participation

A leader's approach sets the tone. Leaders who don't support mentoring in talk and action stifle demand within their organization. If leaders do not acknowledge the value of mentoring and learning and do not recognize those who participate, they send a clear message about the lack of importance of the initiative.

It took verbal arm twisting from the Great Community Bank manager to get the three initial team members to finally agree to participate. It was only when the mentoring experience became personally meaningful to these individuals (who were leaders in their own right) that each moved from being a passive group mentor to a program advocate. Their energy and advocacy inspired others.

Leaders who demonstrate personal commitment rally others around the commitment. Leaders must encourage and invite participation by inspiring a shared vision of what is possible through mentoring. They talk about how it serves the individual and the organization and aligns with vision and strategy. They share their personal stories. They acknowledge and recognize the importance of mentoring by taking the time to talk with others about their experiences.

Strategy

When properly nurtured, demand grows. It takes people and process to nurture the readiness to hear, receive, learn, and act. Without a coherent strategy, proper timing, and sequence, communication is often scattershot and demand is negatively affected. Having a strategy in place to jump-start demand creates the needed momentum to bridge the gap between what is and what we want to happen.

Buy-in

Part of a company's strategy must be directed to developing awareness and understanding. If, in the rush to roll out or implement mentoring (or any other initiative, for that matter), those in the organization make the mistake of omitting these preliminary steps, management should not be surprised at the number of people who do not understand and get on board. Just because "it's good for our people" doesn't mean they automatically want it. Creating demand requires some preliminary groundwork to foster receptivity. Without it, demand proceeds at a snail's pace, if at all.

Patience

Nothing succeeds like success. It takes familiarity, experience, and time to create and sustain demand. Jump-starting the process works only if there is a continuum of effort. People need time to get to the place where they can buy into mentoring. If an organization or team moves too fast, it leaves people behind and often angry.

Inclusion

Lack of inclusion, perceived or real, can produce jealousy and resentment. These feelings are highly contagious; they negatively influence demand and undermine mentoring goals. On the other hand, lack of inclusion can also serve as a motivator, as something to aspire to or as a catalyst for generating other alternative mentoring routes and possibilities.

There is a rhythm to the demand cycle. Its inherent ebb and flow requires monitoring as well as management consciously built into the mentoring implementation strategy. Use Exercise 9.1, Addressing Potential Obstacles, to help you determine which factors are missing or negatively affecting demand in your organization and how you might best overcome these impediments.

How Do Mentoring Hallmarks Contribute to Demand?

Now that we've addressed the importance, impact, and indications of creating demand in a mentoring culture and explored some of the factors that contribute to lack of demand, it is time to consider how infrastructure and the eight hallmarks all work together to create demand for mentoring within an organization.

Each infrastructure component—whether leadership, time, financial resources, technology, human, or knowledge resources—can help support demand. Leaders play a central role in promoting demand within their organization and must regularly step forward to demonstrate their commitment. Financial resources can increase visibility, which in turn creates demand. Technology, when it is well used, is an excellent marketing and promotion device. HR specialists, managers, and supervisors can facilitate and often jump-start demand in conversation with others.

Alignment

Unless daily actions and activity support mentoring, it cannot get off the ground. Mentoring needs to be a clear win-win for business; it must align with business results, or people won't trust it—and won't demand it. A mentoring initiative needs to be aligned with other critical processes that are going on in the organization. Without this alignment, mentoring may meet with disinterest or indifference.

Accountability

Because mentoring champions and advocates play a major role in creating demand, it is critical to clearly define their roles and responsibilities and get their buy-in. Demonstrable progress and results generate enthusiasm and affect demand. Continuous integration of process improvements adds value that influences demand.

Communication

It is tempting to think of communication as the panacea for creating demand. Actually, communication is necessary but not sufficient to stimulate demand. Too much of the wrong kind of communication, and people

Addressing Potential Obstacles

Instructions: If any of the items in the first column are missing, demand will eventually be affected. Are any of these items lacking in your organization? If so, what gets in the way? Develop three strategies for overcoming each potential obstacle. Determine which strategy has the greatest likelihood of success, and develop a plan for implementation.

What Is Missing?	What Gets in the Way?	Three Strategies for Overcoming Obstacles
Credibility		1. 2. 3.
Leader Participation		1. 2. 3.
Strategy		1. 2. 3.
Buy-In		1. 2. 3.
Patience		1. 2. 3.
Inclusion		1. 2. 3.
Other		1. 2. 3.

won't listen. A strategic communication plan that segments an internal market goes a long way in promoting mentoring awareness, understanding, acceptance, and commitment.

Value and Visibility

Value and visibility influence demand. Role modeling is a powerful driver. Reward, recognition, and celebration are opportunities to reinforce the organization's commitment to mentoring and create demand. Sharing positive mentoring accomplishments forces people to pay attention, and when they do they begin to see how mentoring might benefit them.

Multiple Mentoring Opportunities

Demand may be created by felt need (internal), normative need (an externally defined gap), or comparative need (relative to others in the same category). Multiple venues allow people with differing needs, whether internally felt or externally defined, to have their needs met in a variety of ways. At the bank, employees were excited by what they saw happening with the mentoring program. Since there weren't enough venues, they demanded more. This demand signaled a culture shift that resulted in a much more aligned and generative organizational culture.

Education and Training

Education and training foster a level of readiness and receptivity that should motivate people to take the next step for themselves. Many organizations today offer progressive levels of education and training, starting with dissemination of information (awareness) and going on to training (understanding), thus increasing demand for mentoring.

Safety Nets

Safety nets help people feel successful and sustain their interest in mentoring. They avert mentoring casualties that inevitably have an impact on what people feel, say, and do in regard to mentoring. In practice, safety nets help people maintain control and yet enable them to get their needs met. If people feel successful, their success positively affects demand.

Each hallmark is important to demand. In fact, the absence of any hallmark can potentially erode demand, whether directly or indirectly.

Demand: Reflection on Practice

Demand is a hallmark of a successful mentoring culture for very good reasons. As we've seen:

- Demand has a multiplier effect. Indications of this are a buzz about mentoring, increased interest in mentoring, and self-perpetuating participation.

- Demand motivates participation. This is shown by people seeking to strengthen and develop themselves through mentoring, increased interest in learning about mentoring opportunities, mentors becoming mentees and mentees becoming mentors, and people engaging in multiple mentoring relationships. Demand invites volunteers who actively support and advocate mentoring and informally share mentoring experiences, learning, and outcomes.

- Demand spurs conversation and dialogue about mentoring. Both formal and informal discussion about mentoring occur regularly and ultimately engage even those who have been skeptical about mentoring.

- Demand and credibility work together. Leaders authentically advocate for mentoring and become mentoring role models.

- Demand produces momentum. As a result, mentoring continues, despite other priorities and contingencies.

- Demand inspires application of new insights and learning. When mentoring is viewed as a stretch opportunity, individuals request an opportunity to increase their mentoring effectiveness and enhance their mentoring experiences.

Great Community Bank was able to create demand within its organization because it understood the importance of demand and of the other hallmarks of a mentoring organization. As a result, it generated a groundswell of interest, participation, and support. It had, as its base, an infrastructure that supported mentoring and thus was able to nurture demand.

There is a positive and direct relationship between demand and the ultimate success of mentoring. Demand is in the end about commitment to success. We have seen in this chapter that creating mentoring demand constantly requires a delicate balancing of push and pull; it is important to leverage both appropriately, at the right time and in the right place. If demand lessens in a mentoring culture, value must be reinforced.

We turn next to how the demand is met and perpetuated—mentoring in actual practice and the variety of quite specific approaches, types, and options for organizational mentoring.

Chapter 10

Multiple Mentoring Opportunities

Good fortune is what happens when opportunity meets
with planning.

—THOMAS ALVA EDISON

SUBSTITUTE "A positive result" for "Good fortune" in Edison's quotation
and you have a lesson for organizational planning. The potent combination
of opportunity and planning produces remarkable results. In some situations, planning creates the opportunity; in others, it is opportunity that
prompts planning. There must be movement between both to create and
sustain a mentoring culture. This chapter focuses on planning opportunity
and the opportunity to plan; it identifies categories and types of mentoring
opportunities that foster a quality learning experience.

Opportunity, as presented in this chapter, covers multiple approaches,
types, and options for maximizing learning within a mentoring relationship.
The focus is on the opportunity the mentoring relationship presents and the
learning opportunities that flow from it—thus less on organizational mentoring, skill competence, and mentoring knowledge. Being aware of multiple opportunities enriches planning and supports the mentoring process by
helping to identify a range of possibilities and options for learning.

Planning the Opportunity

Although some mentoring activity goes on in nearly every organization
(Kaye and Jacobson, 1996), most need to work at creating a culture that concurrently advances and supports multiple types of mentoring opportunities. A mentoring culture strengthens and supports mentoring in whatever
form it appears, whether informal, formal, or a blend of the two.

Informal Approaches

Informal mentoring relationships are usually described as unstructured,
casual, and natural. Part of their special character is that there is no rule of
thumb; each relationship is idiosyncratic. They are serendipitous, spontaneous,

self-selected, and situational relationships. Typically, informal mentoring develops when an individual offers to give or ask for advice or guidance from another. The relationship is self-directed and proceeds at its own pace and on its own timetable. It is usually based on need and proximity.

Informal mentoring is so deeply ingrained in some organizations that it receives little attention. Informal mentoring is still regarded by many as less significant and less solid than its fraternal twin, formal mentoring, and rarely embraced on an organizational level with the same enthusiasm, seriousness, and support. Its anonymity and hidden character perpetuate erroneous assumptions that lead to inadvertent organizational disregard. One common assumption is that people will get the mentoring they need when they need it and therefore will know how and where to find a mentor. The irony is that those who need mentoring the most rarely find mentors on their own. New employees in particular often don't know how to find the right mentor at the right level and don't want to be viewed as too aggressive or pushy. Young employees struggle with finding the perfect mentor, and as a result they end up without one. Another assumption is that because informal mentoring relationships are individualized, little external support is necessary. In practice, quite the opposite is true. Because informal mentoring relationships tend to be more intimate and idiosyncratic than formal ones, mentoring partners take things even more personally, experiencing unanticipated personal disappointment and hurt feelings.

A mentoring culture is inclusive and intentional in its reach. It offers support and attention to informal as well as formal practices and seeks to enrich all the mentoring that goes on within the organization. Organizations can use any of a range of options for enhancing informal mentoring. They can, for instance:

- Offer guidance, strategies, and coaching for finding a mentoring partner, including specifics on what to look for; steps for selecting a mentor, such as how to scope out possibilities, narrow down choices, and make the approach; and how to get started on the right foot.

- Provide optional mentoring education and training.

- Encourage participation in skill-building sessions.

- Supply specific information about how informal mentoring works and what to expect.

- Furnish an informal mentoring tool kit that includes step-by-step guidelines, tips, and related articles.

- Present lunch-and-learn sessions for individuals interested specifically in informal mentoring.

- Hold networking forums to encourage individuals to find informal mentoring partners.

- Offer mentoring support sessions for mentors and mentees engaged in informal mentoring relationships.

- Develop tip sheets for recognizing signals that it's time for closure or that the relationship is reaching the end of usefulness.

- Offer guidelines on how to close out the mentoring relationship.

- Build a community bulletin board or Website where individuals who are seeking or offering to be mentors post their names and information about what they are looking for or offering to provide.

Organizations that consciously encourage and support informal mentoring enhance its quality and maximize the learning that goes on within such relationships.

Formal Approaches

Formal mentoring partnerships, on the other hand, are usually attached to a specific program, process, or initiative and require conformity to at least some minimal expectation. They are organized around processes, procedures, policies, and functional structures. The amount of structure in a formal mentoring program varies widely. For example, the partner selection process might include self-selection with guidelines, participant prioritization of preselected candidates, or assigned pairing. Regardless of the process adopted, specific criteria frame the selection of mentoring partners.

Formal mentoring includes formal accountability mechanisms. Roles and responsibilities are defined, mentoring partnership agreements are negotiated, milestones are identified, training is required, and evaluation procedures are in place. Usually an individual or team administers, coordinates, and manages the program to ensure ongoing support and promote alignment and accountability.

Program parameters and procedures generate consistency of practice and manage expectations in a formal mentoring process. Here are some options to consider in supporting formal mentoring:

- Clearly communicate the intent, scope, target audience, and significance of the program.

- Build in adequate structures to support development, implementation, and evaluation of the program.

- Plan for leadership development and succession of the key players.

- Integrate and communicate process improvements in a timely fashion.

- Allow flexibility.

- Safeguard confidentiality.
- Offer multiple mentoring education and training opportunities and venues.
- Monitor the process and evaluate results.
- Anticipate contingencies by developing a Plan B.
- Promote ownership throughout the organization.

Informal and formal mentoring are frequently viewed as opposite ends of a continuum. This distinction may have some validity, but it effectively devalues informal mentoring. Exhibit 10.1 itemizes key features of informal and formal mentoring. Note that these are not discrete categories; mentoring relationships are as individual as each of the mentoring partners.

EXHIBIT 10.1

Comparison of Key Features of Informal and Formal Mentoring Approaches

Key Features	Informal	Formal
Common Descriptors	Casual, serendipitous, spontaneous, natural, idiosyncratic	Organized, structured, facilitated, strategic, planned
Finding a mentoring partner	No eligibility requirements Self-initiated Voluntary Chemistry and accessibility valued Individual asks for or offers advice or guidance	Eligibility requirements established Facilitated selection process Voluntary Learning fit and compatibility Person who makes first contact is stipulated
Accountability	Lack of expectation No formal agreement Commitment not required Accountability harder to maintain Self-managed	Roles and responsibilities predefined Structured or negotiated mentoring agreements Commitment required Mechanism for accountability built in Program-managed
Relationship	Personal Unstructured Evolves naturally over time Lack of formal commitment Communication is sporadic	Partnership Structured Milestones defined for each phase of relationship Commitment to each other Communication is ongoing

EXHIBIT 10.1 (continued)

Key Features	Informal	Formal
Learning goals	Broad goals Goals tend to change or evolve over time Just-in-time goals	Broad, generalized goals become more specific and focused Goals are evaluated regularly Development goals
Training	No training required	May be training sessions for mentors or mentees individually as groups or combined sessions
Duration	No expectation as to relationship time frame Relationships organized around immediacy of need Relationships can go on indefinitely or be purely situational	Relationship finite; has a beginning and an ending point Relationship organized around time frame or completion of learning goals Relationships often renegotiated
Evaluation	No formal mechanism Goal achievement ad hoc No required reporting to a third party	Formal mechanism Relationship progress toward goal achievement is measured regularly Required reporting on a program-matic basis

Today's work environment requires diverse and multiple learning opportunities. Organizations need to support mentoring more broadly and become more inclusive in thinking about and planning multiple mentoring opportunities. They need to move beyond an either-or approach. In fact, a mentoring culture embraces a both-and approach. This blended approach promotes quality mentoring interaction within the organization by supporting both informal and formal mentoring. It is more intentional and inclusive in its support of informal mentoring. It seeks to create a mentoring community where best practices are regularly shared, and information and resources are available to anyone who seeks to learn more about mentoring or enhance a mentoring relationship. It encourages individual involvement in informal and formal mentoring. Exercise 10.1, Strategies and Action Plan for Supporting Informal and Formal Mentoring, is designed to assist you in identifying some ways to support both types.

Types of Mentoring Relationships

Some types of mentoring relationships lend themselves naturally to informal as well as formal approaches. Others do not. A mentoring culture seeks a balance of multiple types of relationships—a blended approach. The purpose

Strategies and Action Plan for Supporting Informal and Formal Mentoring

Instructions: The left-hand column includes ten strategies you might want to consider. At first glance, some of the strategies listed may not appear to fit your organizational circumstances. If so, identify an alternative strategy that might accomplish the same purposes in a way that is more appropriate for your organizational setting and context. Use the right column to record action steps to be taken.

Strategy	Action Plan (How Are We Going to Make This Happen?)
1. Encourage participation in both informal and formal mentoring experiences.	
2. Continuously demonstrate specific ways in which mentoring enriches the culture.	
3. Make technology available to support online and videoconferencing mentoring sessions.	
4. Identify venues to showcase best practices in informal and formal relationships.	
5. Hold leadership accountable for formal and informal mentoring relationships.	
6. Find opportunities to include informal mentors and mentees in existing mentoring education and training sessions.	
7. Run open sessions for anyone interested in building informal relationships.	
8. Communicate criteria for mentoring success.	
9. Make mentoring coaching and support available to informal and formal mentees and mentors.	
10. Ensure budget includes a line item to support informal mentoring.	

of this section is not to present all the possibilities in the pantheon but to lay out examples of common mentoring practices so that the possibilities for innovative practice are apparent. Many cultures or fields of practice "invent" their own specific type suiting their needs and setting. In addition, new types of mentoring continue to emerge. In general, the types fall into four categories: one-to-one mentoring relationships, group mentoring relationships, distance mentoring, and cross-cultural mentoring. These categories are not mutually exclusive; there is potential for overlap among them, and in fact some types include elements of all four. For example, a cross-cultural, one-to-one mentoring relationship or a group mentoring partnership might, at any time, become a distance mentoring relationship because of changing responsibilities, personal circumstances, or convenience.

One-to-One Mentoring

The traditional view of mentoring, and the eventual coining of the word mentoring itself, had its roots in the one-to-one, face-to-face relationship between Telemachus (Odysseus' son) and Mentor in Homer's *The Odyssey*. The traditional view has evolved in practice over time, but the basic configuration of the relationship remains two learning partners engaged in a mentoring relationship with each other. There are many variations on the theme, though. The three we discuss here are reverse mentoring, peer mentoring, and supervisory mentoring.

Reverse Mentoring

Jack Welch, former CEO of General Electric, is credited with originating the concept of reverse mentoring in 1999, when he directed a group to gain technical expertise from within the rank and file of the company. The concept has evolved, and today reverse mentoring is sometimes referred to as mutual or reciprocal mentoring. It has become an increasingly popular way of managing knowledge within the organization. Use of these terms captures the essence of the relationship and sets up the fact that the parties involved expect there is something to be learned and taught by each party, as indeed is the case.

Mentoring partners share know-how and perspective, one in exchange for the other. The person with (technical) expertise mentors a less (technically) experienced, organizationally senior, individual. As that learning takes place, the senior individual is learning about how the other mentoring partner (often of another generation) thinks (what his or her concerns and issues are). Senior leaders and managers (who are removed from the trenches) gain technical expertise and acquire a "younger perspective" or different point of view. What they learn helps bridge hierarchical structure and avoid potential conflict in the future. The technical experts have opportunities to interact and develop relationships with senior leaders or managers they may never otherwise get to know, and gain valuable insights about the organization.

Mark and Steve had so many differences that it was a stretch to see how they might engage in a productive mentoring relationship. Steve was convinced that the relationship would never work because of the many organizational layers between them. The mentoring coordinator persuaded him it would not be a waste of his time. In this case, reverse mentoring offered the potential for more positive mutual learning than a traditional mentoring relationship did. Reverse mentoring enabled Mark to get to see the executive floor and, for the first time, gain respect for the company's management. It turned out to be a powerful motivator because it gave him a "vision of the possible," and he appreciated that someone "upstairs" knew who he was. Steve too gained respect for Mark's technical knowledge. He was amazed at how, under Mark's tutelage, he was soon able to grasp and filter information and begin seeing how that information could eventually lead to increased market share for his company's products. He was in awe of the speed and facility with which Mark could retrieve information. Steve learned as much from Mark's teaching as he did from observing him in action. The shared experience enabled them to engage in some meaningful conversation that neither would have had without reverse mentoring. The experience opened Steve's eyes to new ways in which to create a workplace that could better attract and retain a new generation of employees and give him another marketing point of view.

Reverse mentoring promises to encompass far more than just the technological expertise that younger cohorts currently bring to the workforce. We are now beginning to understand that reverse mentoring is often uniquely suited to connecting knowledge and people who may be separated by hierarchical barriers. It offers unique learning opportunities that ultimately build a more connected workplace.

Peer Mentoring

One-to-one peer mentoring occurs when two peers engage in a mentoring relationship. They may be at the same level within a structural hierarchy, or they may hold the same title across organizations. They may be in roughly the same age cohort. It is the equality or commonality of status, experience, expertise, or interest that defines their "peerness." Since it is generally less threatening to learn from one's peers (despite the competition that may exist), peer mentoring is more likely to establish an immediate level of comfort and openness to learning than does being mentored by someone who is in a more senior position within the organization. The configuration of peer relationships varies. In some models, each person plays two roles, mentor and mentee. In others, one peer is the mentor and the other is the mentee.

Peer mentoring relationships are more appropriate to some learning goals than others. For instance, faculty members in the same academic department together might engage in a peer mentoring relationship to learn more about each other's research. If the learning goal is to help an employee become more politically savvy about the organization, and neither peer has had much longevity or experience in the organization, the use of peer mentoring seems inappropriate. A peer might not be able to raise the bar high enough for the mentoring partner since she hasn't had enough experience or learning. It might be appropriate under the circumstances to have a more senior person who has been around the organization for a long time mentor this individual. If the learning goal is to familiarize a new employee with the organization, peer mentoring might be appropriate. Peer mentoring is an ideal way for peers to share information and experiences learned as a result of being in other organizational settings.

Supervisory Mentoring

Supervisors play a significant role in enabling and supporting mentoring partnerships. They encourage employee participation, ensure time for mentoring, suggest learning goals that relate to employee development targets, offer opportunities to integrate new learning, and provide feedback regularly. In addition to their primary support role, supervisors may mentor (formally or informally) those whom they supervise. In contrast to a formal mentoring relationship, the learning that occurs as a result of supervisory mentoring is often informal and additive. It can include situational mentoring moments, mentoring transactions, and learning experiences that take place serendipitously and spontaneously.

Although formal supervisory mentoring can be effective, it is potentially problematic and precarious on a number of levels. The opportunity for role confusion can negatively affect the supervisor-employee relationship. Mentoring relationships depend on the trust and candor of the mentoring partners, yet supervisory mentoring potentially sets up barriers to authentic communication. It is difficult for mentees to be candid and open with someone who also evaluates their performance, assigns work, and determines their bonus. Power and politics create an uneven playing field that makes mentees reluctant to take risks, fearing that information they reveal could later be used against them.

Despite these potential problems, the reality is that many organizations or departments must rely on supervisors (or managers) to engage in formal mentoring relationships with their direct reports. In this case, great care must be taken. It's important to understand that both conscious and unconscious factors can play a role in the success of mentoring relationships. Those who are not part of the supervisor's mentoring relationship(s) may perceive that the supervisor is playing favorites. Similarly, if a supervisor mentors more than one direct report, mentees may become jealous of the time and attention another mentee gets with the supervisor. These and other potential problems must be addressed if an organization intends to create a mentoring culture. The organization must be proactive and cognizant of the pitfalls of supervisory mentoring and plan accordingly. This requires time, attention, and tending.

Since chain-of-command issues can muddy the waters, it's essential to establish a comfortable and trusting relationship. This can be accomplished by clearly defining the supervisor's mentoring role. In addition, supervisors need to be adept at moving in and out of the mentoring role by offering cues for the mentee ("I am going to step out of my role as your supervisor to say something to you that I might not otherwise say" or "Because I am your supervisor as well as your mentor, I think further discussion of this topic is inappropriate"). It is helpful to set aside a regular block of time specifically dedicated to mentoring and not commingle supervision and mentoring time. A supervisor's ability to mentor effectively depends on managing the duality and boundaries of the mentor-supervisor role.

Exhibit 10.2 summarizes the one-to-one types of mentoring presented in this section. In addition, it offers strategies to help support successful implementation of these models.

Group Mentoring

Many organizations find group mentoring to be a good alternative to one-to-one mentoring because they simply don't have enough (or enough qualified) mentors. The diverse perspectives that emerge from group mentoring interactions is a powerful motivator for employee development. Group mentoring encourages a more connected workplace and is a welcome option for those who learn better in group settings.

In this section, we explore several forms of group mentoring, some of which expand on the one-to-one mentoring models already described. In part because there is no universally accepted practice paradigm for these mentoring terms, each term—facilitated group mentoring, peer mentoring group, team mentoring, and mentoring circle—is defined as it is being used here.

EXHIBIT 10.2

One-to-One Mentoring Types

Mentoring Relationship Model	Description	Strategies for Supporting Success
Reverse mentoring	Employee with specific technological knowledge shares that know-how with a senior executive to facilitate the speed with which the individual gains technological knowledge or skill. Relationship bridges the hierarchical structure.	• Put safety net in place to protect senior executive from looking and feeling stupid. • Prepare "younger" people so they have confidence and feel ready to engage in this type of relationship.
Peer mentoring	Peers at the same level of experience, expertise, organizational status, age cohort, etc., form a mentoring relationship; this is appropriate for achievement of some goals and not for others.	• If formal, be explicit about the outcomes. • Be alert to the fact that this type of mentoring works better when peers have differing kinds and levels of experience or expertise. For example, someone who is brand new to the organization should not be mentoring someone about the organizational culture.
Supervisory mentoring	Formal or informal mentoring job and performance-related relationships between a supervisor and a direct report.	• Provide mentoring training for supervisors to prevent role confusion.

Facilitated Group Mentoring

Facilitated group mentoring allows a number of people to benefit from the experience and expertise of a mentor at the same time. It is a structured facilitation that creates a learning group (Kaye and Jacobson, 1995).

The richness of the experience multiplies as each group participant brings personal experiences into the conversation. The facilitator's role is critical. Her role is to make sure that everyone in the group can participate, ask questions to keep the dialogue thought-provoking and meaningful, provide feedback and share personal experience, and serve as a sounding board and reality tester.

Consider, for example, the process that a group of physicians use. Once a month seven of them meet in a private dining room at the back of the hospital cafeteria to talk about issues pertinent to their small subspecialty area of practice. Attendance is pretty consistent because there is no other forum where they can dialogue about these issues. For each session, they choose an outside facilitator (usually a medical academician) depending on the topic they are exploring. Group members enhance their individual and collective practice of medicine by learning from the experiences of their colleagues and the facilitator.

Peer Mentoring Group

Similar in principle to the peer mentoring process described in the earlier section on one-to-one mentoring, a peer mentoring group is composed of peers with similar learning interests or needs. The group is self-directed and self-managed. It takes responsibility for crafting its own learning agenda and managing the learning process so that each member's learning needs are met and group members derive maximum benefit from members' knowledge, expertise, and experience.

One type of peer mentoring that many organizational executives prefer is executive mentoring. It gives them a sounding board of people at their own level, gender, or background, to test ideas; it is a safe haven for preparing for significant personal and organizational transitions. Another peer mentoring group, the mentoring circle, is a circle of opportunity for each individual group member. In one session, it allows each person to tap into the collective wisdom of the group and cull needed expertise and experience to solve problems, improve practice, or advance personal effectiveness. A mentoring circle should be small enough (perhaps four to eight people) so that each person is able to get feedback on a problem, challenge, or situation.

Team Mentoring

Team mentoring offers a methodology for facilitating the learning of an intact team. Together the individuals making up the team actively engage in reaching consensual team learning goals and work simultaneously with several mentors who guide them through a deliberate and deliberative process to facilitate their learning. The mentoring process allows them to be supported and learn from each other's experience and knowledge.

Mentoring Board of Directors

An emerging concept of great value, the board of directors, combines elements of one-to-one mentoring and group mentoring. Advisory boards are extremely popular, particularly among savvy entrepreneurs. The board of directors concept, as applied to mentoring, operates as an advisory board. Two models in particular have demonstrated excellent results.

In the personal board of directors model, the individual learner seeks out and recruits a group of qualified individuals to mentor her as she seeks to achieve specific learning goals. The mentors become her personal board of directors. The learner manages the learning process, calls the meetings, and together with the mentors monitors the learning process and measures results. This model is not for the fainthearted. It requires a lot of self-management, but the rewards reaped as a result far outweigh the time it takes to get started. The selection process is vital to accelerating and deepening the learning.

The junior board of directors model surfaced early in the new millennium as a tool to help senior executives learn directly from junior executives who possessed the technological knowledge they needed in order to inform their decision making. The model has since been used in a number of arenas; it works something like this. Senior executives tap into the knowledge they need by identifying a group of (junior) mentors to help them understand a situation, problem, or area of operation and to gather feedback or test out ideas prior to making a decision. SMART learning goals drive the process and the time frame of a junior board of directors. For example, as Betsy reviews the latest key demographic figures printed out, she realizes that for the first time the company has more thirty-year-olds than forty-to-sixty-year-olds on staff. She pulls together a junior board of directors composed of ten thirty-to-thirty-five-year-olds to help her better understand the needs of this cohort and how the company can address their needs and issues.

Exhibit 10.3 summarizes the models of group mentoring and the mentoring board of directors and offers strategies for organizational success.

Distance Mentoring

For centuries, letter writing was the sole means of building and maintaining mentoring relationships at a distance. The emergence of the telephone in the late nineteenth century changed this. Certainly by the mid-twentieth century people were comfortable enough with the phone (and conversations that were not face-to-face) that it became an effective vehicle for distance mentoring. Today, some organizations rely on electronic or telephonic means for distance mentoring. Others use multiple technologies—mobile, digital, and virtual—to bridge the gap of physical distance.

A mentoring culture promotes and supports distance mentoring by harnessing the power of technology and individuals to facilitate interactive and meaningful learning. Implementation of distance mentoring can be as challenging for an organization as for the individuals within it. If these challenges can be converted into opportunity, distance learning creates a more connected and aligned workplace, establishes relationships that might

EXHIBIT 10.3

Group Mentoring Types and the Mentoring Board of Directors

Mentoring Relationship Model	Description	Strategies for Supporting Success
Group Mentoring		
Facilitated group mentoring	• Individuals learn together and from the experience and expertise of a mentor who facilitates the group's learning experience. • Group drives the learning agenda and asks for what they need when they need it.	• Limit group to eight people. • Reach consensus on group member responsibilities. • Be sure members agree to accept responsibility for the group and that consequences for not following through are clarified.
Peer mentoring	• A small group of individuals who have similar job functions, experiences, interests, or needs form a self-directed group to learn from each other. • Group is self-managed and takes responsibility for crafting its own learning agenda and managing the learning process to meet members' learning needs. • Executive mentoring and mentoring circles are examples.	• Make training and information available to support the group so it can manage itself more effectively. • Provide goal-setting and success-measurement tools.
Team mentoring	• Several mentors team up to offer feedback and guidance to a group. • Mentors promote collaborative learning, enabling members to benefit from each other's experience, knowledge, and support.	• Provide mentor training and support tools. • Make coaching available.
Mentoring Board of Directors		
Personal board of directors	• An individual forms mentoring relationships with multiple individuals who work individually and collectively to help him or her achieve learning goals.	• Furnish guidelines for maximizing your personal board of directors.
Junior board of directors	• This is a methodology for gathering information and knowledge from individual expertise within the organization. • Offers a way to give junior executives or knowledge workers visibility • Promotes informed decision making	• Especially helpful in evaluating technological opportunities • Use as a way of staying on top of trends • Set meeting agenda and timetable collaboratively

never happen, manages and retains organizational knowledge, saves on travel costs, broadens perspectives, and generates more global thinking, as a couple of examples illustrate.

As a condition of admission into her graduate program in organizational psychology, Anne was required to find a field mentor outside the institution to help her satisfactorily complete the requirements for her master's degree. She surfed the Web, talked with faculty, read as much as she could, and narrowed her selection to three candidates, with whom she exchanged e-mails and telephone calls. These telephone "interviews" allowed her to hear and "see" the dynamic of each individual's personality, helping her make up her mind as to which one would best match with her learning style and needs.

Anne and her mentoring partner, Gordon, set up weekly telephone sessions. She gave him periodic updates on her progress prior to each telephone session and sent assignments and papers as e-mail attachments. As she formulated her thoughts and struggled with unfamiliar concepts, she would e-mail him and ask for "chat room" time. He would support her by asking questions and just being there to listen electronically as she came to understanding. Gordon was impressed with her background and would mark up her draft papers and send resources (things he had read, sources he knew of, including links to Websites) via fax from time to time. He would also refer her (through e-mail) to colleagues and set up chat rooms or electronic classrooms (e-learning) to facilitate group mentoring experiences. He was an expert in the field of organizational psychology, working as an organizational consultant; the author of several textbooks widely used in the field; and holder of a lifelong interest in executive coaching (her thesis topic). He loved technology, was well connected, and thought that some of his clients could also benefit from interaction with her. Anne was fortunate to find such a willing and capable mentoring partner.

MentorNet is an e-mentoring nonprofit network for women in engineering and science, sponsored through corporate and academic partnerships, grants, and donations. Through its Website (www.MentorNet.net), it provides a much needed networking vehicle for recruitment and retention of women in science and engineering. In its first six years, more than eleven thousand engineering and science students were matched in structured, one-on-one, e-mail-based mentoring relationships with male and female scientific and engineering professionals. Cognizant of the challenges inherent in e-mentoring, MentorNet supports its one-on-one programs with a system of ongoing coaching via e-mail that furnishes a set of cues and prompts to remind mentors and students to keep in touch regularly and suggests topics for electronic conversation. In addition to its menu of networking and mentoring options, MentorNet offers online discussion groups and a resume database for students seeking employment as well as companies seeking to hire. MentorNet's expertise and experience in distance mentoring demonstrates the power and promise of technology in establishing a state-of-the-art distance mentoring culture.

On a smaller scale, one mentoring matching committee identified twelve pairs to be part of its new initiative, entitled LearnAndEarn. The initiative was focused on breaking down the silos (vertical organizations) within the company. The pilot group was as diverse as it was dispersed. Although people worked in numerous locations, they all regularly attended the same sales meetings several times a year.

Several online orientation sessions were held prior to initial mentoring partnership meetings, during which participants were oriented to their roles and responsibilities. In addition, each participant completed three e-learning skill modules before the sales meeting. Advance preparation and an initial training session at the sales meeting, along with adept use of technology, jump-started the mentoring process and accelerated the learning curve. Before the mentoring relationships formally began, the group was already bonded and felt connected to each other and to the LearnAndEarn initiative. Right from the beginning, the use of technology contributed to the quality and speed of new learning. It helped broaden understanding. The access to and transmittal of additional resources (links, data, courses) throughout the mentoring year promoted unanticipated individual and organizational learning that supplemented the mentoring partner meetings. LearnAndEarn was a safe, just-in-time resource, promoting development of a learning community that broke down preexisting silos and creating a shared vocabulary of mentoring practice.

Meeting the Challenges of Distance Mentoring

As we've seen, distance mentoring can accommodate most types of mentoring relationships, even among people who have never directly met. Distance mentoring also allows an established face-to-face mentoring partnership to continue even after one party relocates. Whatever the circumstance, distance mentoring relationships require clear ground rules, more regular communication than face-to-face mentoring might demand, and a commitment to accountability. Without these assurances, distance mentoring runs the risk of becoming mere information exchange.

Ground rules clarify and establish mutual expectations and consequently lay the foundation on which the relationship grows and develops. Ground rules set parameters around behavior; for example, if one partner never pays attention to instant messages (IMs) on the computer screen and the other gives them priority, the former may feel intruded on while the latter feels ignored. The distinction between regular and frequent communication should also be made clear at the outset. As another ground rule, the level of confidentiality in what should be discussed in virtual space must be agreed on.

Any communication can create potential misunderstanding. Regular communication helps bolster the feeling of connection that is frequently lost through electronic communication. In distance mentoring, communication is often accomplished in sound bites—a quick e-mail, a fax, or a brief conversation—as well as longer conversation. Knowing which form of communication to use, and when, is advantageous—as is regularly evaluating communication effectiveness. Here are three sequential online conversations illustrating just how difficult this can be.

Scenario One

Mentor: Hi there. Haven't heard from you in a long time. You OK?

Mentee: Lot of pressure here. Deadlines. Too much work. Not enough of me to go around.

Mentor: Sounds like you could use an ear. Want to talk?

Mentee: Don't have any time right now. Catch you later.

The fact that the mentor did not follow up and let the mentee close the conversation without any progress is telling. Little is likely to happen unless the mentor ends the conversation with some assurance of accountability.

Scenario Two

Mentor: Hi there. How are you doing?

Mentee: Pretty much the same. All work. No play.

Mentor: Maybe I could help.

Mentee: Hmmmm. I don't see how.

Mentor: Frankly, I'm not sure either, but I'd be happy to make some time for a conversation later this afternoon. What time works for you?

Notice how the mentor's last question opens the door for the mentee and presents an opportunity to set aside time to focus on the task at hand.

Scenario Three

Mentee: Thanks for your time yesterday. You really gave me some perspective.

Mentor: You're welcome. Keep me posted, OK?

Mentee: Cool. Say, by the way, do you have time to review a draft of my memo?

Mentor: When do you need the feedback?

Mentee: Actually, yesterday! Need to know if I'm off base or not.

Mentor: I'll look at it tonight and fax back a marked-up version. That
             work?

Here we see clearly that the mentor is aware that the mentee is overwhelmed; the mentor needs to be responsive to that reality. It took courage and encouragement on her part to get the relationship moving. Online e-mail and IM conversations magnify the challenges of true communication and require persistence, sensitivity, and being able to hear beyond the words appearing on the screen.

As technology changes, the range of available options for distance mentoring constantly expands. Exercise 10.2, Options for Distance Mentoring, itemizes the venues for promoting communication and learning in a distance mentoring relationship that were most in use as this book went to press. Use this exercise to determine which options might work best for your organization. For example, if it has good video conferencing capability, this might make a viable option if time and training are available for the mentoring partners.

Accountability

Distance mentoring relationships have a much better chance of succeeding if assurances of accountability are put in place right at the start. It is for this reason that the relationship tends to take more time, not less, than other mentoring relationships at the beginning. Agreements about shared intention, responsibility, ownership, and commitment as well as about the learning process need to be clearly established. It helps to set SMART goals, clarify mutual expectations, and define mutual responsibilities. To stay on track and achieve positive results, be sure to monitor progress and measure results. Competence in structuring the agenda and project management are most helpful.

Mentoring at a distance fosters multiple opportunities and challenges for even the savviest mentors and mentees. A mentoring culture supports distance mentoring and the productive learning that can result by:

- Encouraging mentoring partners to spend enough time to establish communication ground rules and a regular contact schedule

- Creating value for the importance of holding online conversation rather than information exchange

- Stressing the importance of working on both learning and the relationship

- Advocating use of multiple venues for communication, electronic and nonelectronic

EXERCISE 10.2

Options for Distance Mentoring

Instructions: Some options for distance mentoring are listed in the leftmost column. Space remains for you to add other items. Review the list. If the option is one that you want to promote or support, determine what needs to be put in place to support mentoring partners, and what action is required on the part of the organization to support use of this venue.

Options	Learner Needs	Organization Strategy
E-mentoring (also called cybermentoring or telementoring)		
E-mail		
Chat room		
Instant messaging		
Electronic face-to-face meetings		
Videoconferencing		
PC and Web camera		
E-learning		
Electronic classroom		
Other		
Discussion boards		
Listservs		
Threaded (asynchronous) conversation		
Electronic bulletin boards		
Telephone bridge lines		
Videoconference		
Mail		
Telephone		

- Providing templates for monitoring progress and measuring results

- Allotting adequate time for distance mentoring

- Training to specifically support distance mentoring

- Ensuring a strong infrastructure is in place

- Consciously connecting adult learning theory to the practice of distance learning (for information about related resources, see Appendix Two, Digging Deeper)

- Establishing a supportive learning environment

- Expanding distance learning opportunities as new technology emerges

- Making sure technology is available, accessible, and user-friendly, and that people know how to use it

The accountability and communication challenges inherent in distance mentoring underscore the importance of providing support. Similarly, support is required for cross-cultural mentoring.

Cross-Cultural Mentoring

The need for cross-cultural mentoring is accelerating with the emergence of an expanding global and diverse workforce. Cross-cultural mentoring, whether one-to-one, group, or distance, presents a significant opportunity to leverage diversity and build a more inclusive, globally functional, and productive organization.

At its broadest, most inclusive sense, cross-cultural mentoring encompasses individual and cultural diversity. Some organizations use a definition that focuses on difference in behavior, values, and assumptions that two or more people might find in their cultural backgrounds (race, gender, and ethnicity). This might be a mentoring relationship between an older white male who attended a private school and an African American female who grew up in Chicago's inner city. Another cross-cultural definition focuses specifically on differences in behaviors, values, and customs unique to a particular geographic area or country. Applying this definition, someone from Argentina might have a mentoring partner from the United States. Whatever definition is applied, cross-cultural mentoring adds another layer of complexity and dimension to the learning dynamic that takes place in the mentoring relationship and ultimately adds to the richness of a mentoring culture.

Culturally conditioned behavior affects mentoring relationships in subtle and overt ways, owing to "the political and social hierarchies in which both people live" (Johnson-Bailey, and Cervero, 2002, p. 22). In addition, as Hansman points out, "issues of power may affect how protégés and mentors interact and negotiate their relationship both internally and externally, and ultimately affect the success of formal mentoring programs" (2003, p. 96). Cultural unknowns and false assumptions generate many possibilities for a misstep or misunderstanding, making it more difficult for mentoring partners to establish trust. The challenge is always to facilitate mutual learning while also affirming individual and cultural uniqueness.

Cross-cultural mentoring offers multiple learning opportunities and rewards. Cross-cultural relationships present an organization with the opportunity to become more consciously inclusive, to generate cross-cultural capital, increase the diversity within the organization, and promote equity of opportunity. Those who participate in a cross-cultural mentoring relationship gain diverse and broad perspectives that help them better appreciate and work with cultural differences. As they increase mutual understanding of their cultures, they are able to communicate more openly and honestly and make better business decisions.

Preparing for Cross-Cultural Mentoring

For all its benefits, unless there is a baseline of cultural understanding, cross-cultural mentoring can be quite challenging. Take, for example, the mentoring pair of Jana and Saatchi at a Fortune 500 manufacturing company. No matter how hard Jana tries, she always feels she is bumping up against a glass ceiling. Because of seniority in her department, her employment benefits, and close relationships with coworkers, she is reluctant to leave her organization. Just before her forty-fifth birthday, Jana realizes that if she is ever going to make significant advancement in her career she needs to act quickly. She speaks with several managers to ask how to position herself for promotability. Both managers point out that those who succeed in a big way have mentors to guide their growth and development and expose them to opportunities in the company. She asks for suggestions; Saatchi's name surfaces each time.

From Jana's perspective, Saatchi, a fifty-year-old Japanese American and director of sales and marketing, seems to have it all: seniority, accomplishment, interesting work, and power and influence. Jana is thrilled that Saatchi agrees to be her mentor. She hangs on every word as Saatchi talks about her history with the company and how she worked through the issues of cultural and glass-ceiling barriers. Jana asks lots of insightful questions. She is surprised and taken aback, however, by Saatchi's response to questions about her family and hobbies ("Jana, let's stick with the work issues, please").

As they continue to meet, Jana finds Saatchi's reserved and formal demeanor hard to penetrate. On the few occasions when Jana makes a joke to try to lighten things up, Saatchi doesn't even crack a smile. Jana begins to wonder what she might have done or said to merit such a reaction.

Saatchi, for her part, is becoming concerned about Jana's persistence in trying to get to know her in a deeper way. It makes her personally uncomfortable, and she can see how it might make other people uncomfortable as well. Knowing the importance of relationships in sales and marketing, she fears that Jana might be limiting her own effectiveness. By the same token, she sees great potential for Jana in sales and marketing and wants to be fair to her. Saatchi begins to think that perhaps she is not the right mentor for Jana. The organization's mentoring coach suggests that what she really needs to do is set some clear ground rules and boundaries and come to agreement about how they should promote meaningful learning in the mentoring relationship. The ensuing conversation reveals how their cultural differences contribute to assumptions they are making about the relationship. This mutual discovery leaves them more comfortable and open with each other, and as a result they are able to pursue the learning process in earnest.

This example illustrates mentoring relationship challenges in general and the inherent challenges of creating a cross-cultural mentoring agreement in particular. Cultural assumptions threaten the viability of the relationship. Jana and Saatchi need to spend time in the negotiating phase of the mentoring relationship.

It's clear that cultural assumptions, behaviors, and values drive business practices (such as time, protocols, punctuality, and decision making), affect how people learn and process information, and influence how individuals communicate with one another. These in turn determine how mentoring relationships are formed, maintained, and sustained—all important factors in success.

Meeting the Challenges of Cross-Cultural Mentoring

Successfully meeting the challenges of cross-cultural mentoring requires that those engaged in a mentoring relationship and those who support them extend their cultural antennae, pay attention to differences, and be vigilant about individual learning needs. They must be conscious of their own assumptions and willing to suspend these assumptions, to look beyond cultural stereotypes and honor cultural diversity.

The organization must create readiness for cross-cultural mentoring by becoming more inclusive in planning, implementation, and administration processes. It must adopt a "planning with" approach rather than a "planning for" approach to ensure that mentoring initiatives are culturally sensitive and relevant. Those administering a cross-cultural mentoring program should mirror the diversity it seeks to promote. Multicultural feedback and input are critical to success. Those engaged in implementing cross-cultural mentoring must adequately prepare to assume the role. In addition, to be effective they must also develop a flexible cultural lens.

If an organization is to truly promote cross-cultural mentoring, every effort must be made to ensure that the information presentation is suitable for a multicultural audience. Mentoring materials should be culturally relevant and meet the learning needs of those engaged in mentoring and individuals who support it. For example, even though the same language is spoken, it may not be mutually understood. Even the word mentor can be understood differently. In one cultural context, it might be closely related to teacher, supervisor, or expert; in another, it could carry a negative association because of a perception that seeking or being directed toward a mentor denotes weakness.

Preparing and negotiating the mentoring agreement is probably the most critical challenge for a cross-cultural mentoring partnership. Training is instrumental in overcoming this potential challenge and should include exercises to promote cultural awareness. It should be relevant and applicable to the culture. Using a trainer from the culture in which the training is being delivered helps ensure cultural relevance. Exercise 10.3, Promoting and Supporting Cross-Cultural Mentoring, is a worksheet to help you in planning and supporting cross-cultural mentoring.

From Opportunity to Planning

How does an organization know which type(s) of mentoring to select from the range of possibilities? Organizational need must mesh with cultural fit. Successful implementation requires organizational readiness, infrastructure, and a learner-centered focus. It doesn't require big plans; it demands big thinking.

As a step in this direction, use Exercise 10.4, Identifying and Implementing New Mentoring Models, to stimulate systematic thinking about expanding the types of mentoring relationships in your organization.

If mentoring partners take an active role in planning and designing their own learning opportunities, and their organization joins in the enterprise, the mentoring partners are likely to achieve their learning goals and maximize the learning opportunity. Even so, it is hard work. Several organizational approaches can help facilitate the work necessary to deepen mentoring relationships and broaden the range of learning opportunities:

- During a training session, ask participants to recall outstanding learning opportunities they have experienced and share them with others in the room.

EXERCISE 10.3

Promoting and Supporting Cross-Cultural Mentoring

Instructions: Options for promoting and supporting cultural mentoring are listed in the left column; extra space is given for additional options you might add. Use the right column to write up your implementation strategy.

What Your Organization Can Do	Action Strategies
Become more inclusive	
• Plan with rather than for	
• Gather multicultural feedback	
• Prepare and train planning committee members	
• Develop a more flexible cultural lens	
• Mirror the diversity we want to create	
Accommodate cultural differences through communication	
• Present information so that it is suitable for multicultural audiences	
• Meet the needs of diverse learners	
• Ensure accessibility and compatibility of available technology	
Provide training to manage expectations across cultural differences	
• Conduct a thorough needs assessment	
• Use visuals when there is a language barrier	
• Use terminology that is relevant to the culture	
• Make available plentiful resources and support	
Ensure thoughtful and culturally sensitive cross-cultural pairing	

EXERCISE 10.4

Identifying and Implementing New Mentoring Models

Instructions: Review the models presented in the chapter. Then identify the models that already exist in your organization (column one) and those you'd like to develop (column two). The third column has space for you to write out what you need *to do* to successfully implement each model identified. Finally, itemize implementation action steps for each model in column four.

Models	New Models (What Could Be?)	Strategies for Success	Action Steps
One-to-one			
Group			
Distance			
Cross-cultural			

- Engage in a brainstorming exercise (virtual or live). Ask small groups to brainstorm a list of learning opportunities (internal or external to the organization), and identify their group's top three ideas. Embellish the list of opportunities. Add resources and related items.

- Identify specific ways in which the organization can support those opportunities.

- Compile a list and turn it into an electronic or paper tip sheet, for mentors, mentees, supervisors, and others, for access by the group as a whole, either electronically or in paper form.

- Add to the list of best-practice learning opportunities over time.

- Solicit best-practice learning opportunity stories to be featured in organizational mentoring publications.

Encouraging individuals and organizations to think broadly about learning opportunities deepens learning and enhances the mentoring relationships. Exhibit 10.4, on enriching learning opportunities, presents a list of ideas typical of what emerges from this process, together with possible ways to support the learning.

Exercise 10.5, the Learning Opportunity Checklist, includes a template to help you gauge the degree to which specific learning opportunities offer exposure to new learning, reinforcement of learning, and acceleration of new learning. A balance among these three objectives broadens and deepens the learning experience.

Multiple Mentoring Opportunities: Reflection on Practice

The dance between opportunity and planning within a mentoring culture forms a never-ending circle that embraces individual and organizational learning. The multiple mentoring opportunities and configurations within it extend and enrich the impact of organizational mentoring. The polarized notion of either-or (formal or informal, group or one-on-one, one opportunity or another) is neither functional nor congruent with the ideal of a mentoring culture. Multiple mentoring opportunities are possible and desired because of the inherent inclusivity of a mentoring culture.

The array of options and opportunities for mentoring presented in this chapter offer a springboard and structure to stimulate expansive thinking about how to best provide meaningful learning through mentoring. The challenge is not to be overwhelmed by the smorgasbord of menu options, or fall in love with a single model. Rather, as appropriate, use criteria-based

EXHIBIT 10.4

Enriching Learning Opportunities

Top Ten List	How the Organization Can Support or Enhance the Learning
Simulation	Encourage mentees to be risk takers by experimenting with new ideas.
Sharing information and experiences	Mentors should be encouraged to share failures as well as successes. Check in with mentors periodically to see if there is information they might need to assist them.
Risk taking	Maybe during the next training we should conduct a risk-taking assessment and offer some strategies to help mentees feel more confident.
Shared cultural and sports experiences	We link to this information on the Web. Maybe we should think about actually making tickets available.
Asking questions	This is a slippery slope. We want to encourage asking questions for understanding and to deepen awareness, but there are some boundaries that people need to be aware of. We should think about a tip sheet on this.
Structured volunteer experiences	Let's link up with the Chamber of Commerce here and prepare information and materials to facilitate this for those who feel it would be helpful.
Experimenting	This appears to relate to the theme of risk taking and application of new learning. We need to encourage people to apply what they learn as they learn it. Probably need to bring supervisors into the loop on this.
Field projects	We need to encourage our mentors to bring their influence and networks to bear on making this happen.
Case studies	At our next mentoring management meeting we might want to examine the data we have collected over the years to determine what kinds of case studies would be helpful to mentoring pairs.
Networking	We don't do enough on this topic. A case study wouldn't be bad (see above). In general, our people don't do enough of this. Is it is a case of not knowing, or not wanting?
Outside experts	Here is where our mentors could add value to mentoring relationships. If they use their networks and connections, they could better assist mentees in their weak areas. Mentees should be encouraged to build their own networks, consult outside experts, and bring that new learning to the relationship.
Shadowing	Since so many people identified shadowing as an opportunity, we ought to make sure that people know how to maximize it. Here's a perfect opportunity to incorporate action learning.

Learning Opportunity Checklist

Instructions: List learning opportunities on the left and use checkmarks to indicate which learning objectives each one meets. Review the list; look for gaps and consider how to deepen each learning opportunity.

Opportunity	Learning Objective		
	Exposure	Reinforcement	Acceleration

EXERCISE 10.6

Multiple Mentoring Opportunities Checklist

Instructions: Review these practices. In discussion with others, decide what items should be on your mentoring to-do list.

	Practices	To-Do List
Mentoring approaches: • Informal • Formal • Blended	• Encourage participation in formal and informal mentoring experiences. • Demonstrate specific ways in which mentoring enriches the culture. • Make appropriate technology available. • Identify best practices to showcase informal and formal mentoring. • Offer mentoring education and training to informal mentoring pairs optionally. • Communicate criteria for mentoring success. • Run open education and training sessions. • Provide mentoring coaching and support for informal and formal mentoring participants. • Ensure a budget is in place to support informal mentoring.	
Types of mentoring: • One-to-one • Group • Distance • Cross-cultural	• Encourage multiple types of mentoring. • Multiple options exist for using distance mentoring. • New models of mentoring are encouraged and supported. • Be consciously more inclusive in planning. • Accommodate cultural differences through communication. • Offer training to manage expectations across cultural differences. • Ensure thoughtful and culturally sensitive pairing.	
Learning opportunities	• Best-practice learning opportunities are communicated and supported. • Mentoring pairs are encouraged to look for opportunities to promote exposure to new learning, reinforce learning, and accelerate learning.	
Mentoring menu of opportunities	• Criteria-based decision making is used as a tool.	

decision making for strategic and culturally congruent choices. (Examples of such criteria: alignment with mentoring intent, organizational priorities, infrastructure capacity, organizational vision, and learner needs or learning goals.) Exercise 10.6, the Multiple Mentoring Opportunities Checklist, can be used to identify actionable items for creating and supporting multiple mentoring opportunities within your organization.

Mentoring opportunity is the wellspring of individual and organization learning and thus a key hallmark of a mentoring culture. Education and training, discussed in the next chapter, lay the groundwork for informed mentoring practice.

Chapter 11

Education and Training

Developing in adults a sense of their personal power and self-worth is
seen as a fundamental purpose of all education and training.
—STEPHEN BROOKFIELD (1986, p. 283)

MENTORING EDUCATION AND TRAINING contributes significantly to building a more confident, competent, and creative workforce. It plays a critical
role in establishing organizational readiness and promoting productive and
meaningful learning that ultimately builds individual and organizational
capacity.

At the start, we need to address the semantic labyrinth of education and
training. Although the terms education and training are frequently combined under the rubric "organizational learning," there is a distinction
(albeit sometimes subtle) that can be drawn between education and training. Mentoring training is a planned learning experience (an event or series
of sessions) that focuses specifically on development of mentoring awareness, understanding, knowledge, and skills. Training is probably the first,
most familiar, and most common learning practice implemented by organizations in launching a mentoring program. Mentoring education is a
broader, more inclusive, and strategic term than training. It encompasses a
number of potential mentoring learning experiences (including training)
under its ever-widening wingspan. In a true mentoring culture, the distinction may be moot since there is a seamless continuum of learning experiences that flow together.

Focusing on education or training alone limits an organization's ability
to maintain a viable mentoring culture. Only when learning surrounds, permeates, and transcends a single event or episode can education and training positively affect mentoring success within an organization. In tandem,
education and training reinforce and leverage each other, while at the same
time strengthening and supporting the other hallmarks.

In contrast to Chapter Ten, which focuses on multiple mentoring opportunities for learning outside the formal structure of education and training,
this chapter approaches formal mentoring education and training from the

outside in and inside out. It presents structural frameworks and delves into process components of mentoring education and training that are necessary for creating organizational readiness, effective learning experiences, and meaningful mentoring relationships. It also includes a variety of training exercises that can be used as-is or customized to specific situations. I also illustrate how I facilitate some of the exercises.

Developing a Big-Picture Perspective

At Creative Public Relations (CPR), education and training are woven tightly into the fabric of everyday organizational life. When the decision was made to bring mentoring to CPR, the process of integrating mentoring into the organization's education and training platform was easy and almost seamless. CPR's mentoring orientation program became the gateway to learn about mentoring and the mentoring process.

During CPR's orientation program, a mentoring competency and skill checklist is administered. Those who pass muster are invited to participate in the mentoring training program. Those who lack a skill or competency are encouraged to participate in skill development programs prior to attending the next mentoring training. Throughout the mentoring program year, mentors and mentees have multiple opportunities to identify their own strengths and weaknesses and are encouraged to supplement mentoring training by taking advantage of other existing programs. Upon occasion, these trainings have included businesses with similar development needs willing to partner in creative ways so that they can save money, maximize human and financial resources, and expand their mentoring efforts.

Maintaining a big-picture perspective (as CPR exhibits) enables a mentoring culture to develop the kind of strategic agility that is needed to keep education and training a priority regardless of fluctuating economic trends.

Key Factors at Work

The quality, impact, and value of the learning that results from mentoring education and training depends on the dynamic interplay of context, need, learners, facilitator, learning process, setting, and timing. If each factor is at work, achievement and sustainability of learning outcomes is likely to occur and learner satisfaction is great. These factors constitute a framework for productive planning, implementation, and evaluation of mentoring education and training, regardless of whether the organization is focused on a specific education or training event or a continuum of education and training experiences.

Context

Without sensitivity to context (which includes the situation, social patterns, and culture of the organization), education and training could be perceived as irrelevant or even useless in a specific organization. In other words, if "dialogue and interaction" is an accurate description of how internal business is conducted, training and education should offer opportunities for conversation and interaction rather than a didactic approach. If coworkers are talked at or information is downloaded on them, this is not likely to create value. Similarly, if reams of material are prepared but people only have time for sound bites, the precious time and money spent on producing educational material will show little result.

Need

It is frustrating to spend dollars for education and training only to discover after the fact that it wasn't relevant or applicable. To prevent this, it is essential to understand how learning will be applied every day. In addition, it is important to identify the organization's expressed, felt, and normative needs (Monette, 1977) for education and training. Once organizational needs have been identified, the next step is to explore individual and group learning needs through a needs assessment process to ensure that education and training is relevant and applicable.

Exercise 11.1, the Mentoring Skills Inventory for Mentoring Coaches, is a tool for identifying the needs of "mentoring coach-learners." Using this template based on the mentoring inventory in *The Mentor's Guide* (Zachary, 2000), an organization can identify specific skills, competencies, or content areas and ask learners to indicate their comfort level in regard to each item. An analysis of the data gathered reveals gaps, pinpoints priorities, and identifies starting points. Collecting baseline data is a starting point for meeting individual and group needs and also suggests the approach or approaches most likely to yield results. I often use this inventory as an experiential training exercise on peer mentoring. For example, if someone is quite comfortable in brainstorming but lacks knowledge in problem identification, I might pair that individual with a learning partner who has knowledge and experience in problem identification and is not at ease in brainstorming.

Some skill learning needs can be filled through existing education and training venues; others cannot. Being cognizant of what is already available can avoid duplication of resources—if the existing content and process fit the culture and learning needs and align with a mentoring approach.

Learners

Adult learners bring unique experiences, personal and generational histories, cultural contexts, and diverse sociodemographics (including assumptions, values, and behaviors) to education and training. Understanding the

Mentoring Skills Inventory for Mentoring Coaches

Instructions: Review each skill and indicate how comfortable you are in using it by checking one of the three grids: V = very comfortable, M = moderately comfortable, U= uncomfortable. Then identify an example that illustrates a concrete situation in which you were either comfortable or uncomfortable using the skill. Check each skill that you feel you must improve to develop a level of comfort. Once you have completed the skill inventory, rank your overall comfort level with all twelve skills on a scale of 1 to 5.

Skill	Comfort Level			Examples	Needs Work
	V	M	U		
1. Asking for feedback					
2. Brainstorming					
3. Brokering relationships					
4. Coaching (at multiple levels)					
5. Communicating					
6. Fostering accountability					
7. Goal setting					
8. Managing conflict					
9. Mentoring					
10. Problem identification					
11. Problem solving					
12. Providing feedback					

Overall rating: 1 2 3 4 5

Source: Zachary (2000). Adapted by permission of John Wiley & Sons, Inc.

adult learning market within an organization goes beyond merely identifying individual age and stage of development, institutional department, and organizational band. Accurate knowledge about the target or intended audience of learners helps in developing a meaningful learning experience.

Organizations often develop mentor training programs without giving enough thought to the mentor as a learner. My experience confirms that if mentors meet their own learning and development needs they enrich and enhance their personal effectiveness as mentors. In a recent mentoring training experience for senior leadership within a nonprofit organization, I arrived early to set up and listened carefully to the murmur of conversation in the room. My ears perked up when I heard these comments: "I'm not sure what I'm doing here. I've mentored people all my life"; "I'm showing up because I was told to . . . not sure there's anything new under the sun on this topic"; "I don't understand why we need to set up a formal mentoring program. There's nothing broken that we have to fix. Things seem to be working just fine." The murmurings amounted to some important clues and enabled me to set the stage to validate their prior experiences and immediately engage them because I met them where they were. I opened by saying, "Listening to the conversations going on in the room as I entered, I learned very quickly that some of you have a great deal of mentoring experience. I am going to be counting on your participation because your experiences will contribute to all of our learning today."

In a mentoring culture, the education and training agenda includes renewal opportunities for veteran mentors, honoring and building on past experience and challenging and stimulating further learning. The learners in a mentoring culture transcend the individual mentoring partners and include a variety of other learners, such as supervisors, managers, and trainers. Although they have many common learning needs, each learner category is unique based on experience and work roles, relationships and responsibilities. For example, an "HR manager-learner" might need to know how to support the mentor and mentee without compromising confidentiality; the "mentoring program manager-learner" would need strategies for orienting supervisors to their role in the process, teaching goal-setting skills, and helping supervisors integrate new learning.

Facilitator

A facilitator's values, assumptions, and behaviors influence what is being taught. For example, a facilitator with firsthand mentoring experience has a frame of reference that enriches the learner's experience; one without this experience has a more limited frame of reference. Many organizations require prior mentoring experience and/or intensive just-in-time training to furnish context, content, and mentoring knowledge prior to any required train-the-trainer sessions. Without adequate preparation, a facilitator might misinterpret and therefore misrepresent key mentoring concepts. For example, if a facilitator's experience with feedback has been solely as a remediation tool (critical feedback) or to correct behavior (for performance gaps), he or she could easily overlook the central role of feedback as an enabling mechanism in a mentoring relationship. Those who lead, manage, coordinate, and facilitate mentoring in an organization should be aware of their own assumptions, biases, and behaviors. Self-awareness is a positive first step in creating mentoring culture alignment.

Many organizations do not have the capacity or need to support an internal training staff. Some, particularly smaller ones, outsource all or part of their training. In a specialized area such as mentoring, hiring an external consultant or outside trainer can be an effective way to jump-start the mentoring process and build organizational capacity. Sometimes training departments lack specific mentoring expertise and thus may choose to borrow expertise from those departments that have developed their own internal mentoring expertise. Where this is the case, using such experience and expertise (internal consultants) makes a great deal of sense. The decision as to who should facilitate mentoring training—whether it is someone in organizational leadership, a trainer, a consultant (internal or external), or a combination thereof—is important and should be made in light of the organizational context, need, and learners.

Learning Process

Three adult learning models that are particularly relevant to developing and delivering mentoring education and training are self-directed learning, experiential learning (which includes action learning), and transformational learning. Each has its own distinct body of theory, research, and practice and has contributed to shaping the best practices in adult learning today. They are not mutually exclusive theories of practice; intertwined, they have the potential to enrich one another and produce dramatic and long-lasting results.

Self-Directed Learning

Self-directed learning (SDL), as Malcolm Knowles first introduced it into the adult learning lexicon in 1975, has been a subject of growing interest and ongoing research (Knowles, 1975). Mentoring is the quintessential expression of self-directed learning. At the heart of the definition of SDL (and mentoring) is individual responsibility for learning. Self-responsibility means the learner accepts ownership and accountability (individually or with others) for setting personal learning objectives, developing strategies, finding resources, and evaluating learning. In a mentoring relationship, the responsibility is mutually defined and shared. The mentoring agreement is, in essence, a learning contract that defines the objectives, strategies, resources, timeline, and evaluation methodology of the relationship.

Experiential Learning

Kolb's four-phase experiential learning model (based on previous work by Dewey and others) describes "the learning cycle of how experience is translated into concepts, which, in turn, are used as guides in the choice of new experiences" (Kolb, 2000, p. 1). Kolb's model is constructed around two dimensions. The first focuses on how information is perceived. That is, as one takes in new information, does experience or abstraction dominate? The second dimension focuses on how an individual processes or deals with the information. Is it processed by reflection, or through active experimentation? Although most individuals have a preferred learning style, effective learning depends on a person's ability to use each of the four styles in transforming learning experience. To illustrate how this works, consider that a learner is personally involved in a specific experience (say, participating in a lecture). Then the individual reflects upon the experience, interprets it (makes meaning of the experience), and draws conclusions. These conclusions guide the learner's actions. Program managers or facilitators who are aware of preferred learning styles can then customize education and training activities to specific learning needs.

Learning styles are expressed as part of the culture. Your organization might have what is characterized in Kolb's Learning Style Inventory as an accommodating learning style (Kolb, 1985). If so, employees are encouraged to take risks, seek new opportunities, and become personally involved in projects. Leaders might well be described as "charismatic visionaries" and seem to thrive on crisis and challenge. There is a corporatewide spirit of entrepreneurship, a focus on goals and implementation of initiatives, and a shared sense of accomplishment. The company's mentoring education and training mirrors the learning style. Organizational leaders assist in presenting mentoring training by sharing how mentoring helped them realize their personal vision and potential. Learning resources are always expanding; opportunities for involvement in mentoring exist throughout the organization. Mentees are encouraged to become mentors once they have engaged in a successful mentoring experience. In addition, mentees are encouraged to take risks, experiment, and directly apply their new learning. Weekly group mentoring sessions are a venue for mutual support, continuing education, and celebration.

Even if a preferred organizational learning style is established, it is important to include a variety of learning methodologies that tap into various styles to enhance the learning experience. This approach facilitates more inclusionary learning and helps learners draw on the full range of styles to become more effective in their learning.

Another form of experiential learning is called action learning. It can be summed up as learning by doing in real time. In action learning, a group of people with diverse skills and experience analyze an existing problem, determine new strategic directions, and develop an action plan. Together, they gather new insights as they reflect on lessons learned from implementation. They then apply their new learning and continue the action-reflection-action cycle, striving to continuously improve their desired results. Mentoring networking is an application of action learning. A group of mentors might come together to share best practices and address common problems and issues. By engaging in dialogue, they are able to find new solutions.

Transformational Learning

Transformational learning is facilitated through a process of critical self-reflection (Mezirow and Associates, 1990). A cycle begins as learners become aware of their existing assumptions. Learner self-awareness converts to self-understanding as people begin to challenge existing assumptions. The learning that results from increased understanding enables learners to let go of the self-limiting and unrealistic assumptions holding them back and transform their thinking into new and more productive action and behavior.

The subsequent learning that results from building on and combining these learning models is indeed dynamic and powerful. Because they are mutually reinforcing, they produce more informed, relevant, and generative mentoring practices.

Setting

Setting is the space, place, or environment in which education and training takes place. The setting selected for delivering education and training influences the quality of the learning experience; it can be conducive to learning or present insurmountable learning roadblocks. Setting should never ever be left to chance. It must be deliberate and marry the intent of the event, the needs of intended learners, and the organization's culture. It must invite participation. All aspects of the chosen setting must be conducive to learning. For example, choosing a beautiful setting for an offsite retreat may be a welcome option, but if the microphones aren't working and people can't hear each other, or if the room is too warm and people are uncomfortable, learning will suffer.

Timing

Effective mentoring education and training hinge on the right timing. Mentoring education and training create the need by facilitating mentoring awareness and understanding and debunking negative mentoring myths and assumptions. Individual and organizational readiness to learn signal the right timing for delivering mentoring education and training. Thus, the timing must be strategic to create the point of need and be responsive to it.

Rollout, implementation, and timing should be chosen strategically and based on organization priorities. When too many competing priorities concurrently vie for time, money, and leadership, it is hard to build momentum and the case for mentoring. Mentoring education and training ends up by the wayside.

One client, for example, decided she wanted to bring mentoring into her organization. The organization had "tried mentoring" previously but had failed miserably. To manage expectations, we helped people understand the basic principles and best practices associated with mentoring. As employees moved from mentoring awareness to mentoring understanding, the questions began, and with them arose the need to know even more. Acquiring familiarity with mentoring vocabulary buttressed learner confidence and created multiple and varied learning needs. The bottom line? Generally speaking, people don't know what they don't know. It is unrealistic to expect learners to articulate their learning needs intelligently without a basic frame of reference.

The natural sequence of the mentoring relationship cycle (preparing, negotiating, enabling, and coming to closure) suggests parallel points of need for mentoring education and training. In some organizations, people are vocal about asking for what they think they need. In others, learning needs must be identified through more formal feedback mechanisms, such as surveys, focus groups, and structured conversation. Mentees in one client organization we surveyed stated they were looking for leadership skills, career change options, technical skills, knowledge of how to achieve a win-win mentoring relationship, and the desire to become a better organizational contributor. Much of the information that we gathered was incorporated into the very next training. The mentees felt heard, had their learning needs met, and found the training extremely satisfactory.

Failure to provide learning when it is needed is a missed opportunity. A recent training we conducted gives life to this statement. We were in the middle of a goal-setting exercise when it became obvious that neither mentees or mentors understood the importance of goal setting or how to frame SMART goals. We took a time out from our planned agenda to do basic goal-setting training. After the remainder of the training, we met with those who felt they wanted more goal-setting practice and gave them the opportunity to get feedback and further coaching. Had we not stopped the clock to acknowledge the need for goal setting to give a further explanation of SMART goals, there would have been considerable frustration and floundering, slowing of the learning progress, and diminished relationship satisfaction. In short, forging ahead could have undermined the entire purpose of the mentoring relationship itself: the learning.

The factors of context, need, learners, facilitator, learning process, setting, and timing can be used as a logical framework for productive planning, implementation, and evaluation of mentoring education and training.

Evaluating Your Key Factors

The template in Exercise 11.2, the Mentoring Education and Training Worksheet, presents a way to help you check on the key factors and identify process improvements to strengthen mentoring education and training efforts. Once you have collected individual results for each program or event, you can better identify gaps and opportunities for improvement that would improve and benefit mentoring education and training organizationally.

In a mentoring culture, mentoring education is pervasive and includes an array of education and training opportunities that meet individualized and organizational mentoring needs. Options to engage in formal and informal learning meet diverse learning needs at multiple levels and entry points, whether acquiring basic mentoring information and concepts, mentoring relationship preparation, mentoring skill competency, advanced mentoring, or (for veteran mentors) renewal opportunities.

Even if they lack foundational skills or need to develop specific skills to bring them up to speed in particular areas, learners should have learning opportunities available. The items included on a mentoring education menu need not be flown under a mentoring banner. For example, an individual who needs to shore up listening skills to become a better mentor would benefit from learning opportunities to help fill the skill gap, be it material resources, coaching, classes, or e-learning. Such opportunities may or may not be available in house. If they are not, all is not lost, for appropriate learning opportunities are often available outside the organization or, perhaps, through a strategic alliance.

EXERCISE 11.2

Mentoring Education and Training Worksheet

Instructions: Complete a separate worksheet for each mentoring education or training event or program delivered in your organization. Review each factor in the first column, and identify how it is demonstrated. Then list process improvements that might strengthen your efforts.

Mentoring education event, venue, and activity or training event

Factor	How Demonstrated Needed	Process Improvements
Context: • Process of learning and learning objectives fit with the culture • Design and delivery are relevant and applicable to the context		
Need: • Individual and group needs expressed • Felt and normative needs identified		
Learner: • Diversity of learners explored • Information about prospective learners factored into learning experience		
Facilitator: • "Right" facilitator(s) identified • Learning needs of facilitator clear • Explicit opportunity to reflect on assumptions and biases is part of preparation • Adequate training and coaching available		
Learning process: • Self-directed learning explicitly encouraged • Experiential, action, and transformational learning woven into the learning process		

Factor	How Demonstrated Needed	Process Improvements
Setting: • Conducive to learning • Marries learning intent with needs of learner and culture		
Timing: • Readiness to learn creates points of need • "Curriculum" responds to points of need in timely fashion		

There are many practice models and ideas for delivering mentoring education and training, including some novel approaches. Some organizations adopt an annual thematic approach (usually linked to organizational priorities) to keep mentoring education and training fresh. Some offer introductory, midlevel, and advance mentoring courses on a rotating or cyclical basis. Others have certain fundamental requirements for core courses and electives; they award CEUs (continuing education units) or mentoring certificates for fulfilling these requirements. The possibilities are endless; a few are described in Exhibit 11.1.

Despite the many support mechanisms built into a mentoring culture, many mentors and mentees still don't have access to just-in-time learning opportunities. Even seasoned mentors sometimes have problems understanding the key components and basic concepts necessary to successfully navigate a mentoring relationship. A "mentoring workout center" meets these needs by providing timely technical assistance when mentoring participants are most ready to learn; this helps build "mentoring muscle" within the organization.

The material can be presented in brief sessions that last an hour or two, or in half-day or even daylong sessions. If held as a daylong session, be sure that there are enough mentoring coaches so they can rotate in and out rather than devote their entire day. The format also lends itself to weekly sessions or variations on the theme. For example, an organization might consider holding a mentoring workout session every week during national mentoring month.

Exhibit 11.2, a workout center format, is an adaptation of a model that my colleague, collaborator, and mentor, Martin Parks, and I created. Although this describes an in-person session, the process can also occur virtually.

EXHIBIT 11.1

Mentoring Possibilities

Mentoring Masters (also called mentoring coaches, supermentors, or mentor mentors)	This advanced training program targets individuals who demonstrate mentoring excellence and facilitates their next level of learning. It also creates a knowledgeable cadre of role models and coaches for others engaged in the mentoring program.
Mentoring Resource Center	This concept of a mentoring resource center adds an education and training component to the model as it was first presented in Chapter Seven. The resource center becomes a physical or cyberspace repository of mentoring education and training materials and an education center promoting mentoring education through self-directed learning courses.
Mentoring Boot Camp	Some organizations use the military boot camp model as a vehicle for intensive mentoring training. Whether held annually or on another basis, this model offers skill training, practice, and opportunities for application and feedback.
Mentoring University	The mentoring university concept is based on the corporate university model (Meister, 1998). There are many variations on how the model is presented, but the basic concept is the same, whether it is implemented virtually or in real time. A mentoring university creates a stand-alone central address for organizational mentoring education.
Mentoring in a Box	The need to drive mentoring education and training deep down into the organization and deliver it on a local level or in addition to a corporate level can sometimes be met efficiently by developing a user-friendly turnkey program and toolkit of materials and training resources. These materials—sometimes referred to as "mentoring in a box"—are everything that is needed to deliver the mentoring program. Mentoring education and training is usually required to provide the know-how and technology to best use the box or toolkit.
Integrated Model	In some organizations, mentoring is a seamless part of education and training initiatives and integrated into the content of existing courses rather than a separate curriculum. In others, a separate curriculum for mentoring exists that is carefully aligned with other education and training courses.
Mentoring Roundtable	The roundtable promotes peer learning experiences and peer coaching for a small group. Mentor and mentee participants drive the agenda on the basis of their learning needs and interest. Experts make regular presentations to the group. Each presentation is followed by a facilitated dialogue session to help in the processing and application of new learning.
Strategic Alliances and Partnerships	A group of interested institutions collaborate to develop and implement mentoring education and training with the goal of sharing the cost, expertise, and benefit.

EXHIBIT 11.2

Mentoring Workout Center Format and Process

Room Setup

- A list of ground rules is posted on the entry wall. Ground rules (i.e., "Don't ask a question you wouldn't want to have answered in public"; "Avoid yes-or-no questions") are described to prevent individuals from monopolizing the time. A table sits under the ground rules and has a stack of question cards (and pens). Participants are invited to write one question per card. A question coach is available to assist participants in defining and focusing questions as clearly as possible.
- Each table has eight chairs tight up against the table, two for mentoring coaches and six for MWC participants.
- Coaches are assigned tables and sit next to each other at each table. It is best to pair mentoring coaches together so as to generate diverse perspectives. The remaining six chairs are for participants who are ready with their mentoring question. Behind the six chairs is a larger circle of chairs (twelve maximum) for the observers.
- Off to the side of the room there is a table, called the BrowseAbout. Mentoring information and learning resources are displayed on this table, and an LCD/computer is set up with selected mentoring URLs ready to be accessed.

How It Works

1. Individuals who enter the room with specific mentoring questions write one question on a card and sit at a roundtable. Individuals, in turn, are invited to raise their question; as they do, they hand the coaches their question card. Both coaches respond to each question that is asked. Once the question has been answered, the person can stay at the table as long as no one else is waiting for a chair. If there is ample time and space at a table, participants may ask more questions. Otherwise, they need to move away from the table.
2. Individuals who prefer not to ask questions observe until they are ready to actively participate. They sit in the second row of chairs (away from the table) and listen to the question-and-answer session. When they are ready to formulate a question, they fill out a card and sit down at one of the roundtables when there is room. All participants, regardless of whether they came with a question or not, are encouraged to formulate a question sometime during the session.
3. Each table has a table coordinator who facilitates rotation in and out of the roundtables, so that as many people as possible can access the mentoring coaches.
4. If participants do not have an opportunity to have questions answered, if other questions come to mind, or if they are uncomfortable asking questions in a "public" forum, they are encouraged to submit a question in this alternative manner. The table coaches collect question cards from the individuals; later, cards are sorted according to topic. Answers are published in a FAQ (frequently asked questions) format.

Ideally, mentoring education and training should take each of the seven factors (context, need, learner, facilitator, learning process, setting, and timing) into account in framing an agenda. It should also apply the Keep It Simple and Smart (KISS) principle so that mentoring education and training remains manageable. Exhibit 11.3 presents a sample of what a mentoring education and training agenda might look like in a midsize or large organization. Although a sample agenda in a smaller organization might be on a different scale, it should still include multiple and varied learning activities and embrace the KISS principle.

EXHIBIT 11.3

Sample Mentoring Education and Training Agenda

Learning Activity	Description
Mentoring Orientation Workshop	Open informational session for anyone in the organization who wants to learn more about the concepts, benefits, and practice of mentoring.
Mentoring Training for Mentors and Mentees	Mentoring training curriculum consists of three sessions, repeated yearly. One: relationship preparation and negotiation Two: enabling the relationship and addressing stumbling blocks Three: successful closure
Mentoring Training for Managers	Integrated into employee orientation for new managers; focuses on the mentoring support role of the manager.
Mentoring Masters Classes	Intensive three-day process workshop with practicum experience and follow-up online coaching. Program targets individuals who demonstrate excellence and facilitates their next level of learning. Creates a knowledgeable cadre of role models and coaches for others engaged in the mentoring program.
First Fridays	Early morning breakfast learning sessions featuring a variety of speakers addressing some aspect of mentoring.
Mentoring Learning Center	Virtual format including portals to other Websites, chat rooms, online minicourses, crib sheets, articles, and mentoring success stories. Learners access information at point of need and are notified as new resources are posted to the Website.
Best Practices Newsletter	Mentors and mentees submit success stories and best practices. Newsletter appears quarterly.
Mentoring Speaker Series	Based on the symphony series idea, mentors, mentees, and mentoring coaches are given a list of local lectures and workshops that relate directly or indirectly to mentoring. Participants select their top three (or more) speaker choices. Tickets are available to attend events; when appropriate, mentoring partners attend together.
Annual Mentoring Institute	Keynote speaker addresses some aspect of mentoring, followed by workshops related to the speaker's theme. Skill workshops and modified mentoring clinic are held, as is a recognition and awards luncheon.

Anatomy of a Training Experience

The success of a training experience depends on astutely balancing and blending context, need, learner, facilitator, learning process, setting, and timing with clearly defined learning outcomes. Learning outcomes are derived from the intended purpose (learning objectives) of the training; they should be SMART (once again: specific, measurable, action-oriented, realistic, and timely). Exact focus on what participants will know (cognitive objectives), what they will do (behavioral objectives), and how they will feel (affective objectives) as a result of participating in the training experience is essential.

Without creating mentoring competence, it is impossible to develop and maintain a viable mentoring culture. Max De Pree sums it up this way: "When a leader or a group lacks resources or competence, nothing will save even their grandest vision of the way things might be" (2003, pp. 117–118). The "business" of training is to bring appropriate human and knowledge resources to bear in a disciplined way that facilitates and elevates the learner's mentoring competence and confidence. Unless learners achieve at least a minimum level of competence, the long-term benefit of training diminishes. Since mentoring competence is quite a broad learning outcome of mentoring training, a challenge is defining specific and measurable competencies that the organization needs or wants to have in place.

In discussing the training experience, we cover people, process, content, practice, performance, feedback, and closure. All are necessary, and it is the artful combination of people and process that is a core component of effective training.

People

Facilitators must make available sufficient opportunities for learners to bring their own unique world of experience into the room. Participants need time and space to get to know and interact with each other to tap into the experience. Sometimes, particularly if the training is a multiday proposition, this happens quite naturally over time. More often, the facilitator has to establish the means to bring experience into the room. This may require inclusion of structured activities that invite participants to share themselves and their experiences. The larger the group, the more difficult it is to accomplish this. However, with larger groups there are many more options to break into groups (whether dyads, triads, small table groups, or teams). Small-group sharing is a great icebreaker, but the real payoff and broadening of relationships comes from debriefing and pooling individual group experiences. In this way, the group is exposed to the larger community of people and ideas and can serve as resources to one another.

"Connecting activities" are structured conversation and interaction encouraging people to get to know one another. In many instances the people in the room may already have a history with each other, but they probably haven't established a mentoring connection; they may be unaware of others' past experience with mentoring or in a mentoring role. Establishing connection is an important step in helping to bring a mentoring focus to the relationship.

Process

Process is the core of the mentoring training experience, how the learner becomes actively engaged and the learning is structured. Certain processes have more leverage than others in promoting learning. Here I touch on a few processes related to awareness and assumptions.

Self-Reflection

In the workaday world, we don't routinely make time for self-reflection, whether from time pressure or because we don't see self-reflection as contributing to productivity and results. Yet self-reflection promotes awareness, clarifies thinking, generates insights, facilitates new learning, and promotes individual development.

Whenever mentoring training includes structured opportunities for self-reflection, it promotes experiential learning and generates powerful lessons. To encourage authenticity and build in a comfort level with self-reflection, I prepare a handout or ask a reflection question and then allot ample time for individuals to capture their ideas, thoughts, and insights on paper. I try to make it as comfortable as possible for people to participate, by saying something like this:

> *This training will include some moments for self-reflection (or individual journaling). We do this because we want to encourage more reflective and effective mentoring practitioners. We've also discovered over the years that it accelerates the application of learning. Self-reflection (or journaling) may feel uncomfortable to you at first, particularly if you have not done this before. Each of you brings a wealth of experience. By giving you time to reflect on that experience, we all benefit from your experience. Before we begin, I'd like to suggest a couple of ground rules around confidentiality. First, I will let you know ahead of time which activities we are sharing. Second, share only what you are comfortable sharing.*

Exercise 11.3, Reflecting on Your Mentoring Experiences, is a structured exercise to encourage individual reflection on past experience. Not everyone has had a mentor, but most people have had someone somewhere in the past guide, support, or strengthen them. When I work in a setting where it is likely that people have had mentors, I pose the question to focus specifically on mentors who guided, supported, and strengthened them.

Reflecting on Your Mentoring Experiences

Facilitator Instructions: Make sure everyone has a copy of this handout. Set a minimum of ten minutes for responding to the items. At the end of the ten minutes, invite participants to share their responses with a partner or in a group. Allot fifteen minutes for sharing responses.

Participant Instructions: Think about your past mentoring experiences and write answers to these questions.

1. Who were the people there to guide you, support you, and strengthen you?

2. What did you learn?

3. What made the experience worthwhile and meaningful?

4. What wisdom did you gain?

5. What did this experience teach you about being a mentoring partner?

Once participants have completed the exercise, I ask them to share their stories in dyads, triads, or small groups and then debrief in whole-group conversation. The stories that emerge from responses to "What made your experience so worthwhile and meaningful?" inevitably speak to the power of mentoring. The answers to "What did this experience teach you about being a mentoring partner?" generate behavioral benchmarks that can be referred to during the training session. I find that the debriefing process levels the playing field and creates a common vocabulary and shared set of understandings.

Checking Assumptions

The foundation of transformational learning is developing awareness of unconscious assumptions and testing out those assumptions for accuracy. One of the most eye-opening experiences for mentoring participants is to reflect on their individual assumptions about mentors, mentees, and the mentoring relationship and then check them for validity by receiving feedback from others. I like to ask people to make a list of assumptions they hold about mentees, mentors, and mentoring relationships. I then divide them into groups and ask the mentors to share the assumptions they hold about mentees; once they have come to consensus, they gather around a flipchart and post their results. Similarly, I ask the mentees to focus on the assumptions they hold about mentors. In turn, each group shares its list, and we focus on where there is common ground and where there is not. As a group, we then talk about mentoring relationship assumptions and close the exercise by discussing mutual expectations and implications for action.

This exercise usually results in an "a-ha experience" for learners. For example, mentees might assume that because they have a mentor "in high places" they will automatically be promoted. Mentors, on the other hand, might assume that mentoring is about promotability rather than promotion. The chasm between getting a promotion and positioning oneself for promotability is difficult to bridge and could potentially result in huge disappointment. Getting assumptions out in the open at the beginning of a relationship helps manage the expectations of the mentoring partners.

Content

Training is structured around specific subject knowledge and skills (content). Topic areas flow from the learning objectives and desired learning outcomes. Some general mentoring content areas apply to most audiences; they include, but are not limited to, an operational definition of mentoring, the mentoring relationship cycle, mentoring core competencies (such as goal setting, feedback, time management, interpersonal skills), specific programmatic nuts and bolts and information, role expectations, avoiding and addressing stumbling blocks, and mentoring best practices.

An HR mentoring training with the goal of preparing HR managers to successfully implement new roles and responsibilities in supporting organizational mentoring might have some anticipated outcomes: that participants (1) understand the parameters of their role and their specific responsibilities in supporting the mentoring process, (2) achieve competence in making successful mentoring matches, (3) become more proficient in each of five key support skills, and (4) frame an action plan to further their own development in the mentoring role.

The content or topics that might be addressed include understanding HR's role and the role of others, partnering, making mentoring matches, supporting mentoring relationships, and ensuring personal and professional growth. The amount of time that should be devoted to each topic and the relative emphasis among topical areas is unique to each organization. For example, if there is an absence of feedback within an organization's culture, significant time and attention would have to be devoted to the topic; if feedback is a seamless part of the culture, less time can be spent on it.

Practice

Practice helps ensure immediacy of application, as well as reinforcement, integration, and deepening of the learning. If practice is combined with reflection and feedback (action learning), it strengthens the learning and the learner's confidence. Goal setting offers a meaningful example of how to incorporate practice into training. Typically, the first reaction is to slough off the need to spend time on creating SMART goals. Nevertheless, failure to clearly set learning goals is a major stumbling block to mentoring success.

Setting the stage for practice is critical. We first make the case by saying something like, "The presence of clear learning goals is a significant benchmark for predicting and achieving success in a mentoring relationship. Learning how to set goals takes practice."

We back up the case with stories and examples that bring home the point. Our next step is to give ten examples in a handout and ask participants to review the list in small groups and identify which of the ten are SMART goals. As the group debriefs each goal, key learning points are summarized on a flipchart.

We ask participants to practice by developing a SMART goal with a learning partner. Learning partners share their results in small groups and get feedback on how to strengthen the goal. We close by summarizing key learning points. It doesn't take long for participants to realize that it requires skill to create a learning goal that produces the desired results.

Performance

Effective performance depends on self-confidence, content knowledge, and practice. The opportunity to perform during training helps drive home key learning points and increases the portability, transferability, and applicability of skill, knowledge, and new behavior. Performance offers learners the opportunity to demonstrate ownership of learning by personally engaging with and applying new learning. As a result, it enables the community of learners (those attending the session) to benefit from the experience of diverse actors and learn from that diversity. If performance is couched as a learning opportunity rather than a test, it serves these purposes. Therefore the facilitator must create a safe, open, and nurturing environment where performance is nonpunitive yet still encourages the learner to stretch.

Scenarios and role plays are examples of experiential learning. They support and challenge participants as they try on the learning (concrete experimentation), see how it looks and feels (reflective observation), draw new insights from lessons learned (abstract conceptualization), and apply new learnings to other problems and situations (active experimentation).

Exercise 11.4, a Sample Mentoring Scenario, can be used in large or small groups. Customize the context and setting so learners can readily relate to the setting and issues. The scenarios can be performed in small breakout groups to ensure a safe audience. If the whole group is small, ask for volunteers to perform the roles using what they've learned. The exercise is usually richer if both role play and discussion take place. The opportunity to perform in a safe environment sharpens later performance in a real-life situation. If a group pushes back on the role-playing aspect, simply ask each group to read the scenario and discuss the questions.

A second exercise that brings people, process, and content together in the training experience is found in Exercise 11.5, Stumbling Block Role Plays. It can be used in a number of ways. The content might be taught by first drawing responses from the group about what stumbling blocks they've experienced or anticipate they might face. Next, present a methodology for dealing with stumbling blocks. Ask individuals to form triads. Distribute two cards to each group. Each card should have one of the role plays listed, or another stumbling block you might face in your organization. Instruct participants to apply the methodology, with one person acting as observer. The observer's role is to provide feedback using the "feedback" content presented in the session. In this way, everyone gets to improve performance and practice.

Feedback

As has been discussed in previous chapters, feedback plays a critical role in mentoring relationships and in creating a mentoring culture. Feedback, in this specific context, relates to both the content and the process of mentoring training. Teaching about feedback early on in the training allows people to practice and perfect personal skill. Whenever possible, build in opportunities for individual and group feedback, and set time and guidelines to facilitate the process. Highlight its importance by declaring a feedback break or time-out. For example, stop the activity in progress to call for a feedback break, giving the group time to offer and receive feedback on an experiential activity. Be sure to reserve time for ample feedback opportunity in any performance experience.

Closure for the Session: Pack and Go

It's five o'clock. The third day of your training session started late, and all day you've been playing catch up. You look around the room and everyone appears to be either packing up or looking at a watch. You find yourself doing what you don't want to do: rushing to bring the training session to closure. You apologize to the group, acknowledge the fact that there is no time left, ask them to take responsibility for completing the planned closing exercise on their own, and thank them for the quality and openness of their participation. This scenario is probably familiar for every trainer. Yet an important part of the learning experience is missed whenever you are forced to abort the closing experience of a training.

The pack-and-go feature in Microsoft's PowerPoint program is a helpful analogy because it is so similar to the closure process that takes place at the end of a mentoring training experience. It is important to understand the steps. Pack-and-go prepares a presentation file so that the user can take a copy of a presentation along anywhere. The operative word is "prepares." It takes a few minutes for the "Pack and Go Wizard" to prepare the package file so that all aspects of the presentation remain intact (with animation, sound, and format). The wizard signals its intent and asks for input regarding the file to be packed. The user is instructed to make some choices. The wizard then asks the user to choose where the file is to go (to a disk, DVD, or CD) and asks about the links that need to accompany the file to make it work properly. The final question from the wizard is an inquiry about the new environment where the presentation is to be used. The wizard wants to know if you expect to be in a friendly environment: Is the environment PowerPoint-ready or does it need some additional support (in this case another file) in

EXERCISE 11.4

Sample Mentoring Scenario

Instructions: This scenario is based on content related to the four predictable phases of a mentoring relationship. Encourage people to get into the role and play it out. Make sure that the small groups have adequate time to debrief the role play. The full-group discussion and the questions that are raised serve as a review and position the wrap-up for the session.

1. After the entire group has read the background information about Frank and Charlene, divide into small groups of at least four to eight participants.
2. Groups receive a handout with four scenarios, representing the phases of the mentoring relationship identified in the last part of this exercise. Each group is assigned one scenario.
3. Each group reads its scenario.
4. Given the instruction that they are to apply the information and tools covered during the session, two people role-play the mentoring session according to the information in the scenario.
5. Two people agree to be coaches. One coaches the mentor, and the other coaches the mentee. The rest of the team observe the interaction during the role play as they complete the task indicated.
6. When the role play is complete, team coaches share observations and make suggestions for improvement.
7. Small groups discuss these questions: What issues and challenges did the scenario raise for you? What worked well? What questions still remain?
8. One person agrees to act as team spokesperson and report key learning points from the discussion to the entire group.
9. Review the background information to set the context. Then ask each group in turn to report its findings. Address questions posed by the groups.
10. Summarize key learning points from a big-picture perspective and draw parallels to anticipated mentoring situations.

Mentoring Phase Scenarios

1. Preparing Scenario

   Frank and Charlene have never met. Although there are people in his life who have mentored Frank informally, this is the first time he will be engaged in formal mentoring. Frank is not really sure what is involved or what it is he needs specifically, but he knows he needs the benefits of someone else's insight and guidance. He has high expectations and lots of questions. Charlene has had the benefit of good mentors throughout her career. Currently Charlene has extended her mentoring externally, to some of her business colleagues.

2. Negotiating Scenario

   Charlene sees multiple opportunities to give Frank hands-on learning experiences to get a fuller understanding of the possibilities open to him in developing his business. Frank learns best by taking in information and laying things out step-by-step. He is looking to Charlene for specific how-to information (how to delegate responsibility, and how to balance work inside the office with the need to network and develop strategic relationships outside the organization).

3. Enabling Scenario

   Charlene views Frank as her younger counterpart (her earlier self revisited). She admires Frank's ideas and innovations, and especially his eagerness to please. Charlene is learning too, by seeing small business through a new set of lenses. Frank enjoys the relationship and finds it exciting. His palpable hunger for success is evident as he learns and applies new skills and sees results. He relies on his mentor's judgment more and more. After four months, Charlene is becoming concerned that Frank has lost sight of the big picture and begins to put more pressure on him to find his own answers. The amicable and friendly relationship is beginning to feel less comfortable.

4. Coming to Closure

Frank and Charlene's mentoring relationship has resulted, thus far, in meeting only three of the five learning objectives they set out to accomplish during their negotiating conversation some time ago. When they meet to process the learning and review their progress, they realize that it would be advantageous to continue the mentoring relationship beyond the agreed-on time frame. They talk about what went well for them and what might improve their relationship, and then they renegotiate a timeline for accomplishing the remaining learning goals.

Creating a Mentoring Culture by Lois J. Zachary

Copyright ©2005, John Wiley & Sons, Inc.

EXERCISE 11.5

Stumbling-Block Role Plays

Instructions: Divide participants into groups of four or five people. Assign each group two scenarios. The group has fifteen minutes to read the scenario, discuss the situation, and propose possible solutions. From the list of possible solutions, the group selects the best one. Two individuals volunteer to role-play the solution, which they rehearse using coaching from the small group before they perform for the entire group.

1. The mentee has dropped hints that she is uncomfortable talking with her mentor about how things are going for her.
2. The mentee and mentor can't seem to relate to one another and find common ground. Both sense that their "differences" are undermining the relationship.
3. The mentee feels she has to get everything that is suggested by her mentor approved first by her direct supervisor. This is negatively affecting the mentoring relationship and irritating the mentor.
4. The mentoring relationship is stalled. The mentoring partners have talked to each other several times on the phone but met only once face-to-face. Three months have gone by and no goals have been set.
5. The mentor feels that the time with the mentee is not well spent and has broached the subject with the mentee. The mentee is unable to deal with feedback.
6. The mentoring partner does not understand how important to his partner days off are; he often wants to schedule weekend mentoring meetings.
7. The mentee is focused on personal problems and can't seem to get past them. The mentor is uncomfortable in the role of counselor and feels boundaries have been crossed.

Creating a Mentoring Culture by Lois J. Zachary

Copyright ©2005, John Wiley & Sons, Inc.

order to make the presentation compatible with the new environment so that the PowerPoint presentation can be properly viewed? The wizard helps facilitate the preparation process and allots time for you to respond thoughtfully, ensuring the integrity of the final PowerPoint presentation.

Closure should include time for learner self-reflection, identification of key learnings, consideration of how to apply new learning to a personal or work context, itemization of actionable items, and generation of a list of next steps and timelines. By bringing experiential learning, self-directed learning, and action learning to bear while holding out the promise of transformational learning, the closure process promotes learner self-accountability and helps ensure the portability, accessibility, and application of new learning.

A pack-and-go process (as illustrated by Exercise 11.6, Mentoring Reflection: What I've Learned Lately) is integral to increasing the portability and integration of new learning. It is an opportunity for participants to summarize their learning and think about how to apply new learning after the training session.

Exercise 11.7, a Training Analysis Worksheet, is a handy checklist for making sure all the necessary elements are included in training. It lists the individual elements of the training anatomy, examples from an introductory mentoring seminar, and space so that you can plan and evaluate your own mentoring training to make sure you've included all key elements.

Strategies for Success

Mentoring education and training success rests on an organization's ability to provide rich and varied learning experiences that serve the wide-ranging needs of quite diverse learners. The menu must allow flexibility, promote learner accessibility, maintain consistency of practice, and be guided by principles of adult learning. A systemic and strategic approach maximizes and aligns organizational resources.

Far too often an organization plunges right into mentoring education and training without any consideration of how its existing programs can strengthen, support, and supplement mentoring education and training. Exercise 11.8, Guidelines for Discussion, introduces a template that can be used to frame such a discussion. Taking time to discuss answers to the questions posed there can help you discover innovative ways to maximize financial and human resources, avoid duplication of effort, and ensure internal consistency of knowledge management. It can also reveal mentoring education and training gaps that need to be filled and supplemented through other learning venues. Mentoring education and training includes an array of flexible and ever-expanding learning options. Be sure to choose options that fit the culture.

EXERCISE 11.6

Mentoring Reflection: What I've Learned Lately

Facilitator instructions: Set, at a minimum, five minutes for participants to make notes; ten minutes is better. Once most people have completed the exercise, ask for volunteers from the group to talk about the most significant learning they are taking away from the session. These responses usually amount to a recap of key learning points and validate the experiences of others.

1. You came here with some notions and assumptions about mentoring. How has your thinking changed during this training?

2. What will you do differently now, as a result of what you have learned?

3. What is going to be your biggest challenge in applying your learning?

4. What is your action plan? (List action steps.)

EXERCISE 11.7

Training Analysis Worksheet

Instructions: The first two columns list the six training components, with examples taken from an actual introductory mentoring workshop. Use the third column to list the activities you have included in your training that relate to each component.

Components	Examples	Your Activities
People	• Icebreakers • Group interactions	
Process	• Reflection • Journaling • Partnering • Self-assessment	
Content	• Introduction to mentoring • The mentoring cycle	
Practice	• Initial conversations • Confidentiality • Stumbling blocks • Learning goals	
Performance	• Closure role play • Finding a mentor • Pop quizzes and games	
Feedback	• One-to-one feedback opportunities • Group feedback experiences • Time to debrief learning from feedback	
Pack and go	• Workplan • Lessons Learned	

EXERCISE 11.8

Guidelines for Discussion

Instructions: First identify what kind of mentoring education and training is needed, and then the intended learners. Identify the content, knowledge, and skills to be taught. Consider what you already do that is similar or different. If you are already offering education and training that is similar, how might you align that content with mentoring to maximize use of resources and avoid duplication?

What Kind of Mentoring Education and Training Is Needed?		Who Is the Audience?	What Needs to Be Taught?	How Do We Avoid Duplication of Effort?	How Do We Ensure Consistency and Alignment?
Mentoring Education	Training	Intended Learners	Content Knowledge Skills	Existing Venues	Alignment Required

Education and Training: Reflection on Practice

In a mentoring culture, mentoring education and training requires ongoing commitment. In fact, no hallmark directly influences the quality of mentoring relationships more dramatically than education and training. To ensure mentoring success, learning—on whatever level it takes place, be it for mentors, mentees, managers, mentoring coaches, or administrators—must go deep and wide into the organization. Its results are relevant, practical, and experienced throughout the organization. It is user-friendly as well as usable.

In formulating your mentoring education and training to-do list, consider these questions:

Key Factors

- Are context, need, learner, facilitator, learning process, setting, and timing each considered in planning an event or program?
- Are key factors reviewed annually, systemwide, for mentoring education and training events and programs?
- Do you have a process improvement plan in place, and are you implementing it as scheduled?
- Are you consciously incorporating opportunities for promoting self-directed learning, experiential learning, action learning, and transformational learning into your mentoring education and training?
- Do you consider the timing of mentoring education and training in light of organizational priorities?
- Are your mentoring education and training responsive to learning needs?

Evaluating Your Key Factors

- Are opportunities for mentoring education pervasive throughout your organization?
- Does your mentoring education menu offer an array of learning options?
- Are the opportunities to engage in formal and informal learning meeting the diverse learning needs at multiple levels and entry points?
- Are the mentoring education and training you provide engaging and exciting?
- Do your mentoring education and training adhere to the KISS principle?

Anatomy of a Training Experience

- How well does your training balance and blend context, need, learner, facilitator, learning process, setting, and timing?

- Are there adequate opportunities available for fostering mentoring competence in a variety of skill areas?

- Is self-reflection a purposeful part of mentoring learning experiences?

- Is training structured around specific subject content?

- Are feedback and practice central parts of learning experiences?

- Does the learning environment encourage practice and promote integration of new learning?

- Is the time allotted for bringing the learning experience to closure adequate?

A disciplined and strategic approach to mentoring education and training develops confidence, power, and self-worth for those engaged in learning and elevates the value of continuous learning by ensuring application and integration of new learning as well as creating the opportunity to leverage that learning. As discussed in the next chapter, smart organizations also build in safety nets to support learning.

Chapter 12

Safety Nets

A "good enough" holding environment ... will allow us to consolidate each new sense of self so that we can maintain meaning and coherence in the world and yet remain open to a lifetime of fresh wonders.
—LAURENT DALOZ (1999, P. 185)

A MENTORING CULTURE establishes safety nets so that potential stumbling blocks and roadblocks can be overcome or avoided in a timely fashion and with minimum repercussion and risk. Safety nets are in a real sense holding environments. They provide support that enables individuals, teams, and organizations to continue to move forward coherently. Organizations proactively anticipating challenges that may occur are more likely to establish resilient and responsive mentoring safety nets than are those that do not.

Stumbling blocks are inevitable in any relationship. At one time or another, roadblocks challenge every organization. Yet it is not the block itself that gets in the way of successful mentoring; it is the response to it. Having multiple safety nets in place supports individuals and their organizations as they prepare for and respond to mentoring challenges they face.

Relying on the Net

We thrill at the agility, bravado, and grace of the trapeze artist performing on a high wire above the crowd. The risk sends chills up and down our spine, while the sight of the safety net below reassures us. Yet a safety net does not prevent the trapeze artist from falling. For that, she depends on her skill, wits, and competence. To her, the safety net encourages risk taking; it is tangible evidence to her that something is in place to minimize her personal risk and danger, to help prevent serious injury or death if she stumbles and falls.

The structural integrity of the net is also important. If the net is cut or worn, or its supports are weak, or it is not properly maintained, the net is compromised; as a consequence, risk is increased rather than reduced. Even if the net is strong, if not set properly in place performers can't trust it and won't take risks.

This second circumstance, transposed to the high wire of business, fits the experience of someone we'll call Matt, directly after college. Bill, the senior management team member of a large health care management organization, recruits Matt directly after college, sponsors him, and volunteers to mentor him. Three weeks go by, and Bill informs Matt that he is leaving the organization and that someone else will be assigned to be his mentor. But in the organization's fast-paced, results-driven culture, people don't have much patience for novices and no one steps forward to help Matt, even when he asks. Matt feels abandoned and adrift; he has no one in the organization he can trust and has to rely on his own devices to understand the culture and establish credibility. The cultural expectation that he will perform and know what to do on his own leaves him with no safety net.

Any new employee, no matter of what age, is apt to feel frustrated and disappointed if the one person he trusts abandons him. If the organization had a process in place (safety nets) to assist Bill and Matt in bringing their personal relationship to satisfactory closure and then transitioning Matt to a new mentor, it might have helped retain a high-potential employee such as Matt. Instead, frustration gets the better of Matt and several months later he leaves the company.

In contrast and elsewhere, Gloria, who is by all counts a savvy, sophisticated, and high-energy manager, winds up relying on safety nets that are in place at her company. Everyone thinks she is a natural for the position of corporate mentoring coordinator. This is a highly sought-after position that rotates every three years and carries significant prestige and salary. Gloria considers landing the plum assignment a coup. Increasingly, people turn to her as the in-house, one-stop, mentoring expert. Despite her enthusiasm, it isn't long before she realizes that she is in over her head. As she becomes increasingly aware of the gaps in her own knowledge and experience, her self-confidence begins to wane. True, she has a fabulous track record, but she has little firsthand mentoring experience. She is concerned that her lack of knowledge will soon become apparent to others.

Gloria is fortunate to be part of an organization with a long-standing commitment to the development of its professional staff. The culture has built-in safety nets that support individual and organizational learning and encourage its people to ask for what they need. Having recognized her own vulnerability (evidence of her own internal safety net), she approaches her manager to ask for support. Together they map out a development plan that includes mentoring coaches (internal and external to the organization), additional mentoring material resources, attendance at mentoring conferences, an external mentor, and mentoring skill development. Gloria feels there is minimum risk in asking for what she needs since she has a built-in safety net. The culture encourages people to ask for what they need and provides structures that help them get it without fear of penalty. If she felt there was not an organizational safety net in place to support her, the risk (or her perceived risk) would be far greater.

Gloria's particular stumbling block, as is true in general, is episodic (it comes out of a particular situation), and it takes some work on her part and support from the organization to get past it. Matt was not as fortunate.

When stumbling blocks such as these and others become pervasive in an organization, they create roadblocks that produce a systemic impasse and stop movement around mentoring. They often block more than just an individual mentoring relationship or situation. The larger the stumbling blocks, the more money, time, attention, and other resources are required to deal with them. Obstacles are an inevitable part of the process of embedding mentoring in an organization. A true mentoring culture puts functional safety nets in place to help individuals and organizations deal effectively with mentoring blocks they encounter, individually or organizationally.

In this final chapter, we address proactive and reactive approaches to building safety nets to support people, processes, and structures. The proactive approach anticipates the need for safety nets and builds them into the culture before they are considered necessary. The reactive approach responds in the moment to unanticipated situations that require immediate attention and action. Typically, organizations that use a proactive approach to safety nets factor in the predictable phases in the mentoring relationship cycle and establish safety nets for each of those phases.

Proactive Approaches to Obstacles

Each phase of the mentoring relationship cycle presents significant signposts and potential challenges. These challenges signal starting points for determining what safety nets may be needed in a particular organization at a particular time.

Avoiding Stumbling Blocks

As we've seen, the mentoring cycle is composed of four phases—preparing, negotiating, enabling, and coming to closure—each of which builds on the previous one. They vary in length and sometimes flow into one another. Let us turn to examples of potential stumbling blocks for each phase.

Preparing

During the preparing phase of a mentoring relationship, mentors and mentees prepare individually for their separate roles by exploring their personal motivation and readiness to mentor and be mentored by engaging in self-assessment and reflection. The self-knowledge they gain through this process produces a personal safety net that anticipates potential stumbling blocks by targeting areas for personal development and growth.

The initial conversation that takes place in preparation for the relationship begins the process of building safety nets into the relationship. Mentoring partners explore a variety of topics to establish mutual interest, relationship expectations, compatibility, learning needs, and so on. These conversations serve to build safety nets by managing expectations and helping potential mentoring partners determine if they actually want to work together, and if there is a good learning fit between them. If, on the other hand, people enter a mentoring relationship begrudgingly or because they feel they ought to, they are not likely to fully engage. Eventually the lack of commitment negatively affects the quality of the relationship.

In addition, safety nets should be in place in creating the mentoring pool of interested and qualified mentor candidates. An individual who is in the pool but not selected may feel resentment or anger and wind up undermining or sabotaging the process. Establishing and communicating selection guidelines in advance and communicating the process matter-of-factly in program materials helps keep people from taking rejection personally. Materials might, for instance, indicate this: "Some mentor candidates will not be selected. We have intentionally included more mentors than we will need, since we anticipate we may need to add or replace mentors during the mentoring cycle. If a mentor is not selected, it probably is an indication that there was not a learning fit. We will continue to keep potential mentors in the mentoring pool until an appropriate match is made."

Negotiating

The negotiating phase is critical in establishing relationship safety nets. It is the phase in which strategic and tactical details of the relationship are spelled out. A partnership agreement and workplan, consisting of well-defined goals, criteria and measurement for success, delineation of mutual responsibility, accountability mechanisms, and protocols for dealing with stumbling blocks builds safety nets. Embedding safety nets into a relationship is a critical part of building a successful relationship (Eby and Allen, 2002). Focused conversation about time, goals, and confidentiality builds relationship safety nets and must be addressed in the negotiating phase.

Perceived or real lack of time is a major relationship stumbling block. Partners must build a "time safety net" by agreeing in advance about when and how often they will meet, how to spend their time together, and how to hold themselves and each other accountable if they miss meetings or can't connect with one another to reschedule. Similarly, since learning goals drive the relationship they must be clarified. People might establish goals that are too ambitious, too broad, not appropriate to mentoring, or just not doable. The organization can erect a goal-setting safety net by offering skill-based goal training that prepares people to create appropriate mentoring goals. Tools, guidelines, and examples help ensure that goals are appropriately framed within the context of the mentoring effort. Unless attention is given to goals, the forward momentum of a relationship will be slowed to a snail's pace.

If confidentiality is breached in a relationship, the trust level between mentoring partners will be damaged. A confidentiality agreement sets boundaries about which subjects can be discussed and which can not. Since each mentoring partner probably holds his or her own assumptions about confidentiality, coming to consensus about these assumptions creates shared understanding and builds a confidentiality safety net that both minimizes risk to the mentoring relationship and encourages candor and risk taking.

Enabling

As the longest phase of the relationship, enabling is the time when a relationship is most vulnerable to derailment. The protracted length of this phase can leave a partnership susceptible to burnout and boredom. Mentoring partners often become complacent, conversation grows lackluster, and the relationship just fades out (Dunham, 2003).

One effective safety net for this phase is establishing a regular feedback mechanism. Ongoing feedback helps the partners build and maintain the relationship, monitor process, measure progress, foster reflection, and assess learning outcomes. On an organizational level, facilitated networking sessions can help address the need for ongoing support. Establishing a safe forum for raising questions, sharing concerns, benchmarking progress, and sharing best practices are in themselves safety nets. By asking such questions as "Are we moving as fast as we ought to be? Have we done what we are supposed to? Are we on track? How would somebody else handle this situation?" participants validate their actions. It may also spur them on to consider new options for improved mentoring practice.

Coming to Closure

The closure experience can be a rich developmental opportunity for mentors and mentees to process, integrate, and celebrate learning; redefine relationships; and move on. The act of coming to closure ensures learning even if a relationship ends earlier than expected. In this way, it offers safety nets and makes closure a face-saving, no-fault, positive learning experience.

To a certain degree, closure starts at the beginning of a relationship. During the negotiating phase, partners should talk about what coming to closure might look like. The best way to do this is to consider conditions under which coming to closure might occur (for example, conflict, promotion, end of the year) and agree about how to handle them. The organization can facilitate the closure process by setting up just-in-time training prior to the anticipated time of closure. Providing guidelines for closure, opportunities for role play, and a suggested timeline helps ensure that a mentoring closure conversation takes place.

Exhibit 12.1, Proactive Phase-Related Safety Nets, identifies the focus and key components of each mentoring phase and identifies some of the numerous safety nets that mentoring partners and their organizations might consider putting in place.

Preventing Mentoring Roadblocks

When left unattended, stumbling blocks become mentoring roadblocks, suddenly bringing the mentoring activity to a screeching halt within an organization. A parallel can be drawn to a motor vehicle accident that starts out as simply a two-car collision but through a chain reaction involves a dozen vehicles. In reality, far more than the dozen cars and the people within them are affected. The pile-up creates a roadblock, with cars lined up on the highway for miles going nowhere. Drivers and passengers are confused, anxious, angry, and frustrated.

Safety nets in motor vehicle terms can prevent a roadblock such as this one from occurring, or to some degree at least minimize it. Monitoring of weather systems and road conditions, deploying sanding trucks or snow plows, posting signs, and broadcasting warnings encouraging drivers to stay alert can all help. Once the roadblock has occurred, additional efforts are required to remove the obstacles.

The first step in a proactive approach to obstacles is to consider each of the hallmarks. If any of the hallmarks is missing or weak, it's an indicator of a potential mentoring roadblock. The mentoring culture audit tool (Appendix One) offers a tool to help you focus on the work to be done. The second step is to use the tools presented in each chapter to explore various approaches to addressing potential obstacles.

Reactive Approaches to Obstacles

A successful mentoring culture is resilient and prepares itself to deal with unexpected obstacles when they occur. Resilience makes the difference in the capacity to do so. The right people and the right process at the right time all contribute to the resilience of a mentoring culture. The combination is not possible without an established and disciplined approach for responding to stumbling blocks and roadblocks when they occur.

EXHIBIT 12.1

Proactive Phase-Related Safety Nets

Mentoring Phase	Focus	Key Components of the Phase	Safety Net Examples	
			Mentoring Partners	Organizational
Preparing	• Self-preparation and relationship preparation	• Expectations and motivation • Reflections on mentoring experiences • Self-reflection on learning • Points of connection and common ground • Identification of learning needs and broadly defined learning goals • Awareness of learning style(s)	• Identify areas for personal learning and development. • Hold initial conversation to determine if there is a good learning fit. • Voluntarily participate.	• Establish and communicate guidelines for mentor and mentee selection.
Negotiating	• Establishing relationship safety nets	• Goal definition • Identification of success criteria and measurement • A structure of mutual responsibility in place • Accountability assurances • Protocols for addressing stumbling blocks • Mentoring agreement • Partnership work plan	• Come to consensus about confidentiality, mutual accountability, and use of meeting time. • Agree how to ensure that closure will be a meaningful learning experience.	• Provide tools, models, and training to support mentoring partners in setting up safety nets.
Enabling	• Implementing the relationship	• Support • Challenge • Vision • Feedback	• Ensure ongoing feedback • Revisit mentoring agreements	• Facilitated networking sessions

Mentoring Phase	Focus	Key Components of the Phase	Safety Net Examples	
			Mentoring Partners	Organizational
Coming to closure	• Making closure a learning experience	• Learning conclusion • Integrating learning • Celebrating success • Redefining the relationship • Moving on	• Plan for closure • Pay attention to signals	• Offer training to help mentoring partners bring their relationships to closure in a way that results in meaningful learning for all parties.

Root-cause analysis offers a disciplined approach for making sure that the obstacle itself is being addressed, not just the symptom of the problem. Take, for example, a mentoring coordinator whom no one ever contacts for advice, support, or information. Root-cause analysis requires us to probe further:

Q: Why doesn't anyone call the mentoring coordinator?

A: No one calls her because they think they don't need her.

Q: Why do they think they don't need her?

A: They have no idea what she does.

Q: Why?

A: No one has ever told them.

Q: Why?

A: Her roles and responsibilities have never been clearly defined.

The root cause of the problem (the mentoring coordinator never gets called) is a lack of clarity and communication about the mentoring coordinator's roles and responsibilities. If these roles and responsibilities are clarified and a job description developed and disseminated, the "problem" might disappear; people would use her services, if they knew what she is supposed to be doing.

Overcoming Stumbling Blocks

It is not always possible to anticipate stumbling blocks in a mentoring relationship. Consider the example of Matt and Bill from the beginning of this chapter. Under better circumstances, just-in-time coaching might give Matt the courage he needs to ask Bill to find him another mentor before leaving the company. The organization can also do a better job in helping Bill transition Matt to another mentoring relationship.

Even with ground rules in place to safeguard confidentiality, sometimes it is broken and the trust in a mentoring relationship is undermined. If both partners want to continue the relationship, it may be helpful for one or both of them to look for outside coaching assistance to help them reestablish trust. But if the mentee, for example, does not feel able to confront the mentor and chooses not to deal with the situation, candor may be undermined to such a degree that there is no point in continuing the relationship. In such a case, closing the relationship before it becomes toxic is required. Having the safety net of an agreement already in place to facilitate closure makes it easier.

Mentor burnout is another potential stumbling block. Mentoring burnout can surface for a variety of reasons, often because a mentor attempts to do too much for a mentee, the mentoring relationship becomes too time-consuming, the mentee makes too many demands, or a mentor takes on too many mentees at once. A burnt-out mentor is no longer effective in the relationship. An experienced and properly trained mentor recognizes this and asks for help or to transition the mentee to a new relationship.

The need to address a stumbling block reactively is necessitated whenever the proactive approach is not working. Although the responsibility for dealing with a mentoring stumbling block rests with the mentoring partners, the organization can establish safety nets to help partners themselves deal with the obstacles in the best possible way. The proactive step of offering mentoring coaching and assistance often acts as a safety net.

Clearing Mentoring Roadblocks

As in a multi-car accident, once a roadblock has occurred considerable time, effort, and stamina are required to clear it. People become increasingly anxious, uncomfortable, and irritable with the passage of time. To resolve the situation, state troopers arrive to clear the road to let emergency vehicles through. If it's severe enough, perhaps helicopters bring in water, food, and blankets that volunteers distribute to stranded motorists. To prevent further accidents, roads are sanded and plowed. The coordinated and comprehensive response to the roadblock resolves the situation and generates a proactive response to prevent further accidents. Similarly, in addressing mentoring roadblocks we need to respond in a coordinated and comprehensive way to the immediate situation and learn from the experience to do something differently in the future.

Stumbling blocks slow down or impede forward movement in a mentoring relationship. They require a personal or organizational response or action if one is to move on. Developing proactive and reactive safety nets helps people avert and manage stumbling blocks. Exercise 12.1, Developing Safety Nets for Stumbling Blocks, is an opportunity to review a list of common stumbling blocks and decide which proactive and reactive safety nets you might consider for mentoring in your organization.

EXERCISE 12.1

Developing Safety Nets for Stumbling Blocks

Instructions: Review the list of common stumbling blocks on the left. With your development team, decide which approaches you could take to prevent each block from occurring in your organization and how the organization should respond if it does occur. Be sure to consider who should be involved in both approaches.

Stumbling Block	Safety Net	
	Proactive	**Reactive**
Mentee or mentor moves to another location		
Mentor leaves the organization and mentee is left behind		
Mentee doesn't respond to mentor's concerns or suggestions about a particular issue; mentor doesn't feel valued		
Mentee starts confiding serious personal problems to mentor		
Mentee calls mentor too frequently for advice		
Mentor gets picked for a new assignment that is time-intensive and sensitive		
Mentee doesn't show up or follow through		
Partners feel distance growing between them and just can't seem to communicate in an open and authentic way		
Mentee is too high-maintenance for mentor		
Mentee develops an attitude of entitlement and is frequently disappointed		

Gaps in the Net

Safety nets are not always fail-safe. Mentoring casualties—negative consequences resulting from benign neglect, lack of information, external circumstances, and so forth—do occur. The first line of defense is to be proactive by doing a walk-through of mentoring in your organization or program. Examine the flow of your processes and programs for potential stumbling blocks, roadblocks, and mentoring casualties. Draw or diagram the process and look at the materials; and as you walk through it step by step, determine where the possible gaps might be. To take one simple but illuminating example, does one "apply" to participate in the mentoring program? If so, where are applications available? What is the selection procedure? What happens if there aren't enough mentors available? When are participants notified? When does the training take place? What happens if someone doesn't go through the training? When do mentoring relationships begin?

For each step of the process, detail what happens and in what order. It is sometimes helpful to have people role-play the various steps so that a group can look at the whole picture as well as the detail. Along the way, consider where someone might get lost in your process, and identify potential stumbling blocks and roadblocks.

Next, establish reliable safety nets on multiple levels to minimize the risk to individuals and the organization. Develop a contingency plan for overcoming stumbling blocks and roadblocks. Identify specific policies and procedures. In doing so, be careful to consider these questions:

- Who needs to be involved?
- What is the process?
- What should the timing be?

Once you have completed this process, perhaps in group sessions, use Exercise 12.2, Safety Nets, to record the stumbling blocks and roadblocks you identify. Then identify the people and processes you must put in place if you are to build in an appropriate safety net.

Safety Nets: Reflection on Practice

Safety nets, whether visible or invisible, fulfill a basic human need for security. Their presence enables a mentoring partnership to manage stumbling blocks successfully and an organization to anticipate and deal effectively with obstacles.

Hard work is required to create and maintain strong, stable, and resilient safety nets. It is the powerful combination of the right people

EXERCISE 12.2		
Safety Nets		
Type of Obstacle	**Safety Net**	
	Proactive	**Reactive**
Stumbling blocks		
Roadblocks		

and the right processes coming together at the point of need. Whenever the combination is present, safety nets are highly reliable. Safety nets support individuals and organizations even during a time of great challenge by simultaneously encouraging risk taking and reducing risk.

Under the best circumstances, there are instances where use of safety nets is inappropriate or unwarranted. Their purpose, after all, is not to save or rescue, but only to support and strengthen individuals and organizations as they learn and create a sustainable mentoring culture. The presence of too many safety nets (or the wrong kind) may make it too easy to opt out of a mentoring relationship without doing the real work required to grow the relationship and accomplish the learning goals. The road to learning and growing a relationship can be difficult. Being able to stay on track as the terrain gets a little rough can enhance the learning for both parties. Still, there are circumstances in which it is not in the best interest of the parties for the relationship to continue. In either case, having the safety net of a coach available to provide support and counsel can be beneficial.

Having taken stock of current mentoring efforts and examining the hallmarks of a mentoring culture, we now shift our focus to the future and discuss ways to create a vibrant mentoring culture that enhances, sustains, and renews organizational mentoring.

Moving on: Mentoring and the Future

I choose to risk my significance,
To live so that which came to me as seed
Goes to the next as blossom
And that which came to me as blossom,
Goes on as fruit.

—DAWNA MARKOVA (2000)

THE RESPONSIBILITY for making this a better world for the next generation is the price we pay for living on the planet in this time and place. In a real sense, generativity is our collective bet on the future. It demands that we each choose to risk significance by caring for, being concerned about, and staying connected to each other and to the next generation. This responsibility is a sacred trust and not to be taken lightly. If we truly are to enrich and preserve the quality of life for humankind, we must engage in meaningful learning, deepen individual and collective capacity, and strengthen our relationships.

Mentoring relationships offer an opportunity for individuals to nurture seeds in others so they might become blossoms and blossoms might become fruit, which then nourishes others. When mentoring relationships are rooted in the fertile soil of a mentoring culture, they also enrich the quality of organizational life. The lessons learned there transcend specific mentoring relationships and blossom into fruit in other relationships, both inside and outside the workplace. In its wider scope, mentoring ultimately enriches humanity by helping people connect to a higher purpose that has the potential to change the world.

A mentoring culture fulfills the promise of generativity in many ways. It is a culture of intention and grows out of an organization's conscious desire to continuously improve its business results by building and strengthening the internal capacity of its people. A mentoring culture is one of inclusion and sensitivity; it values, honors and celebrates the uniqueness of the individual. A mentoring culture is a culture of action through learning; it continuously strives to create value at all levels of the organization.

From Seed to Blossom

The presence of a mentoring culture enables an organization to augment learning, leverage energy, maximize time and effort, and better utilize its resources. Individual programs achieve greater long-term impact because a mentoring culture sustains a continuum of expectation, which in turn, creates standards and consistency of good mentoring practice.

An organization doesn't need to be large to be successful at mentoring. However, it must be willing to enlarge its thinking. It doesn't need to possess extensive resources. Rather, it needs to utilize available resources wisely. It doesn't require a lot of work. Instead, it takes a commitment to do the right kind of work. And with this effort come distinct advantages. The ongoing presence of mentoring expands the opportunities for individual, personal, and professional growth and development. A mentoring culture is a powerful mechanism for achieving cultural alignment.

Launching a mentoring program without the presence of a mentoring culture lessens its chances of long-term sustainability and decreases the likelihood that the program will grow and thrive over time. The more anchors that are put in place to support mentoring, the easier it is to sustain a mentoring culture. And the benefits can come quickly: Implementation of a mentoring program often becomes the impetus for creating a culture that is more focused on learning and development.

From Blossom to Fruit

Movement and time are fundamental to creating a mentoring culture. As long as there is movement, however slow, there is progress; without it, there is stagnation. The constant motion inherent in the learning process (for the individual, the group, and the organization) generates organizational momentum.

Similarly, it takes time to cultivate relationships, to build awareness and understanding, and to establish the hallmarks of a mentoring culture. Mentoring time must be allocated by agreement and not begrudged or resented. Although mentoring may, in the short run, seem like just another demand on one's time, the long-term return on the investment is enormous. How long does it take to see benefits? The short answer is the long answer: it depends on where you start your journey and where you want to go. The size, scope, and significance of the mentoring effort will affect the time required to do it well.

Sometimes the pace of the change we experience in our organizations today feels faster than the speed of light. Organizations move from one initiative to another with barely enough time to reflect upon, let alone capture, learning along the way. Consequently, we repeat the same mistakes and new initiatives are not as successful as we would have hoped. A true mentoring culture makes time to reflect on its mentoring practices and identify lessons learned. This adds to the culture's resiliency and flexibility and enables it to effectively respond to and accommodate change as it occurs.

In a mentoring culture people engage in anticipatory thinking. They realistically focus on the future and don't allow themselves to get blindsided by surprises, whether conflicts with projects that might be launched at the same time, economic issues, or regulatory changes, for example.

Cultural Integration: A Caveat

As more and more hallmarks take shape, a cultural shift becomes evident. In time, mentoring becomes embedded into the fiber of the organization and mentoring becomes a cultural expectation. In this process, the mentoring culture becomes flexible enough to accommodate change and establishes clear ownership within the organization on many levels. Along the way, there are a number of points to keep in mind:

- Make sure the scope, magnitude and form that your mentoring culture takes fits your organization.

- Learn as much as you can about your own culture to determine if a match exists between mentoring wants and needs.

- Be open to the process. Expect to make changes along the way.

- Assume that your efforts will take time to come to fruition.

- Think "systems." Consider how you leverage and maximize both people and process.

- Maintain the big-picture approach. The expression "think globally, act locally" holds particularly true here. It helps align and integrate mentoring efforts.

- Prepare to face and deal with the "time-is-money" mantra.

- Seek to combine quality effort with excellence of mentoring practices.

- Keep it simple and manageable. Trying to do everything at once is bound to be frustrating and overcomplicates matters.

- Start where there is the most likelihood of success. Identify the most doable aspects of your plan or a few immediate goals and get some success (and credibility) under your belt. Early success matters.

- Live process improvement. Use what you learn as you learn it to strengthen your efforts and inform organizational mentoring practices.

- Establish ownership for mentoring in the organization.

- Make sure that your leadership is on board and that they are willing to actively support the mentoring effort.

It cannot be overemphasized: leadership is indispensable to success. Leaders must be involved from the very beginning of the effort and stay involved throughout. Far too often, leaders "deputize" others to carry the mentoring banner for them. This may ease their schedules and seem necessary, but it is insufficient to generate significant traction to get the mentoring effort moving. Leaders must be visible and supportive to continuously create value for mentoring. Mentoring leadership succession needs to be addressed proactively; if it is not, an organization is likely to find itself spending the same time, money, and effort over and over again without significant movement. When leadership is not present and accounted for in the mentoring effort, people take notice.

Sustainability requires the attention and time of the organization's leaders. According to Frances Hesselbein (Hesselbein and Johnston, 2002), organizational leaders must:

- Focus on those few initiatives that will make a difference (in this case mentoring)

- Deploy people and allocate resources where they will have an impact

- Plan thoughtfully for leadership transition

- Groom successors

- Disperse the task of leadership across the organization until there are leaders at every level

- Allocate funds for leadership development opportunities as well as resources

With appropriate leadership and time, each of the eight mentoring hallmarks takes shape and a cultural shift begins. Each hallmark adds to the robustness and resilience of a mentoring culture and contributes to sustainability of organizational mentoring efforts. Sustainability allows flexibility and adjustment in response to changing circumstances without losing the integrity of best mentoring practices.

Reflection Is the Practice

Poetry and prose offer a perch for my personal reflections on practice. I have used quotations from a range of pieces throughout the book, hoping to inspire you to think more deeply and reflectively about the mentoring practices in your organization. Here, I offer one more: "Do not now seek the answers, which cannot be given you because you would not be able to live them. And the point is, to live everything. Live the questions now. Perhaps you will gradually, without noticing it, Live along some distant day into the answer" (Rilke, 1954, p. 35).

In writing this book, I wanted to raise questions that would lead you to reflect more deeply about what mentoring might mean in your organization and how you might take your organizational mentoring practices to a higher level. The array of tools I've presented in Creating a Mentoring Culture were designed to stimulate that reflection and enlarge your thinking about what is possible. There are questions that remain that only you, or the people within your organization, can answer. Use the book as a roadmap and the hallmarks as guideposts in your journey. My hope is that they will help you live the questions. For you will need to do so in order to live the culture. Living the questions will, in turn, let your organization "live into answers." The journey will require you to think bigger, bolder, and broader and achieve much deeper insight. The practice of mentoring in your organization can be far richer and more generative than you ever thought possible. It's a journey well worth taking.

Remember there will always be questions. Some you will be able to answer and some you will not. Be patient with the process and with yourself. The seeds will grow blossoms and the blossoms will bear fruit—if you remember to ask the questions and have the patience to live the answers.

Tomorrow will be here before we know it. What is your next step in preparing for that tomorrow?

Appendix One

Mentoring Culture Audit

THE MENTORING CULTURE AUDIT assists you in diagnosing, analyzing, and prioritizing where your organization can best focus its time and effort in creating a mentoring culture. No matter where your organization is—just getting started, in the midst of one or more mentoring initiatives, stalled out in the middle of a process, or needing to evaluate mentoring progress—this tool can add value to your efforts. Completing the audit will help your organization decide how to use the resources provided in this book and on the accompanying CD.

One advantage of this tool is that it can be used to engage people in focused conversation about organizational mentoring practices. Particularly if your organization is large or has a complex structure, it is best to get feedback from a range of people in your organization on the Mentoring Culture Audit. If you don't know for certain whether a specific mentoring practice exists in your organization, you might consider including input from others who are more involved in day-to-day mentoring (trainers, supervisors, mentoring coaches, department managers). The Mentoring Culture Audit can also be used as an informational practice guide to heighten awareness, raise questions, promote systems thinking, and uncover possibilities for mentoring that an organization may not have previously considered.

The Mentoring Culture Audit presented in this appendix (and on the CD, for those who prefer working with an electronic version) consists of fifty of the best practice items that together create a full and vibrant mentoring culture. On the right are four columns. As you review each item, indicate your response by placing a checkmark in the appropriate column. Answer always if the practice is consistently present. Answer sometimes if the practice is present occasionally or fairly often. If the practice is never present, then put a checkmark under the never column. If you are unable to place a checkmark in any of these columns because you don't have enough information or are uncertain, place a checkmark in the don't know column.

Exhibit A.1

Mentoring Culture Audit

	Always	Sometimes	Never	Don't Know
A1. Learning is an established organizational priority.				
A2. Organizational leaders actively promote individual and organizational learning.				
A3. The organization is fully committed to the development of its people.				
A4. The organizational culture supports mentoring.				
A5. Mentoring as practiced in the organization incorporates best-practice models of adult learning.				
A SUBTOTAL				
B6. The right people are in place to support, manage, and coordinate mentoring efforts.				
B7. A mentoring leadership succession plan has been established.				
B8. Mentoring partners are supported in taking time for mentoring.				
B9. Technology and knowledge resources that promote and support mentoring are accessible, up-to-date, and put to use.				
B10. An adequate budget and explicit financial commitment supports organizational mentoring.				
B SUBTOTAL				
I-11. Roles, responsibilities, and expectations of mentors, mentees, and other individuals who interact with and support mentoring relationships are defined and aligned with each other.				
I-12. Mentoring as it is currently practiced clearly aligns with the organization's values.				
I-13. A strategic process for maintaining mentoring alignment is established.				
I-14. Mentoring is aligned with business goals and strategies.				
I-15. Mentoring is linked to leadership development.				
I SUBTOTAL				
II-16. The purpose, scope, and benefits of mentoring are well articulated and linked to business results.				
II-17. Mentoring goals are clearly defined, and criteria for organizational mentoring success are established.				
II-18. Progress toward achievement of learning goals by mentoring partners is monitored.				

	Always	Sometimes	Never	Don't Know
II-19. Mentoring results are measured over time.				
II-20. Mentoring process improvements are timely.				
II SUBTOTAL				
III-21. Mentoring communication messages to stakeholders are consistent, timely, and regular.				
III-22. Mentoring communication is strategic.				
III-23. A shared vocabulary of mentoring practice is consistent throughout the organization.				
III-24. Multiple organizational venues for communicating about mentoring are used.				
III-25. Mentoring communication is sensitive to culture and diversity.				
III SUBTOTAL				
IV-26. Mentoring is consistently creating positive value for the organization and its people.				
IV-27. Best mentoring practices are regularly shared in multiple forms and forums.				
IV-28. Excellence in mentoring is recognized, rewarded, and celebrated.				
IV-29. Senior management visibility adds to the credibility of mentoring within the organization.				
IV-30. Leaders are perceived as mentoring role models.				
IV SUBTOTAL				
V-31. People participate in mentoring relationships enthusiastically.				
V-32. Mentors and mentees engage in multiple mentoring relationships throughout their career.				
V-33. There is positive buzz about mentoring in the organization.				
V-34. Mentors and mentees request additional opportunities to learn how to increase their mentoring effectiveness.				
V-35. Individual mentoring partnerships meet regularly.				
V SUBTOTAL				

	Always	Sometimes	Never	Don't Know
VI-36. Multiple types of mentoring are supported (one-to-one, group, distance, cross-cultural).				
VI-37. Mentoring coaching and information is available at point of need to support individuals engaged in mentoring relationships.				
VI-38. Existing mentoring opportunities are appropriate and broad enough to meet the diverse learning needs within the organization.				
VI-39. The organization supports informal and formal mentoring.				
VI-40. Innovative models of mentoring are encouraged and supported.				
VI SUBTOTAL				
VII-41. Mentoring briefings, trainings, and education sessions are regularly offered.				
VII-42. Training and education are provided for individuals who are at different levels of mentoring readiness.				
VII-43. Next-step training and just-in-time coaching are available for those individuals charged with the responsibility of supporting mentors and mentees.				
VII-44. Individual mentoring training events and education offered by the organization are part of a broad and strategic mentoring training platform.				
VII-45. Mentoring education and training is timely, relevant, and up-to-date.				
VII SUBTOTAL				
VIII-46. Confidentiality of those engaged in mentoring relationships is safeguarded.				
VIII-47. Safety nets help individuals and the organization address mentoring obstacles and stumbling blocks.				
VIII-48. The organization consciously anticipates challenges and assesses opportunities that could affect mentoring implementation or sustainability.				
VIII-49. Mentors and mentees make time for mentoring a priority.				
VIII-50. Mentoring ownership and management are well established within the organization.				
VIII SUBTOTAL				

Reviewing Your Answers

If your organization is just starting a mentoring initiative, it is important to assure that A1, A2, A3, B6, and B10 are in place initially. It may take some time and work to embed A4 as an organizational practice.

If one or more mentoring initiatives have been implemented and are working well, you were probably able to check at least three of the mentoring practices in each category with sometimes or always, especially if your organization has a prior commitment to learning and a solid infrastructure to support mentoring efforts.

If mentoring is stalled out within your organization, you are likely to find whole categories for which you checked sometimes, never, or don't know.

Tabulating Your Results

Record column subtotals for each section in the appropriate column of the scoring grid. Add the number of checkmarks in each column and insert it in the appropriate space at the bottom of each column.

Exhibit A.2

Tabulating Results

Section	Always	Sometimes	Never	Don't Know
A				
B				
I				
II				
III				
IV				
V				
VI				
VII				
VIII				
Column Total				

Understanding Your Responses

- *Always.* If most of the checkmarks end up in the always column, you are already living the mentoring culture. It has become a seamless part of how you do business in your organization, and the results from this audit can help you continue to enhance your mentoring practices. If you have checked some practices as sometimes or never present, or you don't know, then those are areas that may need attention.

- *Sometimes.* If many or most of your answers lie in this column, there is much work to be accomplished to embed specific mentoring best practices in your organization. To do this, you'll need to narrow the scope and focus of the work. The practices you've selected become the broad agenda from which to identify and prioritize action goals and process improvements.

- *Never.* Any checkmark in the never column indicates a specific practice that needs time and attention. If most of your checkmarks lie in this column, know that you have a lot of work ahead of you, particularly if section A and B responses are also never. It is not impossible to create a mentoring culture; just realize that doing so is challenging and will demand time and careful tending.

- *Don't know.* A response of don't know is an invitation to learn from others in your organization. There might be more going on than you realize. Your perceptions may be biased, or others may be privy to information that you don't have. Engaging others in full discussion of these items presents a real opportunity to promote ownership and knowledge about the dynamics of a mentoring culture. If other people don't know, perhaps there is an underlying communication problem that goes deeper than just mentoring.

Note that it is unlikely for every one of these fifty best practices to be present in a mentoring culture at any one time. The more consistently the practices (of each section) are present, the fuller, more robust, and sustainable the mentoring culture is likely to be.

Moving Forward

The Mentoring Culture Audit presents a menu of mentoring best practices that promote sustainability in a mentoring culture. A mentoring culture is an iterative culture that is always in the process of becoming; some things are never completed. The very act of working toward best practices is a best practice. Consequently it is helpful to come back to this tool periodically and use it to track organizational progress.

Two categories of best practices comprise the items in this audit: building blocks and mentoring hallmarks. Building blocks are the preconditions or practices that build the foundation to support the process of creating a mentoring culture: cultural congruence and learning, and infrastructure. Hallmarks are distinctive clusters of mentoring practices that define the salient features of a mentoring culture. There are eight mentoring culture hallmarks in all. Building blocks and hallmarks must be present to create a vibrant and full mentoring culture.

Your checkmarks will help you determine where to begin your efforts. If you found that you have many checkmarks in the never and sometimes columns in a specific section of the audit, focus your effort where there is the greatest likelihood of success.

Exhibit A.3

Understanding Results

Audit Section		Related Chapter Number and Title
Building Blocks:		
A	2	Connecting Culture and Mentoring
B	4	Infrastructure
Hallmarks:		
I	5	Alignment
II	6	Accountability
III	7	Communication
IV	8	Value and Visibility
V	9	Demand
VI	10	Multiple Mentoring Opportunities
VII	11	Education and Training
VIII	12	Safety Nets

Appendix Two

Digging Deeper

CREATING A MENTORING CULTURE is a learning process for those leading and supporting the culture and for the organization as a whole. When learning is limited only to those actively engaged in the mentoring relationships, it inhibits the full development of a mentoring culture.

The titles below will help you extend and expand your learning journey. My purpose is to include pragmatic resources that offer models and tools that complement and relate to the topics covered in *Creating a Mentoring Culture*. I encourage you to consider these as a starting point and add your own resources to the list as you discover them.

The resources are grouped under specific chapter headings, yet the subject matter often transcends those groupings. An overview of each resource presents key insights and practical tips related to mentoring in an organizational context.

Taking Stock

Bell, C. *Managers as Mentors: Building Partnerships for Learning*. San Francisco: Berrett-Koehler, 2002.

> In many ways, Bell's approach to mentoring parallels my own. We share many of the same mentoring metaphors (the journey, for example) and the emphasis on learning. We also share a strong commitment to the development processes inherent in mentoring relationships. Bell's stories are rich and colorful. They are motivating and inspiring.

Zachary, L. *The Mentor's Guide: Facilitating Effective Learning Relationships.* San Francisco: Jossey-Bass, 2000.

> My earlier book takes an in-depth look at the dynamics of a mentoring relationship. I explore the four predictable phases of a mentoring relationship that make up the mentoring cycle and then describe the key components of each phase. *The Mentor's Guide* offers templates, exercises, and tips to help the mentor grow and steer the mentoring relationship in the most effective way to facilitate learning and growth.

Connecting Culture and Mentoring

Cloke, K., and Goldsmith, J. *The Art of Waking People Up: Cultivating Awareness and Authenticity at Work.* San Francisco: Jossey-Bass, 2003.

> "Waking up" describes the process of becoming more engaged, authentic, and productive at work. The metaphor "waking up" builds from the awareness level where information, learning, and evolution of change begin. Cloke and Goldsmith assert that without feedback (what was), coaching (what is), and mentoring (what could be), waking up is hard. This book is a great resource of practical tips, steps, and models that can potentially energize and transform the workplace. The authors' recommendations for rebuilding trust in the workplace, providing effective turnaround feedback, and resolving conflict resonate loud and clear for those engaged in mentoring implementation.

Daloz, L. A. *Mentor: Guiding the Journey of Adult Learners.* San Francisco: Jossey-Bass, 1999.

> Daloz adopts the metaphor of "the guide" to describe the essential role of the mentor in accompanying the learner on a journey. He reflects on his personal stories in guiding the development of adult learners. Daloz's rich metaphors and in-depth descriptions provide a lens to understanding the adult learning process. To help us on our journey, he offers examples and practical approaches for transforming both the learning and the learner.

Marsick, V. J., and Watkins, K. E. *Facilitating Learning Organizations: Making Learning Count.* Brookfield, Vt.: Gower, 1999.

> Implementing a learning culture is not a smooth process; it involves experimentation, close monitoring of results, and making adjustments. This book provides practical insights from the firsthand experiences of leaders who are transforming their organizations into learning cultures. The ability to envision, support, and integrate learning with the

strategic goals of an organization is essential to successfully facilitating a learning organization. Because effective mentoring facilitates the creation and sharing of knowledge, a mentoring culture is often a key indicator of a learning organization.

Schein, E. *The Corporate Culture Survival Guide: Sense and Nonsense About Culture Change.* San Francisco: Jossey-Bass, 1999.

Leaders who want to create a mentoring culture need to understand the behaviors, values, and assumptions that are at play in their organization's culture. Schein demystifies corporate culture by presenting lessons from Atari, Apple, IBM, DEC, and Procter & Gamble that help the reader better understand the challenges of aligning culture with organizational direction. He demonstrates how corporate culture influences corporate performance and provides tools for understanding corporate culture and facilitating change within that culture.

Watkins, K. E., and Marsick V. J. *Sculpting the Learning Organization: Lessons in the Art and Science of Systemic Change.* San Francisco: Jossey-Bass, 1993.

A mentoring culture contributes to individual, team, and organizational learning. Watkins and Marsick describe a set of "action imperatives" that create learning opportunities, promote dialogue, encourage collaboration, establish systems, empower people, and connect with the environment. Their seven C's of a learning organization (continuous, collaborative, connected, collective, creative, captured and codified, and capacity building) provide a template for strengthening mentoring within an organizational context.

Planning Implementation

Caffarella, R. S. *Planning Programs for Adult Learners: A Practical Guide for Educators, Trainers, and Staff Developers* (2nd edition). San Francisco: Jossey-Bass, 2002.

Caffarella's twelve-component model, the "Interactive Model of Programming Planning," underscores the importance of both people and process and offers a useful framework for assisting those who are implementing a mentoring initiative. Each component is supported with clear description, practical tips, and ideas related to concrete tasks. Application exercises are provided to assist the reader in applying the material and can easily be adapted as support material for mentors to help mentees articulate their learning objectives.

Moving Forward: Mentoring at Work

Infrastructure

Charan, R., Drotter, S., and Noel, J. *The Leadership Pipeline: How to Build the Leadership-Powered Company.* San Francisco: Jossey-Bass, 2001.

> This book explores the process of building a pipeline of internal organization leaders by describing the critical passages a leader must navigate and providing appropriate development tasks for navigating those passages. Critical leadership passages include managing self and managing others (manager, functional manager, business manager, group manager, enterprise manager). Each "passage" represents a major change in job requirements that translate into new skill requirements and new work values. *The Leadership Pipeline* is a useful guide for organizational mentoring implementers and those who seek support in their mentoring relationship.

Conger, J. A., and Benjamin, B. *Building Leaders: How Successful Companies Develop the Next Generation.* San Francisco: Jossey-Bass, 1999.

> Leadership is a vital component of the infrastructure required for creating a mentoring culture. Growing the next generation of leaders is one of the most frequently articulated business reasons for mentoring. Conger and Benjamin present proven techniques and discuss common pitfalls to avoid in building leadership talent at all levels. Coaching and mentoring are presented as vehicles for leadership development and are set in the context of adult learning.

Kouzes, J. M., and Posner, B. Z. *The Leadership Challenge.* San Francisco: Jossey-Bass, 2002.

> Kouzes and Posner identify five exemplary practices of leaders—modeling the way, inspiring a shared vision, challenging the process, enabling others to act, and encouraging the heart. Each practice is an essential element in creating a mentoring culture and ensuring future organizational leadership. Each practice influences the others and is necessary to achieve excellence, credibility, and sustainability. Any mentoring program that strives to build leadership capacity must begin by clearly defining and articulating the leadership practices it seeks to support. The authors offer activities and engaging questions that coaches, mentors, and organizational leaders will find useful for triggering deeper reflection, stimulating learning, and ensuring future mentoring leadership.

Merrill, D. W., and Reid, R. H. *Personal Styles and Effective Performance: Make Your Style Work for You.* Boca Raton, Fla.: CRC Press, 1999.

> The ability to build and maintain relationships is critical to organizational success and ultimately impacts workplace satisfaction. The effectiveness of mentoring relationships is dependent on the ability to establish meaningful relationships. Merrill and Reid demonstrate how social behaviors—what an individual says and does—form exhibited and predictable patterns that can be identified and responded to. When these behaviors (driver, analytical, expressive, and amiable) are mutually understood, people are more likely to create productive and significant relationships as well as increase the quality of interaction and learning.

Murray, M. *Beyond the Myths and Magic of Mentoring: How to Facilitate an Effective Mentoring Process.* San Francisco: Jossey-Bass, 2001.

> This revised and updated version of Murray's book offers practical organizational models, checklists, flow charts, and steps for implementing mentoring programs. Murray focuses on "facilitated mentoring," a term she coined and defines as "a series of processes designed to create effective mentoring relationships; guide the desired behavior change of those involved; and evaluate the results for the protégés." Readers will find her set of criteria and processes for qualifying mentors and strategies for matching mentoring pairs particularly helpful.

Alignment

Block, P. *The Empowered Manager: Positive Political Skills at Work.* San Francisco: Jossey-Bass, 1987.

> Block emphasizes the relevance of mission and vision for organizations that seek to realign corporate culture and reenergize leadership. In this now classic book, Block provides practical guidance on how to negotiate support and strengthen alliances, prerequisites for fostering ownership in a mentoring culture. The second section on political skills at work speaks to the realities of the political process in organizations today. It teaches lessons that can be applied to the processes of building support for a mentoring vision.

Carter, L., Giber, D., and Goldsmith, M. (Eds.). *Linkage Inc.'s Best Practices in Organization Development and Change.* San Francisco: Jossey-Bass/Pfeiffer, 2001.

> This comprehensive resource focuses on the topics of change, leadership development, recruitment and retention, performance management,

coaching, and mentoring. It provides a practical framework for design, implementation, and evaluation. Specific guidelines, competency models, forms, and training enable readers to immediately apply many of the parts to their own mentoring efforts.

Feldman, D. C. (Ed.). *Work Careers: A Developmental Perspective.* San Francisco: Jossey-Bass, 2002.

Feldman, together with a panel of experts, explores current theories about how careers develop at different stages of a work life. The basic building blocks of careers (personality traits, vocational interests, skills, and abilities) are examined as they influence choice in career identity. The authors show how personal life issues interact with work demands and affect career decisions. This book helps explain how changes in organizational context facilitate and frustrate individual developmental needs. It also demonstrates the critical role of organizational policy in facilitating or impeding employees' developmental opportunities such as mentoring.

Simonsen, P. *Promoting a Development Culture in Your Organization.* Palo Alto, Calif.: Davies Black, 1997.

Simonsen highlights specific ways to create a development culture—one in which an employee's career development aligns with business needs. She presents examples of how to assess current readiness and needs and how to overcome common objections to promoting a development culture. Specific roles of senior management, managers and supervisors, and mentors are defined. A marketing strategy is provided to identify critical steps for effective implementation.

Accountability

Leider, R. J. *The Power of Purpose.* San Francisco: Berrett-Koehler, 1997.

Many formal mentoring programs focus on the development of career path, leadership, and advancement. Yet, many mentors and mentees find their most satisfying experiences in the arena of personal development and growth. Leider's book is an excellent resource for mentoring partners to explore the deeper meaning of work and life. It is equally useful to those engaged in creating mentoring initiatives and a mentoring culture because of the way it frames the question and the work of purpose. A set of questions and questionnaires work as personal development tools for mentors and mentees.

Waclawski, J., and Church, A. H. *Organization Development: A Data-Driven Approach to Organizational Change.* San Francisco: Jossey-Bass, 2002.

Data-based support is often required for senior management to truly recognize the benefits of mentoring. The authors make a strong case for data collection, analysis, and feedback at the front end of any change process. They identify multiple vehicles for collecting quantitative and qualitative data including multisource feedback, personality assessments, organizational surveys, interviews, and focus groups. These tools are critical to fostering ownership for any change initiative and are particularly useful in building support for organizational mentoring.

Communication

Galpin, T. J. *The Human Side of Change: A Practical Guide to Organization Redesign.* San Francisco: Jossey-Bass, 1996.

Galpin's straightforward "cookbook" assists organizations in creating a mentoring culture. It offers models and templates for promoting organizational communication and readiness for cultural change. The models and topics are relevant and basic tools for creating a mentoring culture. The communication strategy matrix, organizational Johari window, and resistance pyramid are particularly important tools for developing comprehensive mentoring communication. His treatment of feedback, measurement, and reward and recognition is an added bonus.

Morin, W. J. *Trust Me: How to Rebuild Trust in the Workplace.* New York: Harcourt Brace Jovanovich, 1990.

The effectiveness of mentoring, as well as other organizational initiatives, depends on the degree of trust that exists in an organization. Morin addresses the challenge of restoring trust in the workplace by highlighting the shift of responsibility and expectations of the organization, the manager, and employee and how trust is impacted. *Trust Me* focuses on open realistic communication and uses corporate stories to highlight successes and failures. Readers will find the list of responsibilities for manager and subordinate in building and sustaining trust useful in helping mentors and mentees understand the dynamics of trust.

Value and Visibility

Bennis, W., Spreitzer, G. M., and Cummings, T. G. (Eds.). *The Future of Leadership: Today's Top Leadership Thinkers Speak to Tomorrow's Leaders.* San Francisco: Jossey-Bass, 2001.

Bennis has pulled together a group of scholars and experts who represent leading thinkers in management today (such as Charles Handy, Tom Peters, Edward Lawler, Jim Kouzes, and Barry Posner) and Silicon Valley entrepreneurs to present their insights and collective wisdom about the challenges leaders face. The questions that result suggest topics and areas that leaders need to ponder to prepare for the future, particularly with respect to developing organizational talent and creating meaning in the workplace. Discussion about these questions can inform and enrich conversation for mentoring partners and mentoring leaders.

Deal, T. E., and Key, M. K. *Corporate Celebration—Play, Purpose, and Profit at Work*. San Francisco: Berrett-Koehler, 1998.

Celebration is an essential part of the mentoring relationship cycle, mentoring planning, and a mentoring culture. This book makes the case for the central role of celebration in reinvigorating and reinspiring corporate life. Specific examples of corporate celebration are described and can help stimulate your thinking about ways to celebrate mentoring in your organization. "How to" principles and practices are included for making celebration meaningful: setting the stage, orchestrating the details, improvising where necessary, assuring memories, and highlighting the role of key players. The authors even include a section on "Fatal Flaws" to help the reader avoid common pitfalls.

De Pree, M. *Leading Without Power: Finding Hope in Serving Community*. San Francisco: Jossey-Bass, 2003.

Mentoring requires a commitment to realizing organizational potential. De Pree holds that "organizations need people that move relentlessly toward realizing their potential." Mentoring is one vehicle for achieving realized potential in an organization. It offers people the opportunity to learn and grow, and offers the gift of challenging work. It builds the capacity of its people and celebrates individual and collective accomplishments. This inspiring little book is big on ideas, particularly the big idea of establishing a legacy by building competency in establishing and maintaining trusting relationships. It is a perfect book for mentors and mentees to share and discuss.

Koestenbaum, P. *Leadership: The Inner Side of Greatness*. San Francisco: Jossey-Bass, 2002.

Mentoring presents an opportunity to lead by teaching leadership, empowering people, fostering autonomy, providing direction, and lending support. Insights into the characteristics of great leaders and their commonalities reveal that vision, reality, ethics, and courage are required to achieve greatness. Koestenbaum offers a leadership toolbox based on lessons learned that managers can apply to achieve and sustain personal and organizational greatness. He demonstrates that when a leader is both teacher and a learner, the people in their organizations attain a higher level of leadership.

Kouzes, J. M., and Posner, B. Z. *Encouraging the Heart: A Leader's Guide to Rewarding and Recognizing Others.* San Francisco: Jossey-Bass, 2003.

Reward, recognition, and celebration are significant factors in building and sustaining value and visibility for mentoring within an organization. These are some of the factors, according to Kouzes and Posner, that encourage the heart. Leaders have a primary responsibility to motivate those with whom they work by "putting their hearts into business and their business into their hearts." This leader's guide facilitates implementation of the seven essentials of encouraging the heart: set clear standards, expect the best, pay attention, tell the story, personal recognition, celebrate together, and set the example.

Demand

Conger, J. A. "The Necessary Art of Persuasion." *Harvard Business Review,* 1998, *76*(3), 84–95.

Persuasion and influence are important skills for leaders and are critical to the successful implementation of a mentoring program. Mentoring initiatives require management buy-in, cooperation, and participation. Persuasion can pull people together, move ideas forward, galvanize change, and forge constructive solutions. This article breaks down the art of persuasion into four critical steps: establishing credibility, framing goals around common ground, providing evidence, and connecting emotionally. Leaders who master the art of persuasion create value and visibility for mentoring within their organization much more effectively than those who do not.

Lawler, E. E. *Treat People Right! How Organizations and Individuals Can Propel Each Other into a Virtuous Spiral of Success.* San Francisco: Jossey-Bass, 2003.

A mentoring culture does not occur in a vacuum. It requires that an organization treat its people right. Treating people right produces positive long-term payoffs for organizations and the people who work in them. When organizations reward people for performance, they perform better and the organization is propelled to higher levels of performance. The organization is then able to better reward, attract, and retain more talented people. This, in turn, boosts organizational performance. The "virtuous spiral" that is created requires going far beyond simply being nice to people and treating them fairly. It means developing a wide array of human capital management practices, like mentoring, that motivates people to excel and rewards them when they do.

Multiple Mentoring Opportunities

Aragon, S. R. (Ed.). *Facilitating Learning in Online Environments.* New Directions for Adult and Continuing Education, no. 100. San Francisco: Jossey-Bass, 2003.

> Creating an online environment is tricky business, especially given the rate at which technology is changing. This book presents multiple perspectives for creating positive and meaningful online learning experiences that have significant implications for distance learning and for creating online mentoring communities. The book integrates key concepts of how adults learn with the pragmatics of facilitating online learning environments. Topics include instruction, creating social presence, instructional strategy, creating community, meeting consumer need, and lessons learned.

Berge, Z. L. (Ed.). *Sustaining Distance Training: Integrating Learning Technologies into the Fabric of the Enterprise.* San Francisco: Jossey-Bass, 2001.

> This reference examines distance education and training programs in seventeen leading for-profit, nonprofit, and government organizations. The authors describe key processes organizations use to sustain distance training and integrate it across their organizations. The patterns and commonalities revealed offer many options to consider and much food for thought for those committed to building an infrastructure to support and deliver distance and virtual mentoring.

Hansman, C. A. (Ed.). *Perspectives on Mentoring: Trends and Issues.* Columbus, Ohio: ERIC Clearinghouse on Adult, Career, and Vocational Education, Information Series no. 388, 2002.

> In this jam-packed, multiauthor "paper," Hansman melds her knowledge, expertise, and experience with those of her colleagues Vivian Mott, Andrea Ellinger, and Talmadge Guy to present a variegated and critical review of the mentoring literature. Together, they address the broad definitional landscape of mentoring, its institutional context, telementoring, diversity, and power, as well as the realities of mentoring practice today and in the future. The authors consider provocative questions that will ultimately raise the level of mentoring discourse and practice.

Johnson, H. E. *Mentoring for Exceptional Performance.* Glendale, Calif.: Griffin, 1997.

> This book offers a unique perspective on mentoring that focuses on organizational drivers and demands. Johnson, an experienced CEO,

emphasizes the need to enhance performance through individual, group, and organizational mentoring. Learning, leading, and relating contribute to exceptional performance and are essential elements in any mentoring relationship or program initiative. Each chapter in the book concludes with a "mentor's checkup" to evaluate mentoring programs and guide the development and implementation of program objectives.

Murrell, A. J., Crosby, F. J., and Ely, R. J. (Eds.). *Mentoring Dilemmas.* Mahwah, N.J.: Lawrence Erlbaum, 1999.

Mentoring relationships, like relationships in general, face challenging situations. The mentoring dilemmas experienced within multicultural organizations require sensitivity to those challenges. The potential for misunderstanding intensifies as diversity within the organization increases and presents additional challenges on the organizational level, especially around how to match and manage diverse mentoring relationships. Murrell and his colleagues examine mentoring dilemmas (including specificity about gender, race, and culture) from multiple perspectives (theoretical, empirical, and experiential) and use career and psychosocial mentoring functions as a lens for understanding. In addition, they offer specific action strategies for making mentoring work in diverse academic and business organizations.

Education and Training

Silberman, M. *Active Training.* San Francisco: Jossey-Bass/Pfeiffer, 1998.

This generic resource is ideal for those new to program design and training. Even experienced facilitators will find this activity-filled volume a practical resource for enhancing mentoring training. Silberman presents multiple techniques for assessing learner needs, developing training objectives, creating interesting opening exercises, preparing effective lectures, finding alternative methods to lecturing, and using experiential learning approaches. He includes real-life examples, case studies, stories, and activities that can easily be incorporated into new or existing programs.

Silberman, M. *101 Ways to Make Training Active.* San Francisco: Jossey-Bass/ Pfeiffer, 1995.

In this volume, Silberman provides a broad range of time-tested resources to build and deliver dynamic and interactive learning experiences. Those who are starting an organizational mentoring training program, seeking to enhance their existing training materials, or creating innovative approaches for increasing learned participation and enthusiasm will find this a treasure-trove of training options. It contains a multitude of activities and techniques that can easily be adapted to mentoring training. Several chapters are particularly relevant to mentoring training. One provides creative methods for helping groups and pairs get to know one another. Another chapter provides guided questions for learning journals that can be used to stimulate critical reflection on past mentoring experience.

Stewart, J. *Managing Change through Training and Development.* London: Pfeiffer, 1991.

Uncertainty, anxiety, fear, and resistance often follow on the heels of new organizational initiatives or cultural shifts such as mentoring. Training and development departments are often charged with responsibility for coming up with ways to overcome resistance. Stewart's book shows how training and development departments can play a more confident, proactive role in the management of change or the introduction of new initiatives (such as mentoring). He presents practical and varied approaches for the organization, team, and individual. Supplemental self-analysis instruments, organizational-related tasks, case studies, and a rich array of examples make this a valuable resource.

Taylor, K., Marienau, C., Fiddler, M. *Developing Adult Learners: Strategies for Teachers and Trainers.* San Francisco: Jossey-Bass, 2000.

This volume melds theory and practice by presenting an array of field-tested learner-centric strategies for promoting adult learning and development. It includes seventy instructional activities from multiple practitioners in diverse practice contexts that focus on specific learning strategies such as collaborating, inquiring, visioning, and reflecting. These how-to strategies are useful on many different levels and at critical junctures of creating a mentoring culture.

Vella, J. *Training Through Dialogue: Promoting Effective Learning and Change with Adults.* San Francisco: Jossey-Bass, 1995.

This resource will be especially helpful to those who are charged with creating mentoring training or train-the-trainer sessions. Vella applies the principles of adult learning to enhance the learning partnership in designing and implementing educational programs. Six chapters summarize the experiences of different programs and their lessons learned in developing an education program for adults. Trainers learn how to cultivate the critical skills required to generate the kind of active learning environment that a mentoring culture demands.

Safety Nets

Koestenbaum, P. *The Philosophic Consultant: Revolutionizing Organizations with Ideas.* San Francisco: Jossey-Bass/Pfeiffer, 2003.

> Koestenbaum offers endorsement and guidance for mentoring those who strive to develop their leadership. His leadership model (the Leadership Diamond) lends a dynamic framework and elevates both the language and thinking about leadership. At the heart of the model are two vectors whose sum is leadership: competence (skill and ability) and authenticity (character and willingness). Managers and mentors may feel uncomfortable in this arena, but Koestenbaum provides more than enough material to draw comfort from. The questions he raises are particularly relevant ones for those who guide, support, and coach mentors and leaders. His set of journal prompts are excellent for journal activities or for mentoring dialogue.

Moving On: Mentoring and the Future

Fullan, M. *Leading in a Culture of Change.* San Francisco: Jossey-Bass, 2001.

> Creating a mentoring culture requires an ability to mobilize internal and external constituents to do important but difficult work under conditions of constant change, overload, and fragmentation. Fullan presents deep insights about the dynamics of change and the leader's role in managing and sustaining organizational change. He shows leaders how they can effectively accomplish their goals—by attending to broader moral purpose, keeping on top of the change process, cultivating relationships, sharing knowledge, and setting a vision and context for creating coherence in their organizations. Modeling and mentoring are crucial to the change process. Ultimately, organizational performance depends on it.

References

Aragon, S. R. (ed.) *Facilitating Learning in Online Environments.* New Directions for Adult and Continuing Education, no. 100. San Francisco: Jossey-Bass, Winter 2003.

Bell, C. *Managers as Mentors: Building Partnerships for Learning.* San Francisco: Berrett-Koehler, 2002.

Bellah, R. N., and others. *Habits of the Heart: Individualism and Commitment in American Life.* New York: HarperCollins, 1986.

Bennis, W., Spreitzer, G. M., and Cummings, T. G. (eds.). *The Future of Leadership: Today's Top Leadership Thinkers Speak to Tomorrow's Leaders.* San Francisco: Jossey-Bass, 2001.

Benson, R. *The Game.* New York: Tarcher/Putnam, 2001.

Berends, P. B. *Coming to Life: Traveling the Spiritual Path in Everyday Life.* San Francisco: Harper San Francisco, 1990.

Berge, Z. L. (ed.). *Sustaining Distance Training: Integrating Learning Technologies into the Fabric of the Enterprise.* San Francisco: Jossey-Bass, 2001.

Berne, E. *Games People Play: The Psychology of Human Relationships.* New York: Ballantine Books, 1996. (Originally published 1964)

Block, P. *The Empowered Manager: Positive Political Skills at Work.* San Francisco: Jossey-Bass, 1987.

Bolman, L. G., and Deal, T. E. *Leading with Soul: An Uncommon Journey of Spirit.* San Francisco: Jossey-Bass, 1995.

Bradford, R. "Strategic Alignment." *Executive Excellence,* Jan. 2002, *19*(1), 8.

Brookfield, S. D. *Understanding and Facilitating Adult Learning.* San Francisco: Jossey-Bass, 1986.

Brookfield, S. D. *Becoming a Critically Reflective Teacher.* San Francisco: Jossey-Bass, 1995.

Caffarella, R. S. *Planning Programs for Adult Learners.* San Francisco: Jossey-Bass, 2002.

Carter, L., Giber, D., and Goldsmith, M. (eds.). *Linkage Inc.'s Best Practices in Organizational Development and Change.* San Francisco: Jossey-Bass, 2001.

Cervero, R. M., and Wilson, A. L. *Planning Responsibly for Adult Education: A Guide to Negotiating Power and Interests.* San Francisco: Jossey-Bass, 1994.

Charan, R., Drotter, S., and Noel, J. *The Leadership Pipeline: How to Build the Leadership-Powered Company.* San Francisco: Jossey-Bass, 2001.

Cheney, S. "Benchmarking." In C. S. Russo (ed.), *Train the Trainer Guide, Volume 4: Measurement and Evaluation* (pp. 38–54). Alexandria, Va.: American Society for Training Development, 1998.

Cloke, K., and Goldsmith, J. *The Art of Waking People up: Cultivating Awareness and Authenticity at Work.* San Francisco: Jossey-Bass, 2003.

Cohen, J. "Mentoring Undergraduates with Professional and Liberal Arts Goals: The Mass Communication Experience." In A. G. Reinarz and E. R. White (eds.), *Beyond Teaching to Mentoring.* New Directions for Teaching and Learning, no. 85. San Francisco: Jossey-Bass, Spring 2001.

Colvin, G. "The Changing Art of Becoming Unbeatable." *Fortune,* Nov. 24, 1997.

Conger, J. A. "The Necessary Art of Persuasion." *Harvard Business Review,* 1998, *76*(3), 84–95.

Conger, J. A., and Benjamin, B. *Building Leaders.* San Francisco: Jossey-Bass, 1999.

Connors, R., Smith, T., and Hickman, C. *The Oz Principle: Getting Results Through Individual and Organizational Accountability.* Upper Saddle River, N.J.: Prentice Hall, 1994.

Conrad, C. *Strategic Organizational Communication: Toward the 21st Century.* Austin, Tex.: Holt, Rinehart and Winston, 1994.

Conway, C. *Strategies for Mentoring: A Blueprint for Successful Organizational Development.* San Francisco: Wiley, 1998.

Daloz, L. *Mentor: Guiding the Journey of Adult Learners.* San Francisco: Jossey-Bass, 1999.

Deal, T. E., and Key, M. K. *Corporate Celebration: Play, Purpose, and Profit at Work.* San Francisco: Berrett-Koehler, 1998.

De Pree, M. *Leading Without Power: Finding Hope in Servicing Community.* San Francisco: Jossey-Bass, 2003.

Drucker, P. F. "They're Not Employees, They're People." (Reprint R0202E). *Harvard Business Review,* Feb. 2002.

Dunham, K. J. "Mentors May Not Help." *Wall Street Journal,* Sept. 23, 2003. (http://online.wsj.com/article_print,SB106426684111221000,00.html)

Eby, L. T., and Allen, T. D. "Further Investigation of Protégés' Negative Mentoring Experiences: Patterns and Outcomes." *Group and Organizational Management,* 2002, *27*(4), 456–479.

Edwards-Winslow, F. "When Government Works." *Leader to Leader,* 2002, *24,* 6–10.

Feldman, D. C. (ed.). *Work Careers: A Developmental Perspective.* San Francisco: Jossey-Bass, 2002.

Ferguson, M. *The Aquarian Conspiracy.* Los Angeles: Tarcher, 1980.

Fisher, J. R., Jr. "Mentoring Your Way to Greatness." *Executive Excellence,* 1998, *15*(5), 19.

Fullan, M. *Leading in a Culture of Change.* San Francisco: Jossey-Bass, 2001.

Galpin, T. J. *The Human Side of Change: A Practical Guide to Organization Redesign.* San Francisco: Jossey-Bass, 1996.

Gardner, J. W. *Self-Renewal: The Individual and the Innovative Society.* New York: HarperCollins, 1963.

Garvin, D. "Building a Learning Organization." *Harvard Business Review,* 1993, *71*(4), 78–90.

Greene, M. *The Dialectic of Freedom.* New York: Teachers College Press, 1988.

Hall, T. W., Greenberg, E. M., and Zachary, L. J. *Leading Effectively: Men and Women of the Volunteer Board Room.* Denver: Mountains and Plains Region, Council for Adult and Experiential Learning, 1987.

Hansman, C. A. (ed.). *Perspectives on Mentoring: Trends and Issues.* Columbus, Ohio: ERIC Clearinghouse on Adult, Career, and Vocational Education, Information Series no. 388, 2002.

Hansman, C. A. "Mentoring in Teacher Education Programs: Exercises in Power and Interests." Paper presented at the Midwest Research to Practice Conference in Adult, Continuing, and Community Education, Columbus, Ohio, Oct. 2003.

Heifetz, R. A., and Linsky, M. "Leading with an Open Heart." *Leader to Leader,* 2002, *26,* 28–33.

Hesselbein, F., and Johnston, R. (eds.). *On Creativity, Innovation, and Renewal: A Leader to Leader Guide.* San Francisco: Jossey-Bass, 2002.

Honold, L., and Silverman, R. J. *Organizational DNA: Diagnosing Your Organization for Increased Effectiveness.* Palo Alto, Calif.: Davies-Black, 2002.

Isaacs, W. *Dialogue and the Art of Thinking Together.* New York: Doubleday Currency, 1999.

Johnson, H. E. *Mentoring for Exceptional Performance.* Glendale, Calif.: Griffin, 1997.

Johnson-Bailey, J., and Cervero, R. M. "Cross-Cultural Mentoring as a Context for Learning." In M. V. Alfred (ed.), *Learning and Sociocultural Contexts: Implications for Adults, Community, and Workplace Education.* New Directions for Adult and Continuing Education, no. 96. San Francisco: Jossey-Bass, Spring 2002.

Kaplan, D. I. "Leader as Model and Mentor." In K. Shelton (ed.), *The New Paradigm of Leadership: Visions of Excellence for 21st Century Organizations.* Provo, Utah: Executive Excellence, 1997.

Kaplan-Leiserson, E. "Intelligence." T+D, 2003, *57*(7), 14–16.

Kaye, B., and Jacobson, B. "Mentoring: A Group Guide." *Training and Development,* 1995, *49*(4), 22–26.

Kaye, B., and Jacobson, B. "Mentoring: A New Model for Building Learning Organizations." *OD Practitioner,* 1996, *23*(3), 35–44.

Knowles, M. *Self-Directed Learning: A Guide for Learners and Teachers.* Chicago: Follett, 1975.

Knowles, M. S. *The Modern Practice of Adult Education: From Pedagogy to Andragogy.* Chicago: Follett, 1980.

Knowles, M. S., Holton, E. F., and Swanson, R. A. *The Adult Learner: The Definitive Classic in Adult Education and Human Resource Development* (5th ed.). Woburn, Mass.: Butterworth-Heinemann, 1998.

Koestenbaum, P. *The Philosophic Consultant: Revolutionizing Organizations with Ideas.* San Francisco: Jossey-Bass/Pfeiffer, 2003.

Koestenbaum, P. *Leadership: The Inner Side of Greatness.* San Francisco: Jossey-Bass, 2002.

Kolb, D. (1985): *Learning style inventory,* Boston, MA: McBer & Co (800-729–8074).

Kolb, D. *The Facilitator's Guide to Learning.* Boston: Hay/McBer, 2000.

Kotter, J. "What Leaders Really Do." *Harvard Business Review,* 1990, *79*(11), 2–11.

Kotter, J. P. *Leading Change.* Boston: Harvard Business School Press, 1996.

Kouzes, J. M., and Posner, B. Z. *The Leadership Challenge: How to Keep Getting Extraordinary Things Done in Organizations.* San Francisco: Jossey-Bass, 2002.

Kouzes, J. M., and Posner, B. Z. *Encouraging the Heart: A Leader's Guide to Rewarding and Recognizing Others.* San Francisco: Jossey-Bass, 2003.

Kram, K. E. *Mentoring at Work: Developmental Relationships in Organizational Life.* Glenview, Ill.: Scott, Foresman, 1988.

Lawler, E. E. *Treat People Right! How Organizations and Individuals Can Propel Each Other into a Virtuous Spiral of Success.* San Francisco: Jossey-Bass, 2003.

Leider, R. J. *The Power of Purpose: Creating Meaning in Your Life and Work.* San Francisco: Berrett-Koehler, 1997.

Lencioni, P. *The Five Temptations of a CEO.* San Francisco: Jossey-Bass, 1998.

Lencioni, P. *The Five Dysfunctions of a Team: A Leadership Fable.* San Francisco: Jossey-Bass, 2002.

Lewin, K. *Field Theory in Social Science.* New York: HarperCollins, 1951.

Markova, D. *I Will Not Die an Unlived Life: Reclaiming Purpose and Passion.* York Beach, Maine: Conari Press, 2000.

Marsick, V. J., and Watkins, K. E. *Facilitating Learning Organizations: Making Learning Count.* Brookfield, Vt.: Gower, 1999.

McCall, C. "Leadership: The Values Game." In J. Renesch (ed.), *Leadership in a New Era: Visionary Approaches to the Biggest Crisis of Our Time.* San Francisco: New Leaders Press, Sterling and Stone, 1994.

Meister, J. C. *Corporate Universities: Lessons in Building a World-Class Work Force* (rev. ed.). New York: McGraw-Hill, 1998.

Merrill, D. W., and Reid, R. H. *Personal Styles and Effective Performance: Make Your Style Work for You.* Boca Raton, Fla.: CRC Press, 1999.

Mezirow, J., and Associates. *Fostering Critical Reflection in Adulthood: A Guide to Transformative and Emancipatory Learning.* San Francisco: Jossey-Bass, 1990.

Monette, M. "The Concept of Educational Need: An Analysis of Selected Literature." *Adult Education,* 1977, 27(2), 116–127.

Morin, W. J. *Trust Me: How to Rebuild Trust in the Workplace.* Orlando: Harcourt Brace, 1990.

Murray, M. *Beyond the Myths and Magic of Mentoring: How to Facilitate an Effective Mentoring Process.* San Francisco: Jossey-Bass, 2001.

Murrell, A. J., Crosby, F. J., and Ely, R. J. (eds.). *Mentoring Dilemmas.* Mahwah, N.J.: Erlbaum, 1999.

Phelan, B. *Developing Your Company Culture.* Berkeley, Calif.: Context Press, 1996.

Putnam, R. D. *Bowling Alone: The Collapse and Revival of American Community.* New York: Simon & Schuster, 2000.

Rilke, R. M. *Letters to a Young Poet.* New York: Norton, 1954.

Sayles, L. R. "Leaders for the Nineties: Challenge and Change." *Issues and Observations,* 1990, 10(2), pp. 8–11.

Schein, E. H. *Organizational Culture and Leadership* (2nd ed.). San Francisco: Jossey-Bass, 1992.

Schein, E. H. *The Corporate Culture Survival Guide: Sense and Nonsense About Cultural Change.* San Francisco: Jossey-Bass, 1999.

Scott, C. D., and Jaffe, D. T. *Managing Change at Work: Leading People Through Organizational Transitions* (rev. ed.). Lanham, Md.: Crisp, 1995.

Senge, P. M. *The Fifth Discipline: The Art and Practice of the Learning Organization.* New York: Doubleday Currency, 1990.

Senge, P. M., and others. *The Fifth Discipline Fieldbook: Strategies and Tools for Building a Learning Organization.* New York: Doubleday Currency, 1994.

Silberman, M. *Active Training.* San Francisco: Jossey-Bass/Pfeiffer, 1998.

Silberman, M. *101 Ways to Make Training Active.* San Francisco: Jossey-Bass/Pfeiffer, 1995.

Simonsen, P. *Promoting a Development Culture in Your Organization.* Palo Alto, Calif.: Davies-Black, 1997.

Stewart, J. *Managing Change Through Training and Development.* London: Pfeiffer, 1991.

Taylor, K., Marienau, C., and Fiddler, M. *Developing Adult Learners: Strategies for Teachers and Trainers.* San Francisco: Jossey-Bass, 2000.

Tobin, D. R. *Re-Educating the Corporation: Foundations for the Learning Organization.* Essex Junction, Vt.: Oliver Wight, 1993.

Trudell, D. J. "What Stops Peak Organizational Performance?" *Performance in Practice,* Summer 1997, p. 15.

Vella, J. *Training Through Dialogue: Promoting Effective Learning and Change with Adults.* San Francisco: Jossey-Bass, 1995.

Waclawski, J., and Church, A. H. *Organization Development: A Data-Driven Approach to Organization Change.* San Francisco: Jossey-Bass, 2002.

Watkins, K. E., and Marsick, V. J. *Sculpting the Learning Organization: Lessons in the Art and Science of Systemic Change.* San Francisco: Jossey-Bass, 1993.

Whyte, D. *The Heart Aroused: Poetry and the Preservation of the Soul in Corporate America.* New York: Doubleday Currency, 1994.

Wick, C. W., and León, L. S. *The Learning Edge: How Smart Managers and Smart Companies Stay Ahead.* New York: McGraw-Hill, 1993.

Yearout, S., Miles, G., and Koonce, R. H. "Multi-Level Visioning." *Training and Development,* 2001, *55*(3), 31–39.

Zachary, L. J. *The Mentor's Guide: Facilitating Effective Learning Relationships.* San Francisco: Jossey-Bass, 2000.

Zachary, L. J. "Creating a Mentoring Culture." *Executive Update,* Nov. 2002, pp. 30–33.

Zachary, L. J. "Accountability Triggers Results." *Executive Update,* Sept. 2003a, pp. 37–39.

Zachary, L. J. Building an Effective Mentoring Program." *Consulting Today,* 2003b, *7*(1), 1–4.

Zachary, L. J. "Turbo-Charge Your Leadership Through Mentoring." *Leader to Leader,* Winter 2003c, no. 27, 15–18.

Zukav, G. *Seat of the Soul.* New York: Fireside, 1990.

Index

Credits

Chapter One, p. 7: Epigraph used by permission of Lisa Fain.

Chapter Two, p. 15: Epigraph from *Coming to Life: Traveling the Spiritual Path in Everyday Life* by Polly Berends (San Francisco: Harper San Francisco, 1990). Used by permission.

Chapter Three, p. 31: Epigraph from *The Seat of the Soul* by Gary Zukav (New York: Fireside, 1990). Used by permission of Simon & Schuster.

Chapter Five, p. 98: Exhibit 5.2 from *The Mentor's Guide* by Lois Zachary (San Francisco: Jossey-Bass, 2000). Copyright ©2000 by John Wiley & Sons, Inc. Reprinted with permission of John Wiley & Sons, Inc.

Chapter Six, p. 114: Exercise 6.3 from *The Mentor's Guide* by Lois Zachary (San Francisco: Jossey-Bass, 2000). Copyright ©2000 by John Wiley & Sons, Inc. Reprinted with permission of John Wiley & Sons, Inc.

Chapter Six, p. 132: Figure 6.2 from *The Mentor's Guide* by Lois Zachary (San Francisco: Jossey-Bass, 2000). Copyright ©2000 by John Wiley & Sons, Inc. Reprinted with permission of John Wiley & Sons, Inc.

Chapter Seven, p.143: Figure 7.1 from *The Human Side of Change* by Timothy Galpin (San Francisco: Jossey-Bass, 1996). Copyright ©1996 by John Wiley & Sons, Inc. Reprinted with permission of John Wiley & Sons, Inc.

Chapter Seven, pp. 158–160: Exhibit 7.3 and Exercise 7.4 adapted from *The Human Side of Change* by Timothy Galpin (San Francisco: Jossey-Bass, 1996). Copyright ©1996 by John Wiley & Sons, Inc. Reprinted with permission of John Wiley & Sons, Inc.

Chapter Eleven, p. 218: Epigraph from *Understanding and Facilitating Adult Learning* by Stephen D. Brookfield (San Francisco: Jossey-Bass, 1986). Copyright ©1986 by John Wiley & Sons, Inc. Reprinted with permission of John Wiley & Sons, Inc.

How to Use the CD-ROM

SYSTEM REQUIREMENTS:

PC with Microsoft Windows 98SE or later

Mac with Apple OS version 8.6 or later

USING THE CD WITH WINDOWS

To view the items located on the CD, follow these steps:

1. Insert the CD into your computer's CD-ROM drive.

2. A window appears with the following options:

   Contents: Allows you to view the files included on the CD-ROM.

   Software: Allows you to install useful software from the CD-ROM.

   Author: Displays a page with information about the Author.

   Help: Displays a page with information on using the CD.

   Exit: Closes the interface window.

If you do not have autorun enabled, or if the autorun window does not appear, follow these steps to access the CD:

1. Click Start -> Run.

2. In the dialog box that appears, type d:<\\>start.exe, where d is the letter of your CD-ROM drive. This brings up the autorun window described in the preceding set of steps.

3. Choose the desired option from the menu. (See Step 2 in the preceding list for a description of these options.)

TO DOWNLOAD DOCUMENTS

The documents on this disk are duplicated in Microsoft Word files. To download a document, first open it. For Windows users, under the File pull-down menu, choose Save As, and save the document to your hard drive. You can also click on your CD drive in Windows Explorer and select a document to copy to your hard drive.

IN CASE OF TROUBLE

If you experience difficulty using the CD-ROM, please follow these steps:

1. Make sure your hardware and systems configurations conform to the systems requirements noted under "System Requirements" above.

2. Review the installation procedure for your type of hardware and operating system. It is possible to reinstall the software if necessary.

To speak with someone in Product Technical Support, call 800-762-2974 or 317-572-3994 M–F 8:30 a.m.–5:00 p.m. EST. You can also get support by contacting Product Technical Support at http://www.wiley.com/techsupport.

Before calling or writing, please have the following information available:

Type of computer and operating system

Any error messages displayed

Complete description of the problem

It is best if you are sitting at your computer when making the call.

Jossey-Bass books and products are available through most bookstores. To contact Jossey-Bass directly, call our Customer Care Department within the U.S. at (800) 956-7739, outside the U.S. at (317) 572-3986, fax (317) 572-4002, or visit our website at www.josseybass.com.

If you do not agree to these conditions, do not proceed to install the product and contact Jossey-Bass Publishers to arrange for return before any use.